Beyond the Borderlands

Beyond the Borderlands

MIGRATION AND BELONGING IN THE UNITED STATES AND MEXICO

DEBRA LATTANZI SHUTIKA

F159.K26 S58 2011
Shutika, Debra Lattanzi,
1964-
Beyond the borderlands :
migration and belonging in
the United States and Mexico
Berkeley : University of

UNIVERSITY OF CALIFORNIA PRESS
Berkeley   Los Angeles   London

University of California Press, one of the most distinguished
university presses in the United States, enriches lives around the
world by advancing scholarship in the humanities, social sciences,
and natural sciences. Its activities are supported by the UC Press
Foundation and by philanthropic contributions from individuals
and institutions. For more information, visit www.ucpress.edu.

University of California Press
Berkeley and Los Angeles, California

University of California Press, Ltd.
London, England

Library of Congress Cataloging-in-Publication Data

Lattanzi Shutika, Debra, 1964-
    Beyond the borderlands : migration and belonging in the U.S. and
Mexico / Debra Lattanzi Shutika.
        p.   cm.
    Includes bibliographical references and index.
    ISBN 978-0-520-26958-3 (cloth) — ISBN 978-0-520-26959-0 (pbk.)
    1. Mexican Americans—Cultural assimilation—Pennsylvania—
Kennett Square.   2. Mexican Americans—Pennsylvania—Kennett
Square—Ethnic identity.   3. Kennett Square (Pa.)—Ethnic relations.
4. Guanajuato (Mexico : State) —Emigration and immigration—Social
aspects.   I. Title.
    F159.K26S58 2011
    305.8968'72074813—dc22   2010053180

Manufactured in the United States of America
20 19 18 17 16 15 14 13 12 11
10 9 8 7 6 5 4 3 2 1

This book is printed on Cascades Enviro 100, a 100% post-consumer
waste, recycled, de-inked fiber. FSC recycled certified and processed
chlorine free. It is acid free, Ecologo certified, and manufactured by
BioGas energy.

Contents

Illustrations

Acknowledgments

A long-term book project is never the work of a single person. Rather, it is part of a collaborative effort with the assistance of family, friends, colleagues, and institutions. My first introduction to Kennett Square was made possible by a project supervised by Dr. David Hufford of the Hershey School of Medicine at Pennsylvania State University. Thank you, David, for providing the opportunity to find this community. I am indebted to the staff of Project Salud and La Comunidad Hispana, Inc. where I was assisted by a friendly and insightful staff who facilitated my introduction to the Mexican community in Kennett Square and offered invaluable advice and guidance. I especially thank Peggy Harris, Anita O'Connor, Annette Silva, Iris Ayala, Sergio Carmona, Howard Porter, Guillermo Rivera, and Margarita Quiñones.

Many Kennett Square residents agreed to participate in this study; others provided information and insights to the workings of the community. While I am thankful for the guidance of all of the residents of Kennett Square who were thoughtful and generous with their time, I wish to acknowledge several people who were particularly helpful. Joan Holiday offered her unconditional support; I am especially grateful that she allowed me to participate in the Bridging the Community meetings and introduced me to many Kennett Square residents. Vince Ghione arranged introductions and interviews with several mushroom farm owners; he also spoke with me at length about his career in the industry and the community, and thus he provided insights and perspectives that helped me understand the history of mushrooming in southeastern Pennsylvania. Isidro Rodríguez was a tremendous friend who supported my work in Mexico and Pennsylvania. I am forever grateful for his assistance in finding a house in Mexico and introducing me to his network of family and friends on both sides of the border.

I have spent many happy hours in the village I have identified as Textitlán, where I have developed what I hope will be lifelong friendships. Most significant was the love and friendship of the Rodríquez family: Maria and Benjamin, Lucia and Benjamin, Joel, Claudia and Erica, Benja, Diana, and Javier and Lucila. I also thank René Guzmán, Juan Rico García, Emilio and Elvia Guzmán, and the many others who agreed to be interviewed and provided access to archival documents that were invaluable to the success of this project. I also acknowledge Felipe Ortega, an outstanding research assistant and loyal friend. To the people of Textitlán I can only say that I admire you and am grateful for your willingness to share your lives and community with me.

My life and work have been blessed with amazing colleagues. Payal Gupta was an ideal compañera in the field, and Cory Thorne, Guillermo de los Reyes, Solimar Otero, Amanda Holmes, and Charlie Groth continue to be exceptional friends and colleagues. I especially thank Douglas Massey for his steadfast support and encouragement since the earliest days of this project.

At George Mason University, I thank Peggy Yocom for being a wise and devoted mentor. Working with Peggy has been a highlight of my career at GMU. Amelia Rutledge, Tamara Harvey, Shelley Reid, Devon Hodges, Steven Weinberger, Terry Zawacki, Eric Anderson, Robert Matz, and Alok Yadav are wonderful friends and colleagues. Joan Bristol, Zofia Burr, Amal Amireh, and Denise Albanese all read early versions of the manuscript and offered invaluable advice and encouragement. Carol Cleaveland read all of my later revisions; I thank Carol for her keen insights and for believing in me when I was ready to give up. Jason Morris and Kristina Downs were invaluable research assistants. Thank you both for the time and dedication you provided to this project. I also thank Deborah Kaplan for being the best department chair imaginable.

Thanks also to The Mexican Migration Project at Princeton University, which provided the opportunity to collect data for their project in Mexico, and George Mason University for providing the study leave that allowed me to finish my fieldwork in Mexico.

I have been blessed with the support of many friends and family. I thank Viktoria Ironpride for her careful editorial assistance and for serving as my first writing instructor. Marietta Damond provided invaluable support with my statistical analyses and providing play dates for my kids when deadlines were looming. Laura Scott and Dean Taciuch have exceeded my expectations as supportive friends. Thank you for reading this book (sometimes under pressure) and providing your insights as writers and editors. Most of all, thank you for a friendship that I treasure. I thank my mother Frances Lattanzi, my late father Paul Lattanzi, my sister Susan Lattanzi, and my brother-in-law Jeff Kline for doing the things that families do so well—reminding me that there is more to life than work, watching the kids when I needed writing time, and just being there when I needed your love and support.

My children Helen and John provided the much-needed distractions that have kept my life balanced and joyous. Their sense of wonder with every new experience made our time in Mexico among my fondest memories. I dedicate this book to them. Finally to my husband Ken: I cannot put into words what your love, patience, and support mean to me. It has been a long road, but I'm still looking forward to our next adventure.

ONE

Introduction

NEW BORDERS AND DESTINATIONS

THE SHIFTING GEOGRAPHIES OF
MEXICAN IMMIGRATION

Although I live in Virginia, far from the U.S.-Mexico border, in 2005 it felt as if the border had moved into my backyard. That summer I watched the situation in Herndon, Virginia, with fascination and an uncanny sense of déjà vu as a controversy erupted regarding a group of Latino men. For over a decade a sizable group of day laborers, many of whom were from Mexico and Central America, had been gathering in the parking lot of Herndon's 7-Eleven in the early morning, hoping to find work. The space had become an ad hoc employment center for contractors seeking extra workers for a specific job or local residents looking to employ a handyman for small household projects. Herndon's residents were becoming increasingly unnerved by the men who were described as "scary" and "unkempt." Residents complained that groups of men would "swarm on top of [customers]" when driving into the 7-Eleven (Cho 2005, July 18: A1). The residents, American citizens who constituted the local English-speaking majority, insisted that the local officials force the men to leave lest they risk arrest. As an alternative, a local social service provider proposed to develop a day labor center so that men looking for work would have a place to congregate. As envisioned by the planners, the site would offer on-site English classes and job skills training, as well as a place to spend the afternoon when work was not available.

Although this seemed like a good idea to some, the proposal to build a day labor center, to resituate Latinos within Herndon, met strong resistance from the majority population. Many of the same residents who were unhappy with the hundred or so men waiting by the 7-Eleven were similarly incensed by the alternative: using tax dollars to build an official day labor center located adjacent to a residential neighborhood. They argued that funding a day labor center would officially encourage illegal immigration (Cho 2005: T03). Many also feared that a town-supported center might encourage even more undocumented workers to come to Herndon.

I watched the circumstances surrounding Herndon's day labor controversy with more than a casual interest. The events were reminiscent of those that I had begun documenting in Kennett Square, Pennsylvania, the previous decade. Since the mid-1980s Kennett Square had transitioned from a majority Anglo-European small town into a multiethnic community as Mexican families began moving in and around the area. The issues at stake in Kennett Square during this rapid local transformation were nearly identical to those in Herndon: finding a physical and cultural place for the rapidly growing number of Mexican families moving into the community; frustration with failed national immigration policies and the search for local alternatives; and most significantly, anxiety about the changing local character and communal identity of an Anglo-European historic farming village.

Other issues, such as how to maintain ties to distant families and friends, were voiced by Mexicans who were settling in Kennett Square, yet they were rarely acknowledged in public discussions because very few of these newcomers spoke English, most were presumed transients, and some were undocumented. When I began my work with some of these Mexican families in 1995, I asked them what their thoughts were, and their responses reflected concerns about incorporation into the community and adapting to life in Pennsylvania: what I refer to as emplacement and belonging. These men and women had a strong desire to make a home in Kennett Square and to provide more opportunities for their families. At the same time, they wanted to maintain connections to their home community in Mexico and preserve their identities as Mexicans living in the United States.[1] Although my early work with this group of Mexican settlers began in Pennsylvania, it was not long before I realized that their stories of settlement and adaptation in Kennett were, and continue to be, deeply tied to their home community in Mexico, a place that I refer to as Textitlán, Guanajuato.[2] Their ties to Textitlán constitute a complex binational existence that has shaped their experiences in Kennett Square, everyday life in their hometown, and how they find and maintain their place and sense of belonging in both communities.

This book, an ethnography based on fieldwork in Mexico and Pennsylvania, explores the challenges encountered by Mexican families as they endeavored to find their place in Kennett Square beginning in the mid-1980s. It situates the events in Kennett Square in the historical context of the changing geography of Mexican immigration, the oldest and most sustained of all of America's immigrations (Massey 1998; Suarez-Orozco 1998; Durand, Massey and Capoferro 2005; Zúñiga and Hernández-León 2005). *Beyond the Borderlands* provides a ten-year longitudinal window between 1995 and 2005 during the formation of the new destination settlement in Kennett Square and the accompanying changes that took place in Textitlán.[3]

I was trained as a folklorist, so when I began my work with Mexican families in 1995, I was intrigued by Kennett Square's Mexican population and the local responses to Mexican settlement. On the surface, Kennett Square resembled the types of small, localized face-to-face communities that were the subjects of sense of place studies common in folklore scholarship.[4] As this project grew, however, it became apparent that the situation in Kennett Square was deeply multifaceted. Although the total number of Mexicans in Kennett Square was small, as in many rural and suburban communities where Mexicans and other immigrants are settling in the United States, their presence has had an influence disproportionate to their numbers. Their effect on the community's culture and day-to-day life has reshaped Kennett Square's local character. The experiences in Kennett Square for Mexicans and longer-term residents demonstrates that immigrant settlement and incorporation are characterized not so much by assimilating one's culture and identity to "fit in" to a host society but are constituted through diverse experiences that simultaneously integrate newcomers even as their presence reshapes their new community (Alba and Nee 2003, 11).[5] *Beyond the Borderlands* is an examination of the senses of place, and the Mexican sense of belonging, as each evolved in the context of migration between Kennett Square and Textitlán.

NEW DESTINATIONS AND THE CHANGING GEOGRAPHIES OF MEXICAN IMMIGRATION

It was not clear when I began this study in the mid-1990s that Kennett Square was what has been termed a new destination settlement (Zuñiga and Hernández-León 2005). Although Mexican men had been migrating to Kennett Square for years to pick mushrooms, it had only been a few years since these men started moving their families north. By the late 1990s it was apparent that Kennett Square was one of many Mexican settlements emerging in new locations throughout the United States, settlements that were part of a new era of Mexican migration and settlement. What I was witnessing in the field had not been widespread since the classic era of immigration at the turn of the nineteenth to the twentieth century: the formation of new immigrant communities throughout the United States (Massey 2008).

More recently it has come to light that the events in places like Kennett Square are part of a larger national trend in Mexican immigration that has occurred since the mid-1980s: the phenomenon of Mexicans settling permanently in communities outside the border region. At one time the U.S.-Mexico borderlands were the familiar destination of Mexican immigration and immigration controversy. Throughout the 1980s, national headlines documented the problems of the borderlands: the porous yet militarized border; coyotes (immigrant traffickers) and drug smugglers; migrant deaths in the desert; and undocumented workers siphoning public funds were some of the more common issues discussed. Once considered a localized problem, emigration from Mexico has moved beyond its familiar territory in the borderlands and is now dispersed to new and diverse places across the United States (Zúñiga and Hernández-León 2005).

The most striking changes have taken place in American suburbs and rural small towns. These communities, once the exclusive domain of Anglo middle- and upper-class families, are increasingly home to a growing number of immigrant families. Throughout the 1990s, the U.S. foreign-born population grew dramatically—increasing to 11.3 million or 57.4 percent—and by 2000, nearly a third of these new immigrant settlers were residing outside of locations that were the historic gateway settlement states and moving into places with little history of immigrant settlement (Singer 2004: 3).[6] This shift in settlement gave rise to new immigrant gateways that experienced growth rates of more than double the national average. These new gateways included states such as Colorado, Georgia, Nevada, and North Carolina, as well as a number of large metropolitan areas, including Washington, DC, Atlanta, and Denver (Singer 2004: 9–10). Most notably, by 2000 immigrants in these newly emerging gateways were much more likely to settle in suburbs rather than in cities (Singer 2004: 11).

These demographic changes were in part the outcome of the Immigration Reform and Control Act (IRCA), which facilitated the changing social and cultural landscape of Kennett Square. It provided amnesty and legal residency for previously undocumented laborers, primarily Mexican nationals, throughout the United States, allowing former cyclical migrants to settle permanently in the United States (Durand, Massey, and Charvet 2000; Hernández-León and Zúñiga 2000; Massey, Durand, and Malone 2002; Durand, Massey, and Capoferro 2005). Although the numbers of legal immigrants who were moving into nontraditional settlement areas began to rise in the early 1980s, the total number of immigrants living in new destinations increased significantly immediately after the passage of IRCA in 1986, peaking at 25 percent in the late 1980s and then falling back to 12 percent by 1992 (Massey, Durand, and Malone 2002: 127).

The IRCA was not the only event that shaped the changing migration and settlement patterns in the United States. Increased border security in Texas and California ultimately encouraged migrants to stay longer in the United States. Similarly, a rise in anti-immigrant sentiment in California, culminating in the passage of Proposition 187,[7] also contributed to the establishment of Mexican communities outside the historic gateway states along the U.S.-Mexico borderlands (Massey, Durand, and Malone 2002).

The North American Free Trade Agreement (NAFTA) went into effect in 1994. It promoted the integration of the capital markets of the United States and Mexico and thus lowered barriers to the movement of goods, capital, services, and information, but the agreement excluded provisions for labor. NAFTA was expected to create new jobs in Mexico to decrease undocumented immigration to the United States. These expectations were never realized, however (Andreas 1998, 2000; Fernández-Kelly and Massey 2007). In the never-ending pursuit of cheap labor, many of the post-NAFTA U.S.-owned factories in Mexico were shuttered as operations were relocated in China or other Latin American countries. The deregulation of Mexican agriculture and competition from the United States and Canada also forced many Mexican peasants out of agriculture (Fernández-Kelly and Massey 2007). The net effect of NAFTA's economic integration neither decreased the number of displaced Mexican workers nor reduced entry of unauthorized immigrants from Mexico into the United States.

In Kennett Square, most of the pioneer settlers who participated in this study said that they decided to move their families to Pennsylvania after receiving amnesty, but changes in local economic and labor needs also facilitated this process. For instance, the early 1990s saw an expansion of suburban developments throughout Chester County and increased the labor needs in construction and landscaping. These new jobs fueled Mexican settlement in Kennett Square from the mid-1990s onward. In other parts of the United States, the increased demand for domestic assistance (i.e., housekeeping and child care) created a labor market for immigrant women and also promoted a more diverse settlement pattern (Hernández-León and Zúñiga 2000; Hondagneu-Sotelo 2001; Zúñiga and Hernández-León 2005). Whereas it was rare in Kennett Square for Mexican women to take domestic housecleaning jobs, women were more often engaged in informal child care in their homes, working for other Mexican women who were employed outside the home. The few Mexican women working outside the home were most often employed as cooks or waitstaff in local restaurants, and some women also worked at a Kennett Square mushroom packing plant.[8]

As locations of settlement, Kennett Square and other new destinations have had limited or no prior history of a Mexican presence. As such, they do not provide the long-standing social and political support networks that are common in the borderlands. New destinations are also unique in that the longer-term citizen residents are facing a variety of unexpected challenges, such as providing bilingual education and culturally appropriate health-care services, as their communities grow. The changes that accompany growth are often fraught with controversy as the very character of local identity shifts along with the population.

Since the mid-1990s, new destinations have often been at the center of immigration debates, most notably where citizens organize against immigrants in an attempt to "take back" their communities through the enactment of local ordinances (Bono 2007; Ludden 2007; Osterling and McClure 2008; Walker 2008). Anti-immigrant actions have included a range of activities, including the creation of zoning laws that redefine who can live together in a legal household and enactment of ordinances that enable local law enforcement to arrest suspected undocumented immigrants and remove them from the community. Some cases have also included open harassment of immigrants (Osterling and McClure 2008). Such local responses are frequently characterized as reactions to the failure of federal immigration policy, but they are also fundamentally battles about who belongs to the community and the local sense of place. Understanding the dynamics of new destinations is essential to understanding issues of contemporary immigration debate because these communities have become some of the most vocal and influential players in immigration politics.

Among in-depth examinations of new destinations (Lamphere 1992; Fink 2003; Hirsch 2003; Millard, Chapa, and Burillo 2004; Smith 2006; Jones 2008),[9] *Beyond the Borderlands* offers a distinct approach to U.S.-Mexico migration studies because it provides an in-depth examination of the perspectives and influence of both the English-speaking community in the United States and the non-migrating Mexicans in the sending community. This combined approach has uncovered distinct insights into the evolving cultural practices of U.S.-born residents and Mexicans in the early years of the formation of the new destination. It also points to the important influence of the U.S. citizen population on migrants' perceptions of belonging and exclusion in the newly emerging multiethnic community.

In 1995 when I set out to document everyday life for Mexican families settling in Kennett Square, I quickly found that I could not fully understand these events unless I was willing to pay attention to the role of the English-speaking majority in shaping Mexican experiences of emplacement and belonging. My work quickly expanded from a study of a settlement enclave to one about the relationships between the English-speaking majority and Mexican settlers. *Beyond the Borderlands* examines the English-speaking majority's responses to Mexican settlement, which at times seemed paradoxical and contradictory. Although there were overt strategies that appeared to incorporate Mexican families in the community, it was clear that a number of unspoken rules governed who did and did not belong in Kennett Square and that these rules clearly favored the English-speaking majority and marginalized Mexican families struggling to find their place in the community.

Accessing the immigrant community in Kennett Square, however, was not a simple process. In late 1995, I discovered a nonprofit migrant health clinic and a social service agency, Project Salud and La Comunidad Hispana, respectively. These agencies served as my first introduction to the Mexican community, and they were recognized among Mexican settlers as the places to go when in need of health care and social services or to find help negotiating the complex cultural landscape that was Kennett Square. Drawing upon the resources of La Comunidad Hispana and Project Salud, I was also able to collect essential information about Mexicans who were settling in Kennett Square. The agencies collected demographic data on their client population, including where they were from in Mexico, the average age and family size, and where they were living in Kennett Square.

The fall of 1995 was a tense time in Kennett Square, as it was the peak of racial and ethnic tension between Mexicans and their English-speaking neighbors. Since April 1993, when mushroom workers at Kaolin Mushroom Farms went on strike and demanded better wages and working conditions, there had been a noticeable tension in the community.[10] The strike marked the first time that Mexican workers demonstrated that they were no longer the accommodating and often invisible workforce that farm owners and townspeople had previously known.[11] After the strike, small protests erupted from the English-speaking community. Though most of these were largely nonviolent social protests, they offended and alienated many of the town's Mexican population.

These tensions made my early years in the field challenging. I found that many in the English-speaking community were suspicious of my work and my position as an outsider who they feared might unfairly judge their community, and some Mexican settlers were reluctant to speak with an unfamiliar *gringa* who wanted to know so many details of their lives and experiences. To overcome these barriers, I drew upon my previous career experience as a registered nurse and volunteered at Project Salud. In the process of vaccinating children, completing paperwork, and translating for physicians, I became a familiar face to the Mexican community. The administrator and staff of Project Salud had positive and long-standing relationships with mushroom farm owners and Kennett townspeople, and the clinic's willingness to support my research was perhaps one of my greatest resources in the field, as it allowed me to find my own place in this dynamic community.

As I observed Mexican families in their settlement efforts, I realized that many families were also maintaining homes and continuing to build relationships in Textitlán. In 1999, I joined families returning to Textitlán for the fiesta season, and I discovered a startling aspect of their lives in their natal home: as a group, migrants' and settlers' position in Textitlán was tenuous and returning families engaged in significant efforts to maintain their place there. I had expected the opposite, that homecomings would be a welcome reprieve from their efforts to emplace themselves in Pennsylvania. My early observations of life in Textitlán revealed that the non-migrating community often viewed these men and women as defectors of a sort. They were envied for their successes but also criticized for "abandoning" their home community to work in the United States.[12] In short, although Mexicans living in Kennett Square were maintaining ties to both communities, they were doing so only with great effort.

MEXICAN SETTLEMENT AND THE RENEGOTIATION OF PLACE AND BELONGING

My examination of Mexican migration and settlement focuses on the transformation of sense of place in Kennett Square and Textitlán. In both ethnographic contexts, I examine the mobile population of Textitlanecos and their relationships with their non-migrating neighbors in Mexico and the native-born population in the United States. My premise is that sense of place develops as newcomers move into (or out of) a place and is dependent on the types and quality of relationships that they build and maintain in the places where they live (Cresswell 1996; Mulgan 2009).

Place is "space made culturally meaningful"; it is the lived context for all human activity and cultural processes (Low 1994: 66). Examinations of sense of place include an assessment of lived experiences and the distinctive characteristics that are associated with place identities. It also references the subjective and emotional attachments that people associate with a place (Agnew 1987). More important, sense of place considers how humans shape the places they inhabit and how places similarly influence human social interactions and cultural processes (Cresswell 2004).[13] Places are intimately experienced, and the sense of place is often described as feeling rooted, attached, or belonging to a place (Tuan 1974,

1977). It is broader than an emotional and cognitive experience, however. Sense of place includes, and emerges from, cultural beliefs and practices that are embedded within particular places (Merrifield 1993; Basso 1996; Low 2000).

Sense of place also recognizes that locales are not necessarily limited by the physical world but can be bounded cognitively through perceptions of belonging and exclusion. These sensate boundaries constitute what folklorist Kent Ryden has termed the "invisible landscape," which he argues is mapped through the exploration of vernacular cultural practices and narrative traditions (1993). Emplacement and belonging are part of this invisible landscape, but in a new destination the invisible landscape is also problematic because immigrants often engage in a sense of belonging that is not limited to one place and is produced through memories as well as the adaptation of cultural practices that were common in the homeland.[14]

Fundamental to the sense of place are the feelings of belonging that Mexicans and long-term residents in Mexico and the United States associate with the places they call home. Belonging is a basic human need (Baumeister and Leary 1995; Young, Russell, and Powers 2004; Mulgan 2007, 2009), but it is not a naturalized state; rather, it is socially constructed and negotiated. It is a process through which "people reflexively judge the suitability of a given site as appropriate given their social trajectory and their position in other fields" of experience (Savage, Bagnall, and Longhurst 2005: 12). In new destinations, issues of belonging become a twofold challenge. Local social contexts shift with the introduction of the new population, making new destinations "new" for newcomers and longer-term residents alike. New residents understandably struggle to belong, but the same can be true for those who have lived their entire lives in what has become the new destination. In many instances, longer-term residents experience a type of localized displacement, a feeling that their "home" is no longer a familiar and predictable place, thus making it difficult to embrace the changes taking place around them.[15] Kennett Square's longer-term residents reacted to the changes in their community with a sense of privilege. Because they were "here first," they frequently assumed that their residential longevity justified local divisions of power and the subordinate position of Mexican settlers. As a group they dominated social relations, controlled local resources, and determined which residents would have access to various places in town and the circumstances of that access.

It is in this context that Kennett Square's longer-term population enacted a variety of spatial practices that were employed to manage and limit Mexican settlers in their attempts to shape the local sense of place. Spatial practice refers to space that is appropriated and inhabited by people and institutions though quotidian practices, behaviors, and activities (Lefebvre 1991: 8; Merrifield 1993; Cleaveland and Pierson 2009). Examining spatial practice forces a recognition that sense of place emerges and is shaped by the structure and hierarchy of social relations (Soja 1989; Lefebvre 1991; Massey 2005). It includes the privileging of some according to social class, educational attainment, and facility with the English language and the subordination of others who lack these attributes. In the chapters that follow, I analyze spatial practices in order to reveal the mechanism of privilege operating within the dominant population in the development of sense of place in Kennett Square and Textitlán and to demonstrate how Mexican settlers contest these arrangements through narrative and cultural practices (Scott 1990; Lefebvre 1991).

New destinations such as Kennett Square offer an exceptional opportunity to see how events and practices shape the development of sense of place. By adopting this approach, *Beyond the Borderlands* addresses one of the limitations associated with many sense of place studies: representing "place" as a homogeneous local community while at the same time de-emphasizing the pathways through which sense of place develops. Too often sense of place studies emphasize "memory, stasis, and nostalgia," and relegate place to "an essentialist concept which held within it the temptation of relapsing into past traditions, of sinking back into (what was interpreted as) the comfort of Being instead of forging ahead with the (assumed progressive) project of Becoming" (Massey 1994: 119).[16] These interpretations emphasize place stability and minimize place-making as a process, and at the same time they assume a core local identity that is constant and has a long-term historical presence. Even more problematic is the idea that there can be only one sense of place and that all members of a community experience place equally (Massey 1993: 65; Massey 2005).[17]

Folklorists often take one of two perspectives in their analyses of place: drawing on narrative studies, they reconstruct a sense of place that is rooted in the past and is frequently characterized as threatened by a social or economic transformation.[18] They have also analyzed narrative accounts to reconstitute a present-day sense of place that appears to be stable or unchanging. In both instances, these sense of place studies celebrate place stability rather than examine how, and under what circumstances, sense of place emerges and transforms. One reason for this is that folklorists' work emphasizes the emic perspective of their informants, who in some cases have already constructed an idea of place stability. Thus the folklorist reconstitutes the sense of place as it is interpreted by his or her informants: bounded or isolated, unchanging, and rooted in the past.[19] This is exactly what I encountered when I began working with Kennett Square's English-speaking population.[20] Although I document the sense of place that was described by the English-speaking majority, I also argue that this account of sense of place largely ignores local power relationships and minimizes the fact that residents always actively construct places and local environments that are continually transforming.

Folklorists are not alone in the tendency to emphasize place stability. Doreen Massey's aforementioned comments on the problematics of place are an assessment of the work of human geographers, a critique reiterated by others in her field (Pred 1984). The classical texts of anthropology are also sometimes "cited to justify popular conceptions of place homologous with ideas of boundedness, homogeneity, and exclusion" (McKay 2006a: 198). Similarly, Gupta and Ferguson's (1992, 1997) work on the politics of difference critiques the study of space and place in anthropology, particularly those studies that assume that the "distinctiveness of societies, nations and cultures [is] . . . based upon a seemingly unproblematic division of space, on the fact that they occupy 'naturally' discontinuous spaces" (1992: 6).

Sense of place is the product of ongoing negotiations, and as such, when it is assumed that places are stable, it effectively diminishes the role of power relations and the ways in which conflict, hierarchies, and exclusion are created and maintained. In new destinations, it is common for longer-term residents to accuse newcomers of changing *their* communities, often for the worse.[21] In these instances, concerns about community change are drawn upon to create discourses of local identity and history that establish who belongs and to legitimize the exclusion of immigrants (Harvey 1996).

Newcomers are likely to meet different types of welcome, or opposition, to their arrival depending on how they fit into the accepted ideas of local identity. These responses are mediated by established residents and community leaders and their perception of the newcomers and include their preconceived ideas of who the newcomers are as a group, how new arrivals will transform the community, and how they wish to enact their position as longer-term residents to shape the identity and direction of the community. Recently settled migrants, for instance, might be characterized as a threat to the local sense of place (Lattanzi Shutika 2005) or as a local asset that can revitalize a community (Grey and Woodrick 2005; Hernández-León and Zúñiga 2005), or they may be met with ambivalence (Rich and Miranda 2005; Lattanzi Shutika 2008). It is also possible that settlers can provoke all three responses, at different times, in the same community.[22]

David Harvey (1996) posits that place and its interpretations become more significant in the context of expanding global market forces as they reshape perceptions of space and time, and they have distinct bearings on local power structures. Resisting the taken-for-granted notion that mobile capital and expanded mass communication necessarily render places less distinct or that sense of place is less important to human experience (see Meyrowitz 1985), Harvey argues that places are actually more significant in the context of globalization. This is because even as the globalized world may seem smaller and less distinct, people are more likely to think about their place in the world and have a greater appreciation of the places where they live and work. The restructuring of spatial relations through globalization certainly poses particular challenges to places, but it neither destroys them nor lessens their significance.

Instead, expanding global markets compel residents to see their place as actively competing with other places for mobile capital, making residents become more aware, and often concerned, about what their place can offer. They are also more likely to have a heightened focus on what makes their place exceptional: who lives there, how residents affect the appearance and quality of the community, and how local resources might be engaged to attract outside business and investment. Concomitantly, residents are likely to become hostile or defensive toward people and events that are viewed as a threat to the distinctiveness of their place (Harvey 1996).[23]

In Kennett Square, the introduction of a rapidly growing Mexican population forced longer-term residents to take stock of their community. When Mexican settlers were few in number and largely invisible, their presence caused little concern for the English-speaking majority. When the population expanded to the point where their presence was obvious and they began to reshape the sense of place, many in the majority population expressed concern that Mexicans would diminish, or perhaps destroy, their historic community.

CREATING AND MAINTAINING A SENSE OF BELONGING

The sense of belonging is constituted through shared meanings and a sense of social alliance between people and the places where they reside: it does not necessarily reference a geographic location but can include places that are physical, virtual, or imagined. A sense of belonging enables people to feel like they belong to a place, which in turn allows them to rely on cultural practices to establish and maintain social, political, and economic relationships. The development of the sense of belonging is the result of the activities that people employ to emplace themselves in new and everyday situations; it is a process that consists of multiple strategies that newcomers draw upon to develop relationships and form social networks. These social networks in turn promote cultural expression and social support. Drawing on a framework of emplacement and belonging, we can consider Mexican settlers' relationships to one another, to the citizen community in the United States, and to their homeland. It redirects attention from internal, bounded local processes to the construction sense of place as a multifaceted dynamic processes that acknowledges that there is no solitary place identity but rather a multiplicity thereof, and that boundaries between places are constructed and maintained through social processes that are the product of human construction and not natural features of the social or physical environment.

Though this study explores the Mexican experience of immigration in order to illustrate the process of immigrant incorporation, it is important to recognize that the emplacement and belonging experience is not exclusively the project of the newly arrived immigrant; it is a shared process between newcomers and longer-term residents, and it reveals how local populations are simultaneously transformed as migrant settlers establish themselves in the community and become part of it. Indeed, anyone experiencing a recent move to a new place can feel a sense of displacement while adjusting to and fitting into the new locale. Belonging can be distinguished from popular notions of assimilation, a process associated with transformation and shedding one's cultural heritage; assimilation is often expected of immigrants as a condition of belonging to a local community or to claim a legitimate place in American society.[24] Belonging, in contrast, is constituted through human connections to the places one inhabits and is influenced by the newcomer as well as his or her longer-term neighbors and their shared experiences (Buonfino and Thompson 2007; Mulgan 2007, 2009).[25]

Living in the suburbs of Washington, DC, I have observed some of my neighbors, particularly military families, exhibit an impressive ability to situate themselves and establish a sense of belonging. Military families stationed here are regularly uprooted (typically every two to three years), so in order to feel at home and survive the emotional upheaval that accompanies frequent moves, they must learn to engage each new place and establish connections quickly. When my friend Kelly Wallace, the wife of a career Army officer, moved back to Virginia she explained, "When we move in, I unpack and get everything set up [in the house] right away. We've done it so often that I can typically get my house set up in two weeks; then we start to get involved with our neighborhood, the school."

In everyday life, people actively engage one another to confirm and reaffirm their sense of belonging in ways that are often unnoticed. Indeed, our consciousness of our efforts to belong all but disappears in many everyday situations. It is the unanticipated transgression of belonging, for instance, recognizing a person who is seemingly in the wrong place, adjusting to living in a different town, or feeling out of place when living in a new apartment after a divorce, that forces our recognition of not belonging and how we work to adapt to our surroundings. This is sometimes the case in neighborhoods where many of the homes are rental properties. When people are constantly coming and going, concerns about belonging are often minimized or put off for the time when life is more "permanent."

The social practices that encompass the sense of belonging include initiation rituals and ceremonies that mark rites of passage. Belonging can be expressed through institutional structures, such as the observance of the Roman Catholic sacraments throughout the life cycle. It also includes informal behaviors that are not mandated but nevertheless expected if one is to maintain ties to the people and places where one lives. Activities such as maintaining regular contact with friends and neighbors, attending company picnics, joining the school P.T.O., and otherwise keeping up with one's social "obligations" are in themselves essential to maintaining a sense of belonging to one's neighborhood or group.

BELONGING AND THE TRANSLOCAL

When I entered Kennett Square for the first time it was immediately obvious that the town was in the midst of a transition. The sense of place had become unpredictable as English-speaking and Mexican residents sought new ways to interpret their community. As Mexicans settled in greater numbers, it seemed that the community was changing dramatically; it was also apparent that neither group could rely on old assumptions regarding how to interact with its neighbors.

One might assume that the effort involved with developing a sense of belonging after a move would ensure that it could rarely be produced in more than one place. Certainly, once one has moved from one community to another it is rare to maintain deep or significant connections with the majority of people who have been left behind. Yet many of the Mexican families in Kennett Square that I observed were engaged in a form of multilocal belonging: the process of immersing themselves in and maintaining ties to Kennett Square and their natal community simultaneously. For this reason, Textitlán cannot be characterized as simply a migrant "sending" community, because it continues to figure prominently in the day-to-day lives of Mexicans who have settled in Kennett Square, and it is in many ways the center of Mexican life. Many Mexican families return, as often as possible, to visit their families and friends. However, Mexican settlers still consider Textitlán home, not simply a place to visit. These families often maintain houses in Textitlán, and they regularly return to participate in the social and spiritual life of the village, even as they actively build their lives in Kennett Square.

In this respect, the ongoing connections between Kennett Square and Textitlán can be characterized as creating a transnational community, that is, a group of people for whom everyday life centers on the simultaneous engagement in the social life of two places. Kennett Square and Textitlán constitute a type of "transnational social space" (Basch, Glick Schiller, and Szanton Blanc 1994; Pries 1999; Faist and Ozveren 2004; Smith 2006), but I do not use the term "transmigrant" to identify these men and women in the conventional sense. The terms "transnational" and "transmigrant" carry specific associations and meanings about the nature of social and cultural processes within immigrant populations, and many of these are not reflective of this particular group (see Glick Schiller, Basch, and Szanton 1992 and Rouse 1992 for a review of the more common definitions of "transnationalism" and "transmigrant"). For instance, most studies define transmigrants as a group of people that self-identifies as a single community that lives in two distinct places.[26] This is clearly not the case in Textitlán or Kennett Square. Textitlán is a large township with an economically and socially diverse population of forty-eight thousand, of which over half of the adult population has elected to migrate to the United States at least one time for work.[27] Similarly,

Kennett Square's Mexican population, although largely from Textitlán, has also attracted small numbers of Mexicans from San Miguel Arcángel,[28] several other townships that are adjacent to Textitlán, and a small number from Toluca, located in the state of Mexico.[29]

The connections that Mexican settlers maintain within Textitlán and Kennett Square are also much more fragile than those typically described in the scholarship on transnational communities; the experiences on the ground in Kennett Square and Textitlán reveal a complex expression of binational existence that does not easily fit into the conventional understanding of transnational processes. In neither Kennett Square nor Textitlán can these men and women rest on the assumption that they have a taken-for-granted place or that they truly belong. In this respect, *Beyond the Borderlands* stands apart from other binational studies of Mexican migration in that it highlights the precarious situation of these men and women as they maintain their connections in two places. The Mexican settlers in Kennett Square are in a sense transmigrants based on the fact that their lives are a series of journeys between two locales, but at the same time, lived experiences and cultural practices common in Kennett Square and Textitlán have evolved into a distinct binational existence (Hirsch 2003; Smith 2006). Their experiences in Mexico and the United States are also shaped largely in the context of each community's local milieu; this book explores their efforts to belong to two distinct, but deeply connected, places.

Textitlán and Kennett Square do not form a conventional transnational social space, but instead form one that can more accurately be described as translocal: a local-to-local spatial dynamic (Ma 2002). Translocal places are those whose social relations and local communities have been reshaped through transnational dynamics (Conradson and McKay 2007). I use the term "translocal" to acknowledge that the local is an important ongoing source of meaning and identity for Mexican settlers, that migrants form multifaceted connections that link them to Kennett Square and Textitlán in distinct and complex ways and as a result generate a set of discursive and spatial practices that can reconfigure and transform the cultural landscape and power relations in both locales (Mandaville 1999; McKay 2006b).

In order to uncover the translocal processes of emplacement and belonging, this study examines the migration sending and receiving communities, Textitlán and Kennett Square, as coequals. There were multiple benefits of conducting this study in these communities. Fieldwork in both locations provided ethnographically informed insights to Mexican life across borders. The multisite approach also provided access to a broader range of cultural practices: I was able to witness settlers reconstitute their lives in both cultural fields and in a variety of social contexts. *Beyond the Borderlands* explores three questions about the nature of belonging and sense of place in the context of Mexican settlement: How is belonging, particularly multilocal belonging, produced through daily experiences? How is sense of place structured through spatial practices during settlement in new destinations as well as sending communities? How are ideas about belonging utilized at particular moments to explicitly establish collective identities or to legitimize claims to territory?

FIELD SITES

Kennett Square: The Mushroom Capital

The first time I drove into Kennett Square in October 1995, I was looking for Mexicans. I wanted to begin an ethnographic study of the effects of migration on family life, and my friend Dona, a lifelong Philadelphian, had told me there was a Mexican migrant community in nearby Kennett Square.[30] Dona explained that Kennett Square was locally known as the "Mushroom Capital of the World," and the industry depended on Mexican labor. I decided to drive to Kennett one rainy afternoon, but as I surveyed the town I found no indication of a Mexican presence. There were no Mexican restaurants or grocery stores, and I did not see anyone who was identifiably Mexican on the streets. What I did find was a quaint rural town, one obviously wealthy and well maintained. I had no trouble finding indications of the local mushroom industry, however, including a prominent mushroom museum along U.S. Route 1. There were images of mushrooms just about everywhere, but there were no signs of, or allusions to, how the mushrooms were harvested and by

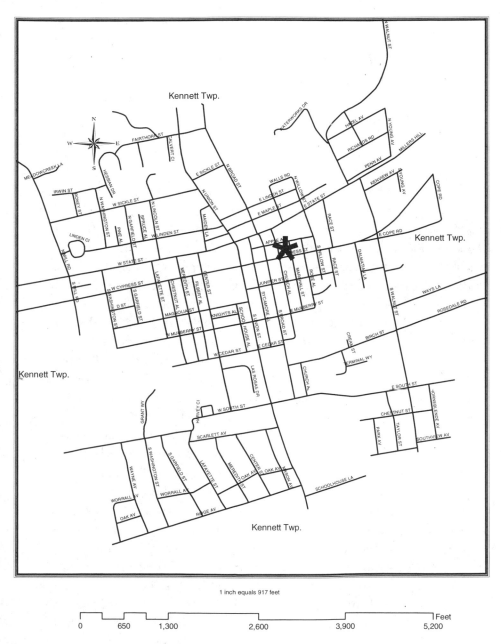

Figure 1. Borough of Kennett Square

whom. When I returned to Philadelphia that afternoon, I called Dona and told her that she must have been mistaken; there were no Mexicans in Kennett Square. She chuckled and said, "Now you know why the Mexicans are known as Chester County's best-kept secret."

During the following months I returned to Kennett Square often, and through my persistence I eventually discovered where Mexican settlers lived and worked. I had come to Kennett expecting to find seasonal migrant workers, mainly young men, who had come to work and left their families in Mexico. Instead, I found a growing population of Mexican families who had decided to settle permanently in Kennett Square, as well as a number of single men who were migrating seasonally but also considering moving their families north. At that time, most of the Mexican residents of the village lived in trailers; some lived in the dilapidated apartments on the edge of town. Single men most often bunked in farm barracks, tucked neatly away from the casual observer. They were living in Kennett but were not part of the town in any real sense.

Although Mexican residents seemed invisible, I realized that their marginal place in Kennett Square was part of a historical precedent for mushroom workers in the town. Like other communities in the United States that depend on migrant farm labor, the Kennett Square workforce has historically consisted of persons who have few employment options. Mushrooming, like other forms of agricultural production, is a labor-intensive endeavor and requires a steady supply of able-bodied laborers who are willing to work all night in the dark, dank buildings where mushrooms are grown. Thus it is not surprising that the workforce historically has drawn from recently arrived immigrants and the working poor: Italians at the turn of the century, African Americans, low-income Caucasians from Appalachia, then Puerto Ricans, and most recently, Mexican nationals from the state of Guanajuato (Bustos 1994a,b; Garcia 1997).[31]

Kennett Square is situated thirty miles southwest of Philadelphia and twenty miles west of Wilmington, Delaware. Located in Chester County, one of Pennsylvania's wealthiest counties, Kennett Square has been the home of the nation's largest commercial mushroom industry for the last century. Despite its rural ambiance and history as a farming community, Kennett Square is a sophisticated town that is home to a number of upscale boutiques and restaurants and maintains its own symphony orchestra. The village is approximately one square mile, and it is home to 5,273 residents of whom 1,154 were Mexican (U.S. Census Bureau 2000).[32] Politically, Kennett Square, like surrounding Chester County, is known as a conservative community and Republican Party stronghold. Founded as a Quaker settlement in 1855, Kennett also has a local reputation of being a more socially progressive community than its neighbors, a point that is frequently emphasized by local residents. Locally produced histories of the town, for example, often emphasize the role the community played in the Underground Railroad (Taylor 1998, 1999; Kashatus 2003).

Kennett Square is governed by an elected borough council, which in turn selects the mayor (a non-salaried official).[33] Kennett Square was an aging town, with 75 percent of the population eighteen years of age or older (U.S. Census Bureau 2000). Of the 3,621 students enrolled in the Kennett Consolidated School District in 2000–2001, 68 percent were white, 24 percent Hispanic/Latino, 5 percent African American, and 3 percent unspecified. Kennett's diversity, a point of pride for many local residents, stands in stark contrast to the neighboring Unionville/Chadds Ford School District.[34] In the same year, that student body consisted of 95 percent white, 2.89 percent Asian American, 1.3 percent Hispanic/Latino, and 0.76 percent African American students (Pennsylvania Department of Education Statistics 2000–2001).

The first large-scale mushroom farm in Kennett Square was owned and operated by J. B. Swayne in the late 1800s. Swayne's business was successful, and his neighbors in the county began to follow his lead—initially producing mushrooms in converted greenhouses that were adapted to the needs of mushrooms. More mushrooms are produced within a ten-mile radius of the town than in any comparable place in the world, which is why it is known as the "Mushroom Capital" (Weiss 1995: 6J).

Modern mushroom farms are referred to as "mushroom houses." They are windowless single-story cinder block buildings equipped with elaborate temperature and humidity controls, which make the air in the mushroom houses dank and stale year-round. Mushroom cultivation requires a dark cool environment and the malodorous mushroom soil.

The soil is seeded with mushroom spores, from which the mushrooms grow (Weiss 1995: 6J). When they are ready for harvest, pickers must clear all the mushrooms from the house in one day. Most mushroom houses consist of three tiers (from ground level to eight feet above). Though this arrangement allows for the maximum growth area in each house, it makes the job of cutting the mushrooms physically demanding. Workers must both stoop and climb as they pick mushrooms, all the while balancing on narrow catwalks or standing astride two beds while they pick mushrooms on the higher tiers. In general, mushroom pickers reported being paid by the bucket (approximately five gallons of mushrooms) rather than the hour. The men reported that they preferred this arrangement, as it enabled a fast picker to earn more money. The mushroom pickers, or "hongeros," I interviewed reported making between $8 and $10 per hour and working between twelve and fourteen hours in one shift, six to seven days per week.[35]

When I began this project in the mid-1990s, mushrooms were the number one cash crop in the Commonwealth of Pennsylvania, as they are today (Clark 1994: 1; Stefanou 2008). But Kennett Square's success as a mushroom producer has little to do with some of the common reasons that regions become successful in agriculture: it is neither the climate nor the soil that makes mushroom production amenable to this part of Pennsylvania. Rather, it is its location, near the largest market of mushroom consumers in the country—the Boston to Washington, DC, corridor—that makes Kennett Square and the surrounding county an ideal location for mushroom production (Redd 1994: 19). At the time of this study, there were approximately eighty farms in the Kennett Square area, which produced 40–45 percent of the mushrooms consumed in the United States (Clark 1994: 1).

Mexican migration into the community began as early as 1958 and evolved into a steady pattern of seasonal migration to the area between 1968 and 1972 (Lattanzi Shutika 2005).[36] Beginning in the late 1960s, Kennett Square and the surrounding county saw a slow but steady increase in the population of Mexican men who have come to work in the mushroom industry. Then, in the late 1980s, the population of Mexican settlers surged dramatically, as women and children began reuniting with their husbands. The majority of Mexicans working in Kennett are from the industrial town of Textitlán, Guanajuato.

For years, Kennett Square residents viewed having men who would travel into Kennett during the peak mushrooming months between October and March as an acceptable and a desirable consequence of being the hometown of a thriving agribusiness. The majority of the laborers between 1968 and 1990 were men who were housed out of sight on farm property in trailers or barracks, where they worked, ate, and lived together. While many of these men worked in Kennett for years, sometimes for a decade or more, their families and lives remained in Mexico. In this sense, although they were an essential part of the mushroom industry, most of them never considered Kennett Square "home." Oral histories I collected from the earliest migrants to Kennett emphasize that their lives were entirely work centered.[37] At times working twenty hours a day, seven days a week, these men accepted the hardships and poor working conditions as a matter of course. One migrant recalled his early years as an *honguero* (mushroom picker): "I worked hard, my life here was pure work, but I knew it would end. I could rest at home [in Mexico] and I would have money for my family" (Camacho interview January 20, 2000).

These seasonal migrants fit well into the hierarchical social structure of Kennett Square. In this sense, the local body politic has always situated the Mexican labor force in a liminal position in the community, a place that has been more or less rigidly fixed. Migrant workers were routinely excluded from community events, like the annual Mushroom Festival. "We knew our place well," said former *honguero* Joel Luna of his early years in Kennett Square on the fringe of the community (quoted in Corchado 1999: 1). Mexicans "belonged" to fulfill a specific purpose, picking mushrooms, but otherwise they were considered transients, and therefore were never intended to be fully accepted members of the local community. Similarly, most of these men never intended to stay.

After they received amnesty and legal permanent residency in 1986, many of the then-seasonal migrants elected to settle in Kennett Square and the surrounding county, and shortly thereafter were joined by their wives and children. Why did these seasonal workers decide to bring their families north? Settling in Kennett Square became an attractive option for these men, and for Mexican migrant workers throughout the United States. Durand et al. (1999) note that the IRCA offered these seasonal migrants the possibility of establishing a secure and legal family and work life in the United States at a time of severe inflation and unemployment in Mexico. Similarly, the IRCA included several provisions that compelled former migrants to stay in the United States for extended periods, such as English and civics classes that were required in order to obtain their permanent legal residency papers (Durand et al. 1999, 2000). Innovations in mushrooming allowed more farms to offer year-round employment; these events coalesced to transform the long-established seasonal migration pattern in Kennett Square into widespread settlement of former migrant workers and their families.[38]

Since 2001, the Mexican population has transformed considerably. Most notably, there have been younger, undocumented families moving into the area. These men and women are often the children of career migrants. In many cases, their parents were legal permanent residents of the United States, but these adult children were not able to procure work visas. They have decided to live permanently in Pennsylvania with the hope that they will have an opportunity to become legal residents in the future. Although their stories are important, their arrival began just as my fieldwork was ending. For this reason, I have not included them as part of this study.

TEXTITLÁN, GUANAJUATO: *PUEBLO TEXTÍL* (TEXTILE PUEBLO)

Textitlán, the original home of many Kennett Square workers, sits at the far southwest corner of the state of Guanajuato. The *municipio* (county)[39] consists of a central pueblo (village) surrounded by some thirty rural farming communities called *ranchos*. The pueblo hosts a population of forty-eight thousand (Instituto Nacional de Estadística, Geografía e Informatica de Mexico 2000) and is home to a thriving garment industry. Textitlán was founded in 1805 as an unincorporated settlement. The territory had been part of the Purépecha (Tarascan) territory, but indigenous

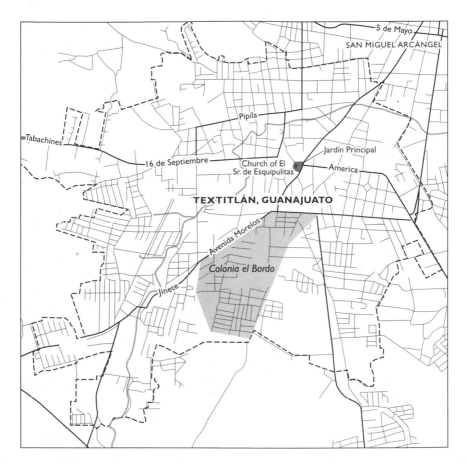

Figure 2. Textitlán, Guanajuato Mexico, and Colonia El Bordo

peoples had moved out of the area well before the nineteenth-century resettlement began.

Textitlán is known throughout the Mexican republic as a producer of the *rebozo*, the traditional shawl worn by Mexican women. In the 1980s, local rebozo producers began expanding their textile production to include acrylic fabric for sweaters and children's apparel. Within a decade Textitlán became one of the leading manufacturers of domestic apparel in Mexico (Gúzman-Zavala 1985).

The garment industry has transformed the pueblo into a major industrial center, drawing thousands of Mexicans from neighboring states and municipalities to purchase clothing for personal use or for sale in retail stores in other parts of Mexico. The textile and garment industries have made Textitlán one of the wealthiest municipios in the state of Guanajuato, and there is little doubt that cash earned in the United States helped develop and sustain these industries. Although wages for textile laborers and seamstresses during the time of this study were high, ranging between 800 and 1,000 pesos per week ($80–$100 U.S.), the wages earned in the United States by migrants were still significantly higher. For this reason, many of the owners of textile and garment businesses are former migrants who worked in the United States long enough to raise money to initiate, or in some cases expand, their businesses.

In many respects, Textitlán is atypical of migrant sending communities in Mexico.[40] For now it is important to understand that the success of the garment industry makes it possible for residents of Textitlán (Textitlanecos) to live a relatively comfortable life in Mexico. Thus the decisions that Textitlanecos make as they move north are usually prompted by factors other than poverty. These include raising money to build a house or capital to start a business, but perhaps most significantly, many of the Mexican settlers in Kennett Square have expressed a desire to transcend the social and economic hierarchy into which they were born. The Textitlanecos whom I have met in Kennett Square could be described as distinctly ambitious; the fact that most do not need to migrate to move out of poverty is something that I believe colors their ongoing relationships with their homeland.

CHAPTER OUTLINE

Beyond the Borderlands's ethnographic present spanned the years from 1995 to 2005, the main period of my fieldwork and the height of conflict over Mexican settlement and the debate about migration in public life in Kennett Square. This time frame also coincided with the bicentennial of the founding of Textitlán, which ushered in a three-year period of celebrations and homecomings as well as debate about the pueblo's identity as a migrant community. Because it would be difficult to understand the everyday challenges of Mexicans living in the United States without a clear understanding of their homeland, I begin the book by describing essentially the midpoint of my fieldwork. The process of living alongside returning families, becoming a participant in their homecomings, and experiencing Textitlán firsthand illuminated my own understandings and insights to Mexican experiences in Pennsylvania. In Mexico I had expected the settlers' way of life to be a sharp contrast to what I had observed in Pennsylvania, but as I followed these women and men to their home community I was able to witness their efforts to re-emplace themselves in their natal community, observe the local conflict between migrants and their non-migrating neighbors, and become accustomed to the daily rhythms of the village. After I got back to the United States I also felt the pull to return to Textitlán, an experience that many Mexican settlers in Kennett Square had described during my previous years of fieldwork.

This account begins in Textitlán with my first long-term introduction to this community during the holiday season from December 1999 through March 2000. It historicizes the influence of immigration in this small industrial pueblo from the Bracero era (1942–1964) to 2005, examining how it emerged as a prosperous industrial town as a result of a strong entrepreneurial spirit and remittances from the United States. Chapter 2 offers an in-depth look at everyday life in Textitlán, outlining the history of the pueblo and the emergence of its prosperous garment industry. It also examines the relationships of Textitlán's residents in relation to the United States, as well as the social relationships between migrating and non-migrating neighbors. Drawing upon statistical data collected in 1999, this chapter presents a detailed portrait of migration and family life, but it is not a "data chapter" that relies primarily on statistical analysis. Rather, it is a statistically informed ethnographic account of Textitlán that is interspersed with historical data I gathered from oral histories and the pueblo's archival sources.

Chapter 3 explores issues of home and homecoming and the structure of migrant emplacement and belonging through *casas vacías*, vacant or abandoned houses. Many migrants leave their homes uninhabited for years while they work in the United States, but rarely are the houses empty. Instead, they are fully furnished and are maintained by a non-migrating family member who visits, cleans, and watches over the house regularly. While Textitlanecos are settling with their families in Pennsylvania, the casas vacías represent a material tie to their community and reveal much about the way the concept of "home" is defined by families who have settled in the United States. These houses play an important role in the lives of Mexicans who use the structures to maintain connections and develop social and familiar ties with their communities on both sides of the border.

The next two chapters return to the early years of Mexican settlement in Pennsylvania from 1995 to 1999, a time when Kennett's citizen population could no longer ignore the influence of the Mexican residents in their community. Chapter 4 provides an in-depth examination of daily life of Mexicans in Kennett Square and the emerging sense of place. It identifies three distinct periods of Mexican emplacement and belonging: Early Settlement and the Evolution of the New Destination (1994–1998), Being and Belonging (1999–2000), and finally Adaptation and Incorporation (2001–2005). It also describes how Mexican families negotiated their place in Kennett Square and eventually were able to restructure their social and cultural worlds and develop a sense of belonging.

Chapter 5 examines Kennett Square's English-speaking population's influences on Mexican belonging through organized social action, particularly through an exploration of the origins and effects of the grassroots social movement Bridging the Community. The Bridging movement was formed in response to community protests against Mexican settlement and was conceived as a means to integrate the rapidly diversifying Kennett Square community. However, the English-only forums and organizational structure of the movement made it largely inaccessible to local Mexicans. Drawing on the Bridging example, I explore the relationship between collective identity and social action to demonstrate how the English-speaking community's notions of the local body politic shaped the social movement so that it reinforced the English-speaking population's dominant position in the community and had a limited influence on encouraging Mexican emplacement and belonging.

Chapters 6 and 7 examine the functions of the festival in creating belonging and a sense of place for Mexicans in Kennett Square and Textitlán. Chapter 6 explores the spiritual lives of Textitlanecos within the context of return migration. Although returning to Textitlán is much anticipated by those who live in the United States, the economic affluence of migrants makes their homecoming uncertain. Thousands of *hijos ausentes* (the town's absent sons and daughters) return to the pueblo, creating tension and a local challenge to the pueblo's elite citizens: wealthy business owners and professionals who have never migrated. This return is examined as a journey in which Textitlanecos come together through their shared devotion to Esquipulitas, the town's patron. By participating in the annual pilgrimage in honor of Esquipulitas, the pueblo is able to reunite as a single community and find a place for those who return during the fiesta season.

In Kennett Square, the Cinco de Mayo festival initiated in 2001 was promoted as a means of welcoming Mexican settlers as members of the community. Chapter 7 traces the history of the event, which provided a public means of demonstrating acceptance of Mexican settlers, and as such was a turning point in local ethnic relations. Although Kennett Square's American residents were in charge of organizing the Cinco de Mayo festival, it nevertheless provided an occasion for Mexicans to have access to the public life of the town. This facilitated the process of belonging and opened the possibility that Mexicans could shape the sense of place in Kennett Square. Three years after it was initiated, however, the organizers moved the festival from Kennett's main street to back alleys and parking lots. This move, along with other festival changes, reflected a growing ambivalence on the part of the English-speaking majority toward their Mexican neighbors and the place they will eventually have in the life of the community.

In exploring the translocal ties between Textitlán and Kennett Square, it is possible to develop a sense of the Mexican families and their lives, particularly the multifaceted experiences of these contemporary immigrants in new destinations and their ongoing relationships with their homeland. Like Kennett Square, the United States is in the midst of a transition, and with it comes a heated, and often reactionary, debate about emigration from Mexico and Latin America. Amid the cries for radical changes to protect the nation's borders and the clamor to find the "roots" of local communities, there has been little substantial discussion about the changes in new destinations and what they mean for these communities.[41] Even less frequently discussed are the consequences the changes in these communities will bring to the nation.

As a nation of immigrants, the United States is at a crossroads. It has long been our custom to jealously guard our nation and local identities and to complain that the most recent group of newcomers threatens the very idea of American identity. Many communities across the United States today seem to be echoing the same message that immigrants at the turn of the early twentieth century also heard: you are too numerous, you are changing the very essence of American society, and we are not sure we want to accommodate you here. At the same time, there is a strong call by many to move these men and women quickly toward citizenship, assimilation, and ultimately to be more "like us."

As I reflect on the "border" that erupted in Herndon, and others that emerged in Manassas and other locations in the eastern United States that are so close to my home, I realize that yesterday's Kennett Square is in some ways today's Herndon or Manassas. Though we may anticipate where new destination communities will arise, it is less clear what potential local problems will spring up as a result. Kennett Square is not a perfect example of how a community should respond to a new destination settlement, but its story does provide many lessons about how these new immigrant communities can emerge and adapt. By examining the process of belonging for Mexicans in Kennett Square, *Beyond the Borderlands* also uncovers perhaps one of the less understood aspects of immigration: how newcomers find their places in their new home and maintain their places in the old and how the native-born population eventually adapts to their presence. Situated in the midst of national debate that seeks to determine the course of immigration to the United States for years to come, Kennett Square is an important example of how one community handled this transition. For other similar communities who are ready to face the reality of a changing and changed America, *Beyond the Borderlands* offers a model for how to approach the immigration "problem" and work toward creating a common belonging by understanding the translocal experiences common among Mexican immigrants in the United States today. In this sense, the story that follows is not a universal picture of what life in every new destination community might look like, but as Mexican (along with other Latino) populations increase in new places throughout the United States, it is likely that similar issues of place, identity, and belonging will emerge.

METHODOLOGY

This project began as a short-term undertaking, one that I expected to be a straightforward investigation into an emerging Mexican settlement in an unusual location. From this beginning, the project grew into a ten-year binational ethnographic study of belonging and the sense of place. It is based on long-term ethnographic fieldwork, oral history, and survey research. Because there were few book-length examinations of new destinations when I began, it was necessary to draw upon a number of research techniques to create a multilayered account of how the connections between the two communities affects belonging and the sense of place in each location.[42]

OBSERVATIONS

The ethnographic observations in Kennett Square were conducted between October 1995 and May 2001, with additional two- to three-day field visits in September 2001, May 2002, and May 2003. Although I returned to Kennett Square for these follow-up visits, my regular fieldwork in Kennett Square ended in May 2001 when I began systematic research in Textitlán.

In Kennett Square, the dispersed location of Mexican residents required that I select a number of field sites for observation. I began by observing the comings and goings of what was identified as the only community center, the migrant health clinic Project Salud, and the social service agency La Comunidad Hispana, which were housed in the same building. Although neither facility offered programs or space for social activities, they were widely recognized by the Mexican population as the first place that most newly settled families would visit, particularly families. I also attended community meetings and forums that addressed issues that directly related to the Mexican settlement.

Because I am a registered nurse and was licensed to practice in the Commonwealth of Pennsylvania, I was invited to observe in the office waiting rooms, to serve as an interpreter for English-speaking physicians during office visits, and to accompany community health workers during their outreach programs in the community. These informal observations were followed by a period of six months were I formally volunteered as part-time clinic nurse. When I was not working in the clinic, I conducted fieldwork in the apartment complexes where Mexican families lived, and when Buena Vista Townhomes opened in December 1998, I began fieldwork in that residential community as well. I continued to work in these sites until I left to conduct fieldwork in Mexico in December 1999. I returned from Mexico in March 2000 to complete fieldwork in Kennett Square through April 2001. Throughout my time in Kennett Square, I conducted fieldwork three to five days every week.

After my first field trip to Textitlán in 1999–2000, I made seven additional trips there for periods of one to four weeks to complete follow-up work during the times that immigrants are most likely to return: the fiesta season (January 8–31 each year) and during the summer months when their children are not in school. During these times I observed community events, including *jaripeos* (bull riding exhibitions), dances, masses, and street fairs. I was also invited to a number of private occasions hosted by Mexican families such as Christmas celebrations, posada processions, family dinners, birthday celebrations, and civil and religious wedding ceremonies.

INTERVIEWS

After a few weeks of observation in Kennett Square, I began to conduct formal tape-recorded interviews using a semi-structured instrument that employed oral history interview techniques. The questionnaire elicited information about family history, migration history, social history, education history, and job history, as well as specific questions about living in the United States and Mexico. Though I asked all informants the same set of questions, the interviews were open-ended and ranged from forty-five minutes to three hours in duration. I used a modified questionnaire for U.S.-born informants that elicited family and community history as well as opinions about migration, the mushroom industry, and community change.

I completed a total of 103 interviews during the term of the project. Of that total, fifty-five were completed with Mexican informants who lived in Kennett Square and fourteen were with members of Kennett Square's English-speaking population. The majority of Mexican interview subjects, forty-eight in all, were first-generation setters in Kennett Square. I interviewed slightly more women than men, fifty-four and forty-nine, respectively, and when possible, I interviewed spouses together. The fourteen interviews conducted with the English-speaking included long- and short-term residents: people who had lived in and around Kennett Square for as few as six years and as long as an entire lifetime, with the longest being ninety-three years. This group included doctors, nurses, social service workers, current and retired mushroom farm owners, and Kennett Square teachers and principals.

In Textitlán, I completed twenty-two semi-structured interviews. Of that group, six informants had never migrated to the United States. I also completed an additional twelve comprehensive oral histories for a total of thirty-four interviews. These interviews followed the same questionnaire that I used in the United States. The majority of oral histories were conducted with informants who were over forty years of age and had been migrating between Textitlán and Kennett Square for at least ten years.[43]

All informants, unless otherwise noted, are identified using pseudonyms. In some cases, informants specifically asked that I use their real names and I have honored those requests here; others who are identified by their real names are local public figures who were quoted here from published accounts, but were also willing to grant interviews for the project.

SURVEY RESEARCH

I traveled to Textitlán, Guanajuato, for a week in September 1999 to find housing, then embarked on a three-month field trip between December 1999 and March 2000 to complete survey and ethnographic research with the assistance of Payal Gupta, then a sociology doctoral student at the University of Pennsylvania. Working for the Mexican Migration Project (MMP) at the University of Pennsylvania and the Universidad de Guadalajara,[44] together we completed 168 household ethnosurveys of the work, migration, and family histories of a random sample of Textitlanecos who returned for the 1999–2000 holiday season, using the survey instrument and following the research protocols developed by the MMP.[45] The households were selected at random from a total of 1,440 households in the neighborhood where I was living.

The MMP employs an ethnosurvey instrument that follows a flexible semi-structured interview.[46] The MMP protocols stipulate that all researchers obtain identical information for each informant, but question wording and ordering are not fixed; the researcher is free to determine the precise phrasing and timing of each question based on the circumstances of the interview. The gathered information is cross-checked with local informants to ensure its validity.

The ethnosurvey elicited multiple types of information: basic social and demographic data for all people in the household and a year-by-year life history for household heads, including histories of childbearing, property and housing, business, and labor. It also collected information about the household head's most recent experiences in the United States, including border-crossing, relatives and friends who may have accompanied him or her, and relatives who are already present in the United States. Finally, the survey also elicited data on the household head's social ties with U.S. citizens, facility with the English language, occupational characteristics, and use of U.S. social services.

When the surveys were completed, they were sent to the Universidad de Guadalajara where they were coded by MMP staff. Once coded, the data were checked for informational and clerical errors. When all necessary corrections were completed, the data collected were released as part of the MMP 118 dataset, which includes two data files: the persfile, which includes individual level data and the housefile, which includes household level data. All of these data are available online at http://mmp.opr.princeton.edu/.

ANALYSIS

The methods and procedures employed for this project produced different kinds of data that required several forms of data analysis. The taped interviews were transcribed and coded, and a content analysis of field notes and interview transcripts was completed. The majority of survey data points used for analyses were nominal in nature. For example, these data were used to determine whether or not a descriptive characteristic of Textitlán compared to its neighbor, San Miguel Arcángel. Thus, nonparametric analyses were required. For ordinal data, chi-square analyses were used. For the few data points for which arithmetic means could be calculated, t-test analyses were conducted. Higher order analyses were not employed for this data set.

Although I collected and refer to statistical data in this study, it is at its core an ethnographic account. The statistical data should be considered a supplement to, not a substitute for, the ethnographic data. Conducting the survey door-to-door was valuable in that it brought me into contact with informants from all walks of life in Textitlán. The combined analyses produced a series of themes and theoretical classifications that allowed me to reconstruct a more nuanced picture of Mexican life in Textitlán and Kennett Square, which further shed light on the multiple ways that belonging and the sense of place develop in the context of migration.

TWO "I give thanks to God, after that, the United States"

EVERYDAY LIFE IN TEXTITLÁN

Textitlán sits in the far southwestern corner of the state of Guanajuato. The two-lane road that leads to the pueblo from the airport in Silao winds up and down steep hillsides before entering a wide valley that reveals a vast, sparsely populated countryside. Textitlán borders the pueblo of San Miguel Arcángel,[1] a smaller but older community; the two villages have grown together over the years, so today it is difficult to determine where Textitlán ends and San Miguel Arcángel begins. The pueblos have distinct governments, churches, and identities, however. Textitlán is neither a picturesque Mexican town nor a tourist destination, but this is not to say that the town lacks pleasant features. Resting on a mountain plateau at 5,938 feet (1,810 meters), there is an unobstructed view of the mountains surrounding the pueblo from nearly every rooftop, and the fountains and gardens in the central plaza are beautifully maintained.

In September 1999, I visited Textitlán for the first time. Although I was enthusiastic to know more about the hometown of the Mexicans with whom I had been working in Pennsylvania, I was also unsure of what I would find. Mexican settlers in Pennsylvania often reminisced about their hometown, but often these recollections provided only vague descriptions. "Everything is so beautiful there, the weather, they way we live. Here [in the United States] we're always working; in Textitlán we enjoy life," recalled Anita Gonzalez at the end of an interview one afternoon. The pueblo at first appeared to be a conventional, quiet Mexican village, but it is actually a multilayered social world that reflects the connections of the transnational experiences of its inhabitants. Immersing myself in the settlers' natal community allowed me to understand the complexities of adjustment and belonging in Kennett Square; it also revealed the unique ways Textitlanecos who live in Kennett Square develop multilocal belonging.

The detailed ethnographic portrait of Textitlán that follows is informed by demographic data about the village and its residents. This description is based upon my cumulative experiences in Textitlán from 1999 through 2005 and is intended to give a detailed picture of day-to-day life in the pueblo, particularly for anyone who has never explored Mexico beyond its well-known beaches and colonial tourist destinations. Although Textitlán shares some commonalities with other migrant sending villages in western Mexico, it differs in several important respects.[2] Most significant, it is a large, economically stable community of some fifty thousand residents that hosts a population of migrating and non-migrating families, some of whom are middle-class or wealthy *comerciantes* (business owners) and educated professionals, whereas the majority consists of working families of various means. The source of Textitlán's local economic stability is its garment industry, which provides many jobs and subsequently draws in new residents from other parts of Mexico who are looking for work within the republic. Also, since 2003, a small but increasingly visible population of Korean immigrants has also settled in the pueblo and has established its own garment manufacturing businesses.

It is the dynamic nature of Textitlán's garment industry that sets this village apart from other migrant sending communities. Although many

Textitlanecos have ventured to the United States in search of a better life, their economic successes rarely transfer into significantly increased social status in their home community, which is also different from the experiences of other Mexican sending communities. For instance, Luin Goldring (1997) notes that it is typical for returning migrants to have enhanced social status in their home communities, and that this is one of the more common reasons immigrants maintain ties to their home community.[3] This is a clear difference between Textitlán and other Mexican sending communities, for although immigrants return to the village wealthier, they are not centrally involved in local affairs, and their social status is little changed within the larger social milieu of the pueblo.[4]

Among the non-migrating population in Textitlán there is considerable ambivalence about migration to the United States, although there is little doubt that migration and its accompanying remittances have benefited this pueblo in many ways. Most obviously, households with a family member working abroad are often supported by remittances and as a result are wealthier, but returning Textitlanecos also infuse the local economy with migradollars (money earned in the United States) when they purchase goods and services upon their return, and others use their earnings to invest in local businesses and house construction. Although many of these same processes are at work in other sending communities, local investments have allowed the garment industry to flourish so that Textitlán's economy is not wholly dependent on remittances, nor has it become a "nursery and nursing home" community where the majority of young adults have left to find work in the United States (Rouse 1992). Migration to the United States has benefited and shaped this community in a unique way, which in turn has also influenced the experiences of returning Textitlanecos.

This chapter outlines everyday life in Textitlán and how Mexicans who have settled in Kennett Square and who return work to belong in both communities. The sense of belonging is always based on a particular social context and grounded in the human perception of familiar lived experience (Mulgan 2009). To understand how belonging and emplacement works, one must first understand how the familiar is distinguished from lived experiences that seem strange or unknown. I expound the day-to-day cultural practices that make this town "home" for Mexicans who have settled in Kennett but also highlight the distinctions between Textitlán and other Mexican communities with a history of migration to the United States.

AHORA YA NOS ENTIENDES
(NOW YOU UNDERSTAND US):
LIVING AND LEARNING TEXTITLÁN

Although they had never visited Textitlán, Americans who live in Kennett Square would often speculate about the living conditions in the pueblo, especially after I told them I would be living there with my family. "I can only imagine that it must be pretty bad there, considering the conditions that they live in here," a Kennett Square citizen told me one afternoon. "I mean, it's pretty terrible, the Center Street and Lafayette apartments [in Kennett Square],[5] and I know things *have* to be better for them here." Why, after all, would anyone give up something good in Mexico to live in inferior conditions in the United States? This assumption was fairly common among Kennett Square's English-speaking population, but it was far from accurate. Mexican lifestyles are quite different from those in the United States, but it would be inaccurate to interpret them as substandard or impoverished. Textitlanecos were often less concerned about amassing material wealth than they were in building strong family ties and maintaining their cultural traditions. During the term of my fieldwork, Textitlán's local economy was robust and provided ample employment for its residents for two reasons: the thriving garment industry that produces clothing for retail markets in the United States and Mexico and remittances from the substantial number of men and women working in the United States. What I found, then, was that most of the families were living comfortably, albeit modestly, and few were forced into migration to escape poverty.

I arrived in Textitlán for my first extended field visit with my husband Ken and our three-year-old twins Helen and John, along with returning migrants and settlers, in early December 1999. I was told it was a good year to be in Textitlán, as many more people had decided to come home and wait out the millennium than had been typical in years past. We moved into a house that we rented from a family I had known well in Pennsylvania. Our landlords, Mario and Ofelia, had put the care of the home in the hands of Ofelia's mother, Doña Elena, who became our first contact in the community.

Renting Ofelia's house was fortuitous in that it initiated my long-term relationship with Ofelia's parents and the extended Fernández family. Ofelia's brother, Omar, picked us up at the airport, and later her parents would become instrumental in assisting me with my work in Textitlán. I had never met Omar before arriving in Mexico, although I would have recognized him because of his resemblance to his siblings whom I had known in Kennett Square. Omar's heart-shaped face with its wide, friendly smile was immediately identifiable as a Fernández face. Still, Omar did not risk that I would not find him. When we passed through the customs doors burdened with our suitcases, boxes of research equipment, and two small children, Ken and I saw Omar standing just beyond the doors with a large sign that read "DEVORA." I waved to acknowledge him but felt a pang of discomfort. Years before I had realized that my name, Debra, was difficult to pronounce in Spanish and the alternatives, either Deborah or Debi, would be much easier for my Spanish-speaking informants. As I had long outgrown using the diminutive of my name, I settled on Deborah, overlooking the fact that the letters "b" and "v" are phonetically identical in spoken Spanish. The moment I saw Omar's sign I realized that in Mexico I would be known as "Devora," which in Spanish means "she devours." It was an association that I clearly did not relish. As it turned out, however, most everyone in Textitlán mistook Deborah for "Barbara," a more common name, when I introduced myself.[6]

Ken returned to his job in Philadelphia at the end of December, and by then the children and I felt settled into the house and neighborhood. I had started my survey work, the children were enrolled in the local public preschool, and I had hired Erica Ramírez, a pleasant, responsible young woman who was the daughter of a career migrant, to work for me as a full-time nanny and housekeeper. I was nervous about living alone with the children, certainly, but I also knew that I had support from Doña Elena and her family.

During the following months, I visited Doña Elena and her family in the evenings nearly every day. The children quickly became bored in our small rented house, and I was anxious for adult company after a long day working in the *colonia* (neighborhood) El Bordo, where I was doing door-to-door survey research.[7] Right before my husband returned to the United States, Doña Elena and her adult children made it clear that I should consider their home my own. One evening when the children and I were visiting, our former chauffeur Omar, who was an American citizen who continued to migrate seasonally, asked me to move in with his mother and father. "You really should think about living here with Mamá after your husband returns to the United States, Débora," he insisted. "We don't like the idea of you being in Ofelia's house alone." I appreciated Omar's consideration and the family's generosity, but I could not understand why they were so concerned about my living alone. I had already met many of my neighbors personally or I knew them through my connections with their extended family members in Pennsylvania. In my previous years working with Mexican migrants and settlers, I had always been treated with kindness and respect. The Mexican men in Pennsylvania were gentle, humble folk, so the warnings I received about being alone, or more commonly, that I should watch out for the men of Textitlán, seemed overstated.

For this reason I wasn't comfortable with the idea of moving in with the Fernández family at first. Their home was warm and inviting, but it was also always full of people, neighbors and family members visiting from the United States, and the Fernández adult children and grandchildren were forever coming and going. I doubted that if I did live there I would ever get any work done, and I knew I would never have privacy. Moreover, Doña Elena was a skilled raconteur. She and I spent many hours chatting together as it was, and I felt that I needed my own space and time alone to think, write, and review the materials I was collecting.

Once Ken returned to the United States, however, there were times when I questioned whether or not I had made the right decision. Helen and John were attending a Mexican preschool each day and were asleep by eight o'clock most evenings. Once they were in bed, I was alone in the house with little to do. From time to time a neighborhood woman would stop by to chat, but most evenings I was by myself, reviewing the oral history interviews and surveys I had completed that day or writing my field notes.

Although I found that most everyone in Textitlán was friendly, my closest friends were naturally the members of the Fernández family. Doña Elena and I became very close, and I often visited one of her two daughters who still lived in Textitlán. Doña Elena's eight children were of my generation, ranging in age from thirty-two to forty-six years, but I also found that I had much in common with her grandchildren, particularly the college students and those who had lived for a while in the United States. As was the case with me, several of the granddaughters in the Fernández clan were among the first to attend college. Adela and Celia, for instance, were first cousins; Celia had lived in the United States for five years and Adela was still waiting, along with her mother and four siblings, for her documents to be processed so she could join her father in the United States. Celia was studying at Penn State University, while Adela had entered dental school at the university in nearby Morelia, Michoacán. Though their opportunities and experiences were expanding, their parents often felt ill at ease about the young women's growing independence, which in turn was a source of frustration for Adela and Celia. When we would get together to talk about college life, they would often express frustration with their parents. Why, they would ask, were their parents so concerned about them going away to college or being more independent? Recalling my own college days of more than decade earlier, I told Adela and Celia that my parents had reacted similarly, and that eventually they adjusted, as I assumed their parents also would. I welcomed their visits, as it was fascinating to hear about their college experiences, which were remarkably similar considering they were attending colleges in the United States and Mexico.

Adela's older brother, José (who preferred to be called "Joe") also often joined our conversations. Joe and his first cousin, Celia, were Doña Elena's first grandchildren, and they were in many ways the family favorites. Celia and Adela, despite living in different countries, were also very close friends. When they were all in Mexico together, Joe and the *muchachas* (young women) were often together attending dances and *jaripeos* (bull riding events).

Ken and I had met Joe our second week in Textitlán. Despite the fact that over half of the adult population had visited the United States at one time or another, when my family and I arrived in 1999 we were viewed as somewhat of a novelty. No American family had ever come to live in Textitlán before, as word spread quickly through our neighborhood that an American family was renting Ofelia's house on Avenida Morelos. Our neighbors stopped by to introduce themselves, and the elderly señoras on my street doted over my *güerito* (blond with a fair complexion) children. Because of his limited proficiency with Spanish, Ken sought out men who spoke some English to spend his time. He found the situation trying, however. Most of his interactions were mediated through me, which meant that his interactions with others were limited to the times when I was not working. His inability to communicate left him understandably frustrated.

One afternoon when I returned from doing survey work, I found a young man sitting next to a motorcycle talking animatedly with Ken as my children danced along the sidewalk. His English was perfect, and I wondered by what good fortune Ken had found him. He introduced himself as "Joe" and told me that he was Ofelia's nephew and the grandson of Don Pedro and Doña Elena. Joe was back in Mexico temporarily. He had fractured his skull in a serious automobile accident in the United States six months before and had nearly died. When he was released from the hospital, his father sent him back to his mother in Textitlán to recuperate. He was happy to meet us, he said, simply because he loved the United States and wanted to speak English. "I love the United States, you know," he said animatedly. "I was born here, but I feel like the United States, it's my country."

Stepping back and surveying him more carefully, I could see that Joe bore the marks of a young Textitlaneco who had lived in the United States. His ears were pierced, and he wore diamond stud earrings and two large gold chains around his neck, one bearing his full name, José Luis. He also wore several large gold rings and a Philadelphia 76ers jersey, baggy white jeans, and expensive athletic shoes. Joe was not an overly handsome young man, but he had a warm smile, a Fernández smile that was nearly identical to that of his sister, I noted. His hair was shaved close to his scalp, revealing the thin surgical scar that went across the top of his head and formed a perfect line from one ear to the other. He grew a pencil-thin beard across his chin that lined up perfectly with the hairless scar line, and the two together framed his face.

As we sat talking to Joe on our stoop that afternoon, he told us that he had gone to the United States when he had finished secondary school.[8] He was a good student but decided he wanted to join his father and work in Pennsylvania. He took a plane to Tijuana and slipped across the border using a fake passport that a coyote had lent him for a fee of $500. From San Diego he took a bus to Los Angeles and then a plane to Pennsylvania, where his father and uncles picked him up at the airport.

Joe spent his first six months enrolled in Kennett High School, where he learned English quickly, then became bored. He decided to quit school to work full-time at his uncle's restaurant. There he worked long hours and impressed his family and coworkers. "I wanted to make money, maybe start a business," Joe recalled to us that afternoon. He washed dishes and cut meat in the restaurant and was well liked by his coworkers. Later one of his uncles would recall Joe's time in Pennsylvania fondly and explain that his friendly, approachable demeanor made him accessible, and his ability to speak English well and to work hard made him popular with many of the single Mexican women who worked at the restaurant.

In October 1999, Joe was driving alone along a quiet country road near Kennett Square late at night. He lost control of his car and crashed, totaling the vehicle. Later Joe told us that he could not remember what happened before the accident. He was flown to a trauma center in Delaware where he remained unconscious for over a week. No one knows exactly what happened that night. The police ruled it a single car accident, although Joe's father once told me that he suspected that perhaps someone had intentionally run Joe off the road that night. "It was a clear night, and he hadn't been drinking," he recalled. Joe came to the United States barely sixteen years old and had been extremely successful in a short period of time. His success, particularly with women, drew the ire of some men in the Mexican community in Kennett Square, particularly those who had not shared in a similar good fortune. Regardless of the cause of the accident, however, his family collectively gave thanks that he survived. "I sat up a lot of nights in the hospital with that kid," his uncle Ernesto recalled. "We really weren't sure he would make it, or if he'd be okay if he did live."

Joe's brush with death did little to deter him from his youthful exuberance. If anything, he was more determined to make his own decisions, even if it meant making mistakes. Joe, taking after his grandmother, was an avid storyteller. He spent many hours recalling his and his family's tales of migration and adventure. He was one of the few people I had met (or would ever meet) in Textitlán or Kennett Square who had a clear understanding of the distinctions between Mexican, American, and migrant (hybrid) cultural practices. Joe also had very sophisticated insights about U.S.-Mexican migration and how it was likely to change individuals and families.

Joe's remarkable bicultural competence made him an excellent informant, and I found myself asking him questions about social situations where I knew I was missing something. At the end of one particularly frustrating day, when I was unable to complete even one survey or interview, I stopped by Doña Elena's house to ask Joe what I might be doing wrong. He surveyed my appearance and replied, "You might want to wear makeup and fix yourself up a bit more. People here don't like it when a woman appears too manly." He was referring to my field attire: I wore jeans, boots, and a cotton T-shirt and kept my face clean scrubbed with no makeup. Although I bristled at his suggestion, the following day when I went back out I put on some makeup, and to my surprise (and dismay) I found that people were more willing to talk with me when I appeared more feminine.

Although my research interests did not explicitly include issues of gender, the matter about my appearance was not the only gender complication that I encountered in the field. Not only did nearly all of the women in the village frequently warn me to watch out for the men of Textitlán, but also Doña Elena made certain that I understood that life for women in Mexico was different than in the United States, particularly for any woman living alone with her children. "Débora," she told me one afternoon in her kitchen, "you should never let a man in the house when you're there alone." At first I thought she was referring to men I did not know well, but when I assured her that I would never let a stranger in the house, she made it clear that no man, even one whom I might know and trust well, should be invited in the house unless my babysitter, Erica, or another adult woman was there with me.

Though I found Doña Elena's warnings parochial at first, later I came to understand the guarded nature of male-female interactions in Textitlán. Any dealings between people of the opposite sex would be monitored by what Doña Elena called the *gente decente* (decent or respectable people). Men and women occupied separate social worlds. There was no context, professional or otherwise, for male-female friendships, and all interactions between unrelated and unsupervised men and women would probably be interpreted as romantic or sexual encounters. As I went door to door to complete surveys, several men who were home alone asked me to return to their houses later when their wives or daughters would be present. Otherwise, they would not allow me to enter their houses. One morning, I was in the middle of an interview with a former migrant, and his wife had to leave the house on an errand. A lively discussion took place between them regarding what to do about me, as the señora was unwilling to leave the house while I was still there. She eventually decided it would be acceptable for her husband to continue the interview as long as the front door was open and her husband and I were clearly visible, sitting across from one another, for anyone to see who walked by on the street.

The restrictions on my movements within the pueblo were among the more frustrating aspects of my work. I knew many of the men and women (or their extended family members) whom I interviewed in Textitlán from my previous work in Pennsylvania. Nothing I had experienced with the settler population in the United States had prepared me for the guarded attitudes I encountered toward women's roles and their work lives. In the United States, Mexican women clearly worked out of necessity, but most of the families in my acquaintance wanted their daughters, as well as their sons, to be educated and to work after they finished high school. Overall, these families were extremely pragmatic. They wanted their children to have the best opportunities possible, regardless of their gender.

Many women in Textitlán work, although the majority still consider themselves *amas de casa* (housewives). When asked what they do for a living, married women typically responded "housewife," but when questioned further they often added that they also worked for wages, most often as seamstresses in the thriving garment industry. Every morning the streets of the neighborhoods would bustle with young men on motor scooters carrying large bags of cut fabric to the homes of women. Most women owned their own commercial sewing machines and completed piecework during the day, as they had time. These *coseras* (seamstresses), however, were first and foremost dedicated to the care of their families and homes. [9]

In this regard, Textitlán's garment industry is ideally suited to the lifestyles of migrating families. The industry centers on decentralized *fábricas caseras* (cottage production), and although there are a number of factories where men and women work on-site, the majority of garment production takes place in the homes of seamstresses who set their own schedules. Marta and Juan Reyes, for example, are a young couple who own their own children's clothing company. Married only two years, Marta, a skilled clothing designer, and Juan's family had moved to Textitlán a decade earlier from Mexico City to start a garment factory. The two work in their apartment, where Marta designs the clothing, and then Juan purchases fabric, cuts it, and delivers it to their seamstresses in the pueblo.

The salary of these coseras is based upon the skill level of the work and how much they complete during the week. Seamstresses who work on the overlock machines make more than those who work on straight stitch sewing machines, and those who do *terminados* (finishing work), sewing buttons and beading sweaters, make the least.[10] Within this system, women are able to earn money while their husbands are working in the United States, but they also have the freedom to structure their own schedules and care for small children, which is the role expected of them as wives and mothers.

Despite the fact that many women in the pueblo lived alone with their children for substantial periods of time each year while their husbands worked in the United States, the fact that I was a professional, and that my husband was willing to leave me alone for several months to complete my work, was an anomaly for most of the people I encountered in Textitlán. Most residents were delighted that I was interested in knowing more about the pueblo and was planning to write a book about them and their experiences, but my role as a woman researcher was problematic for some. When completing the survey work door to door, for instance, many women were friendly and helpful, but a fair number were also suspicious that I was in Mexico looking for a man or that I might have designs on their husbands. After one interview, a woman apologized that she had been discourteous when I first came to the door and asked to speak with the *jefe de casa* (man of the house).[11] "I thought you were here from Pennsylvania because you were interested *in him*," she explained. Her statement was in part a reflection of the general fear wives of migrants have of American women in general. Everyone in the neighborhood knew of at least one family who had been abandoned when a man decided to start a new family with another woman in the United States.[12] Similarly, many of these women had no prior experience with professional women who were also mothers, and they clearly saw these roles as incompatible.

The men of Textitlán also had a difficult time understanding my role as researcher. My neighbors explained that we were the first American family to live in the pueblo, and although many people had some experience with migration to the United States, most had limited interactions with Americans while they lived in the north. Many times I was asked if I was a mushroom farm owner in town to recruit laborers. I once knocked on the door of a man who later told me he was struggling to get his garment factory afloat and was considering a trip to the United States to raise capital to enhance his business. When I told him I was from Pennsylvania, he asked, "Are you from *Hongos Calidad Superior* [a large, well-known mushroom farm in Kennett Square]?"[13] I was surprised by the question, as we had already established that he had never been to the United States, and it was unusual for a non-migrant to know such specific information about Kennett Square. He went on to explain, "I heard a commercial on the radio this week. The Calidad Superior mushroom farm is hiring Mexicans to pick mushrooms. I thought you might be here to hire workers, since you're from Pennsylvania."

Overall, being mistaken for a mushroom farm recruiter was a minor, and somewhat comical, misidentification. Whereas some of my neighbors and informants found my domestic arrangements curious, others saw this arrangement as essential for understanding women's lives in Textitlán. Toward the end of my fieldwork, Samuel Fernández (son of the elder Pedro Fernández) told me, "I know that being here alone has been hard for you, but you really understand what our wives go through when we're working in *el Norte*." Samuel was correct on both counts. As a mother managing my children and household alone, I could see the difficulties that Mexican women faced when their husbands were away, and the experience was invaluable. Although most of the residents of Textitlán were generous and kind, it was difficult living in a community that was very male dominant. I found the *muchachos* (young single men) a timid lot, as they immediately backed down from their macho bravado, whistles, and catcalls when confronted directly. They were frustrating and annoying in that they constantly marked my presence in the street when I would have preferred to go unnoticed. More problematic, however, were the married men. Eduardo, for instance, the husband of a friendly neighbor on my street, took to following me on his motor scooter and asking me out for a drink while I was going door to door to conduct surveys. Undeterred by my refusals, Eduardo followed me until the day I finally agreed to meet him for a drink, provided we did so in his house with his wife, Lola.

On the whole, day-to-day living in Textitlán was peaceful and slow paced. During my subsequent field visits from 2000 through 2003, I left my family in the United States and lived with Doña Elena, Don Pedro, and their adult daughter, Rosa. Although I was the only person in the house to use an alarm clock, the family was up and about in the house by 7:30 a.m. most mornings. Doña Elena would start the day by purchasing fresh-squeezed orange juice from a neighbor's *juguera* (juice bar) across the street and fresh sweet breads for breakfast from a man who walked through the neighborhood with a large cart full of fresh-baked items. We would gather at the table by eight o'clock to have coffee, juice, and bread and then get about our daily work. For Doña Elena, this was cooking *almuerzo*, literally "lunch," but a meal of meat, beans, rice, and tortillas taken around 11 a.m. Don Pedro would set out to the market to purchase freshly butchered meats and vegetables that he would prepare and sell at his *taquería* (taco stand) that night. Rosa would begin the day's housework. The dry and breezy climate produced mounds of dust and required that the Mexican homes be cleaned thoroughly every day, which included sweeping, mopping, and washing dishes. Twice a week we would all gather to do laundry. Doña Elena's children, six of the eight who live in the United States, had provided her with two washing machines. These machines are not like conventional washing machines common in the United States but instead resemble the wringer washers common in the United States a generation ago. We would hand-wash the clothes, run them through the washing machine, rinse them in clear water, wring them again, and then put them on the line to dry. I must admit that laundry was an arduous task that I never mastered fully. In the end, Doña Elena gently suggested that I hire her sister Sofia to do my laundry for me.

After the morning chores were complete, most family members left the house to undertake whatever daily tasks were set before them, such as shopping, running errands, or visiting friends. The family gathered again between two and four o'clock for *comida*, the main meal of the day. Doña Elena's grandchildren, returning from school, along with their parents and the rest of the household, gathered together at her table for the large meal. Comida is a quiet, relaxed meal that marks the end of the school day for the children and offers a midday break for the rest of the family. All of the shops and businesses throughout town, save restaurants, close during comida. By five o'clock the town reopens and everyone is back to work until eight.

As the afternoon shadows draw long and the day draws to a close, Doña Elena, Don Pedro, and Rosa are busy doing the final preparations for the taquería, which will open as soon as the sun sets for *cena*, the last meal of the day. Cena literally means "supper" but is a light evening meal.

Textitlán has many mom-and-pop-style taco stands scattered throughout the pueblo's colonias. There is no regulation of these food stands, and this low barrier to entry provides a business opportunity for families who have a spare room facing the street that can be converted to a taco stand. Don Pedro's taquería is a small twelve-by-fifteen-foot room at the front of his house. He installed a large metal door (much like a garage door) that he opens every night. The wide welcoming entrance allows anyone walking or driving by to see that he is vending tacos, but his reputation as a master tacquero alone draws in hundreds of patrons every week.

Although anyone in Don Pedro's household eats free, often his grandchildren decide to eat elsewhere when they are bored with tacos. Textitlán's streets also host a number of vendors with portable food carts not unlike those found in the streets of major cities in the United States. Many of these vendors sell tacos, but just as often they sell Mexican-style *hamburguesas* (hamburgers with a distinct Mexican flavor), hot dogs, pizza, or tostadas.

As eleven o'clock approaches, fewer people come to the taquería, and the food runs low. Don Pedro closes his door and his assistants, daughter-in-law Lucy and neighbor Marta, start clearing whatever food remains and cleaning the equipment and tables. As midnight approaches, everything is cleaned and piled at the sink to drain. By the time Pedro and his family go to bed, the streets outside are deserted and still.

Textitlán's long history of migration and return has influenced the local economy significantly, although this is something that is debated by locals who have never migrated to work in the United States. Instead, they insist that the robust local economy is the result of simple hard work and determination, and that the regular infusion of U.S. dollars is insignificant in the local economy. My research goals for my extended stay in 1999 were twofold: I was there to complete a survey of families with a focus on migration and work histories and to complete ethnographic work in order to understand the effects of migration on the Kennett Square Mexicans' home community. Shortly after I arrived I began to document El Bordo,[14] and I completed a survey on the work, migration, and family histories of a random sample of the households in the colonia.[15] It was a difficult time; going door to door to ask people a long list of extremely personal questions was intimidating, but there were also pleasant surprises. I sometimes found familiar faces from Pennsylvania behind the doors of what I thought were the homes of strangers, and many times I was invited to eat with the family who completed the survey.

El Bordo covers a large area of nearly a square mile, so for Christmas 1999 Ken bought me a bike to speed up my travel to and from the house. I kept it in Mexico and used it every time I returned. Bikes were one of the more common forms of local transportation in Textitlán, used by those who lacked the resources to purchase *motos* (motor scooters) or cars. Families who could not afford automobiles were able to convert their bicycles and motos into multi-passenger vehicles. It was not uncommon to see a father driving a moto with his wife behind him holding a baby and a toddler standing by the handlebars in front of him. Those with bikes added child seats to the front and back and screwed steel bars into the back wheel hubs so that another person could stand behind the cyclist with their hands on his shoulders and ride along. Textitlán is a small city, and the bicycle is extremely functional for most travel within the pueblo.

In the end, the survey work proved to be an invaluable experience. The work put me in touch with a random sample of the community, something that is not common with traditional ethnographic field methods. It also allowed me entrée to nearly two hundred households and provided a much clearer insight into the lives of immigrants and non-immigrants alike, as well as the social and economic influences of immigration in Textitlán and San Miguel.[16]

DE CAMPESINOS A EMIGRANTES (FROM PEASANT FARMERS TO MIGRANTS): TEXTITLÁN'S EMERGENCE AS A MIGRATION PUEBLO

Settled nearly two hundred years ago, Textitlán is known throughout Mexico as *la pequeña ciudad de la gran industria* (the small city with the big industry). Since 1980 it has emerged as one of the major sweater producers in the Mexican republic (Vangstrup 1995). Textitlán's entrance is marked with a large traffic circle that directs visitors to different places in town. The center of the circle is crowned with three large spools of sweater yarn, one of the many industrial images of this *pueblo textíl* (textile pueblo) that are located around the city.

Textitlán's central plaza retains only a semblance of local historic architecture. Most of the older homes and storefronts have been modernized with contemporary façades and brightly lit signage. Like other Mexican towns, the center of the pueblo is the heart of the community. The central plaza, or *jardín*, as Textitlanecos refer to it, is by far the loveliest place in the pueblo with well-maintained flower beds and a bandstand that offers an unobstructed view of the Parish of Saint John the Baptist, a large Gothic-style church located near the plaza.

The jardín is a local gathering place. On weekday afternoons, older men gather there to meet and talk with one another while children run around the gardens and around the central bandstand. On Sunday evenings the entire jardín is filled with families, young adults, and vendors selling a variety of foods and novelty items, and always there will be a band playing. Young women walk (*pasear*) around the perimeter of the plaza hoping to be noticed by the young men, who congregate in groups on the benches and nearby in their cars. If interested, a young man will begin to walk alongside a girl and ask if she would like to join him. Many of the married couples in Textitlán met and began courting in the jardín on a Sunday evening.

The jardín is surrounded by commercial storefronts on four sides, which are covered with arched porticos. These *portales* have expansive sidewalks that are dominated by restaurants and cafes and frequently bustle with patrons. From the pueblo center there is a large commercial area that extends northward and houses hundreds of clothing shops, the products of the local garment industry. During most of the year Textitlán is a quiet pueblo. The markets are typically crowded with shoppers from the municipio of Textitlán as well as others from neighboring states, but once businesses close at seven o'clock there is little foot or automobile traffic. By ten o'clock the streets are silent. Everything changes, however, in early December, as seasonal migrant workers and those who have settled in the United States begin to return, crowding the streets with extra cars and people.[17] Textitlán sits adjacent to its neighbor San Miguel and the two are, in a real sense, twin cities. The two have grown into one another so that it is difficult in some places to know whether you are in Textitlán or San Miguel; in fact, in 2003 a dispute broke out between the pueblos after San Miguel's mayor said that, with the exception of the central *jardín* (plaza) all of the property that constituted Textitlán was actually the possession of San Miguel. It turned out that on some streets the residents admitted that they were not certain where they officially live, each household having decided that they lived in one pueblo or the other without official authorization.[18]

The distinctions between these pueblos are also maintained through everyday discourse. During my first trip to Textitlán, I stopped by a stationery store to purchase a street map and asked the clerk if I could also purchase a map of San Miguel. He replied, "If you want to buy a map of San Miguel, you have to go to San Miguel." Incidentally, the street maps of each pueblo do not make reference to their neighbors. Residents from both pueblos are fiercely proud of their hometowns and local heritage and are quick to point out that theirs is the superior pueblo. San Miguel residents emphasize their colonial history and long-standing connections to the historical development of the region; Textitlanecos are proud that theirs is the wealthier of the two pueblos and that the regional garment industry originated with them. Although the pueblos have distinct histories, patron saints, and local governments, they are tied together geographically, economically, and socially, and for this reason San Miguel is included in much of the discussion that follows. The pueblos differ in one very significant respect, however. Textitlán has had a much longer and sustained history of migration to the United States, a feature that is the source of other distinguishing aspects that set these pueblos apart.

From the central plazas of both Textitlán and San Miguel, the pueblos branch out into colonias in all directions. There is always a significant amount of new construction in Textitlán, although the overall population has remained steady at approximately forty-eight thousand residents for the last decade. Nevertheless, there is a housing shortage in Textitlán that is due in part to migration and settlement in the United States. Rarely does a Mexican family sell its family home in Textitlán; most prefer to hold onto the homes and leave them in the care of a family member.[19] As families immigrate to the United States, there is a steady influx of people drawn to work in Textitlán's thriving garment industry. These residents move in from rural areas and other communities within Mexico.

Although residents of Textitlán and San Miguel work hard to distinguish themselves from one another, demographically they are nearly identical. They are both young communities, with 55 percent of the total population thirty years old or younger. Similarly, the level of educational attainment is nearly identical for both communities.

Adults in Textitlán have completed on average 4.87 years of education, 4.63 in San Miguel. Figure 3 shows the educational distribution for each community. The low level of educational attainment is a reflection of the fact that families of limited means often have children who start their working careers at an early age. Migration to the United States is also a viable career option for young people in both communities, particularly among those who are not academically inclined. Boys begin to think about joining their fathers in the United States by the time they reach twelve to fourteen years of age, coinciding with the time they finish primary school, although some quit much earlier. Migration and work in the United States is not viewed as an acceptable option for girls or women not accompanying their fathers or husbands to the United States, and in some families this has provided opportunities for women to continue their educations beyond the community average. Overall, however, women and men in Textitlán have completed the same number of years of education, with women on average completing 4.83 years and men 4.91 years.

Vicente Zavala, a prosperous restaurateur in Kennett Square, recalled that when he decided to go to the United States, he quit school. "I went to school, the third grade, [but I] never finished third grade. So I quit. I think it was my age, that I always want[ed] to come to America. . . . 'Cause I always want[ed] to have money . . . that's why I came here . . .'cause of the money. [S]eeing the other people [migrants] coming and going back. And we grow up . . . not poor but I mean like kind of poor. And you would see the other people have money so you want . . . I want to do the same thing. That's why . . . one of the reasons I came here."[20]

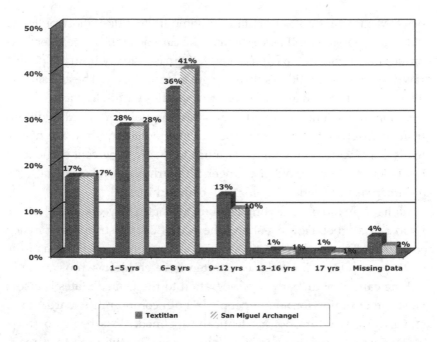

Figure 3.   Education Distribution (Source: MMP 118 [persfile], http://mmp
.opr.princeton.edu)

Textitlán historically has been a migrant "sending community," and
like many of its fellows in western Mexico, the pueblo has a long and
sustained history of migration to the United States. In Textitlán, 62 percent of all respondents in 1999 reported at least one family member had
migrated to the United States.[21] The pueblo's earliest migrants worked in
the United States seasonally as part of the Bracero Accord, a temporary
visa program developed to bring in the harvests, first during World War
II and continuing through 1964. In the course of my fieldwork I interviewed several former Braceros. These men were *campesinos,* poor sub-
sistence farmers, whose only source of income was what they were able
to produce and sell from their small farms. Temporary migration was
a means of earning cash that was needed to move their families out of
poverty. Textitlán's Braceros thus initiated what has been termed the
social progress of migration and work in the United States. After Bracero

laborers were recruited by the United States government to fill agricultural labor needs, migration between Textitlán and the United States took on a self-sustaining character, a pattern that continues to this day.[22] After several years of migrating, many former Braceros moved their families off their farms and into the pueblo of Textitlán, purchasing houses with the money they earned in the United States. "With the money I earned I was able to finish [building] this house and to help my children," Pedro Fernández recalled."[23]

When the Bracero Accord ended, migration to the United States from Textitlán clearly did not. Instead, many of the same Textitlanecos who had participated in the program continued to migrate without documentation on an occasional basis. Figure 4 shows the numbers of undocumented workers migrating from 1964 through 1985 (just prior to the passage of IRCA) increasing steadily. Pedro Fernández went to the United States for the first time in 1955. His trips varied in duration and location. As he recalled, "I went to Mercedes, California, once, then to Texas, Arizona, three times, and other parts of California. . . . We would work for forty-five days or two months, three months; it was for very short periods—they wouldn't give us any more."[24] Like many men of his generation, Don Pedro started migrating because, "I was poor and recently married." Don Pedro's seasonal migration to the United States ended when he reached his mid-sixties; as he said, "I'd had enough of *el Norte.*" Still, he does not diminish the economic benefits of his time as a migrant worker. "When I think of what we have here [his house and material goods], first, I give thanks to God, after that, the United States."[25]

Alfonzo Ramírez is the son of a former Bracero. A generation after the Bracero Accord Señor Ramírez also began migrating for much the same reason as his father. He recalled, "I was born in '47; how can I describe my youth? It was sad because when I wanted to get married, I didn't have enough money to pay for a wedding. I was married in '69 and I left for the United States in '70, illegal, breaking the American law."[26]

In the process of migrating to other areas of the United States, workers from Textitlán like Fernández and Ramírez informally learned by word of mouth that there was work in southeastern Pennsylvania in the

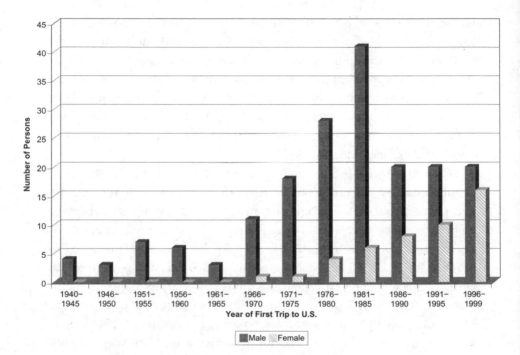

Figure 4.   Textitlán Survey: Year of First Trip to United States (Source: MMP 118 [persfile], http://mmp.opr.princeton.edu)

mushroom industry. Pedro Fernández recalled, "When I went back [to the United States], I went to Pennsylvania. . . . I had friends and relatives who had been there and they said, 'Let's go to Pennsylvania,' so we went. When I got there, there were no Mexicans; it was all Puerto Rican then. . . . But I went back, because I liked Pennsylvania better [than California or Texas]."[27] Textitlanecos' preference for Kennett Square is reflected in the overall choices of those going to the United States. Kennett was a clear first choice followed by Chicago and Houston (Figure 5). Most of the people I interviewed indicated that they preferred Pennsylvania mainly because it was quiet and a rural community, potentially offering a lifestyle not unlike the ranchos that they had left in Mexico. In addition, in the early years of migration to Kennett (1970–1985), men reported that there were fewer problems with *la migra* (immigration

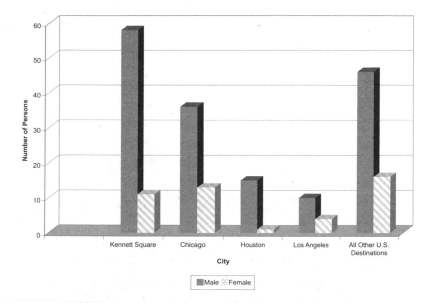

Figure 5. Destinations for First Trip to United States (Source: MMP 118 [persfile], http://mmp.opr.princeton.edu)

officials) in Pennsylvania. Most significantly, Textitlanecos went to Kennett to work with their extended family members and friends who were already working there.

During the work of the survey, I found that the social process of migration has long-standing roots in this sending community, so that those who are currently migrating or have settled in the United States are much more likely to have many friends and family members who also have experience living and working there. Conversely, people who have never migrated tend to be from families that do not have a history of migration (Figure 6). This fact was borne out time and again in the survey data and was true of both Textitlán and San Miguel. This split between migrating and non-migrating family members is one of several social divisions between Textitlán and San Miguel.

For this reason it was not uncommon that non-migrating Textitlanecos were often as misinformed about the hardships and experiences of migrant families as were the citizens in Kennett Square.[28]

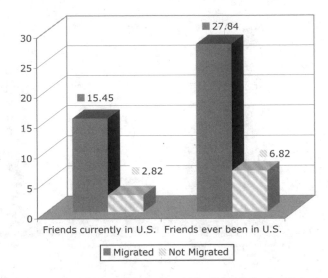

Figure 6.   Social Networks in Textitlán: Friends in the United
States (Source: MMP 118 [persfile], http://mmp.opr.princeton
.edu)

The bidirectional influence of U.S.-Mexico migration was apparent
in Textitlán on several levels. Most obviously, migration to the United
States has provided families in these communities significant social mobility that is reflected by the household amenities that are common in
homes of people in both communities. Textitlán holds no veneer to obscure the day-to-day lives of normal Mexicans. It is a place that exists to
meet the needs of the people who live there, and although it takes some
time to accustom oneself to its daily rhythms and routines, there is a
depth of experience, particularly the connection that its residents have
with one another, that overshadows the lack of some conveniences that
are readily available in Mexican tourist destinations. Textitlán is *puro
Mexicano* (fully Mexican), but it bears the mark of an imported American
influence. Because these cultural changes are the result of migration to
the United States, they are influences that have been interpreted by Mexicans. So although the streets of Textitlán reflect associations with United
States culture, from the numerous *casas de cambio* (currency exchanges) to

Mexican-style *hamburguesas* (hamburgers), hotdogs, and pizzas sold by local street vendors, American culture has been reinterpreted *a la Mexicana*, producing a distinct cultural hybrid.

The number of businesses that market directly to Mexicans who have acquired tastes for American foods and goods is staggering, but just as significant is the manner in which these businesses go about re-creating their products. The Textitlán hamburguesas and pizzas, for example, typically are seasoned with jalapeños and fiery salsas and bear little resemblance to their counterparts commonly found in the United States. An *especial* (supreme) hamburguesa is loaded with ham, jalapeños, and pineapple. Pizzas are often made without tomato sauce, but are laden with chorizo (a spicy Mexican sausage) and other savory meats. These adaptations are significant in that they demonstrate Mexican influence on what might otherwise be mistaken for the insidious nature of American cultural hegemony. Far from usurping traditional foodways, locals have transformed the American cuisine into forms more palatable and recognizable to local Mexicans than to most visiting Americans. These subtle adaptations and inclusions of American culture allow Textitlanecos to characterize U.S.-Mexico migration as an everyday occurrence but not necessarily something that threatens local customs or erodes Mexican culture.[29]

The social distinctions that mark those who have worked in the United States from those who have not are not limited to the social networks mentioned above. Textitlán is a prosperous community, and this fact is obvious from the moment one enters the pueblo. Most houses are in good repair, and even as new houses are being built, older ones are being expanded and improved. There is no consistent pattern of development in either Textitlán or San Miguel, although the most desirable addresses are closest to the central plaza.[30] It is common to see large extravagant residences alongside humble one- or two-room homes. Because wood is scarce, it is not used in building construction; homes are constructed of cement and brick with stucco interior and exterior walls. Houses have flat roofs made of cement or corrugated aluminum. In addition to the *tinacos* (water tanks) on the roofs, wealthier and migrant families usually have satellite dishes as well.

Home interiors can be humble or elaborate, depending on the wealth of the occupants. Wood is often used in fine furnishings, and it is not uncommon for a wealthy family to have a wood staircase in their home. Many homes have balconies that overlook the street, but most Mexican residences do not have elaborate exteriors or curbside ornamentation. Instead, the homes are securely hidden behind vibrantly painted exterior walls with steel doors and barred windows. By American standards the interiors of Textitlán's homes are modest in size and are sparsely furnished with everyday necessities: sofas, chairs, dining tables, beds, and chests of drawers or a chifforobe. Although modest, most of the dwellings are homey and comfortable. Dishwashers and clothes dryers are virtually nonexistent, and the absence of these appliances means that day-to-day housework is more labor intensive.[31] There are small *tienditas de abarrotes* (grocery stores) on nearly every street in every neighborhood. If there is no refrigerator in the home, a family purchases perishable items such as milk and eggs only when the family has need of them. Most women wash dishes and clothes by hand in an outdoor sink. Though doing laundry can be a demanding task, young girls are enlisted to help their mothers at an early age and are generally proficient at the task before they reach their teenage years. Clothing is dried on a line that is usually located on the roof of the house. The dry, crisp air ensures that most clothing that is washed in the morning is dry before evening.

Local prosperity is also evident in the presence of a substantial number of household amenities. All of the houses in these pueblos have electricity and nearly all have running water and access to municipal sewage, as well as stoves and televisions.[32] Some household items that Americans consider essential are not as common in the average Mexican home. For example, refrigerators are less common in Mexico than in the United States. However, 86 percent of the homes in Textitlán and 79 percent in San Miguel have one. Clothes washers are also less common in Mexico, with 70 percent and 68 percent of the homes reporting these items in Textitlán and San Miguel, respectively. Although there are no statistical distinctions between Textitlán and San Miguel with essential household amenities, there is a distinction for nonessential household items that indicate differences in prosperity between the two communities.[33] Residents of

Textitlán are significantly more likely to have telephones, stereos, and sewing machines in their households than residents of San Miguel. Telephones are not essential to daily living in these pueblos, as nearly all social interactions take place face to face. There are no strict social prohibitions to simply "dropping in" when you want to see a neighbor or relative; similarly, when someone in the household needs to see a physician, the patient typically shows up at the office to see whether an appointment is available that day. In addition, the national Mexican telephone company, Telmex, is known for its painstaking inefficiency; it can take several months to get a new phone line installed in a home. Although the prevalence of the garment industry means that sewing machines are considered not as luxury items but as necessities for employment by seamstresses, they are still not common in all households.

The most common indicator of prosperity in the pueblo is access to nonessential technology: cellular phones, Internet access, and stereos. In each year since my first visit in 1999, there has been an observable increase in the number of cellular phones, mainly by younger Textitlanecos. Similarly, the number of Internet cafés in the pueblo has expanded significantly. There were three Internet stations in 1999; each was modest with four to six computers. Each time I visit the pueblo I see more Internet stations than before; these are typically larger and better appointed and have up-to-date computer equipment. As with cellular phones, the most common patrons of the Internet cafés are young Textitlanecos, typically those under the age of twenty. Stereos are also considered luxury items and, like all electronic equipment in Mexico, are prohibitively expensive.[34]

The differences in nonessential items in the household are indicative of the wealth in the two pueblos. Another is the overall size of homes and the materials with which they are constructed. In Textitlán, the average number of rooms in a home was 3.97, whereas in San Miguel it was 2.76. Homes in Textitlán were also more likely to have finished floors of tile or carpet (48 percent versus 25 percent) and were more likely to have been financed with money earned in the United States (29 percent versus 17 percent). Homeowners in Textitlán also acquired their residences earlier than those in San Miguel (1987 versus 1994). The economic differences between these adjacent communities are related to the degree of migration from each. The statistical analyses show that Textitlán, a community with significantly more migrating experience, has benefited economically from this experience. Although the percentages of migrating family members in both Textitlán and San Miguel are high, the overall total of migrations and accumulated months of migration experience differ significantly between the two communities, a fact that explains in part the disproportionate level of affluence in Textitlán compared with San Miguel.[35] Men from both communities began migrating in the twentieth century as Braceros. The average year of the first migration in Textitlán was 1982; in San Miguel it was 1987. Adults in Textitlán have migrated to the United States an average of 2.51 times, whereas the residents of San Miguel have migrated an average of only .52 times. Similarly, adults in Textitlán have spent on average 32.03 months in the United States as compared with 14.66 months for adults in San Miguel.[36] So whereas both of these communities are migrant "sending" communities, Textitlán has a longer and more substantial connection to the United States through labor migration. In addition, as a community, Textitlanecos have a greater number of household amenities and have greater experience with financial options, such as bank accounts and credit cards, in the United States. They have larger and higher quality homes and are more likely to have acquired their homes through money earned in the United States. These results suggest that migration has had a positive impact on the Textitlanecos' standard of living.[37]

The data presented here, however, does not directly compare migrating households with non-migrating households. Statistical analyses conducted within Textitlán confirm a significant difference between the wealth of migrating and non-migrating households. Migrating families are significantly more likely to own their own homes than those who have never migrated. They are also likely to have larger homes that have significantly more household amenities. Families with a history of migration also own larger homes that they acquired earlier, and they are more likely to acquire their homes with money earned in the United States. Taken together these data demonstrate the positive impact of migration on the economic lives of Textitlanecos.

The statistical research and resulting data provide a thorough empirical picture of many aspects of life for Textitlanecos. However, there was no parallel to having lived alongside these men and women, spending hours talking and participating in the social life of their community. It was in Textitlán that I realized what Mexicans in Kennett had to give up and why they felt compelled to maintain their ties to their hometown. The next chapter addresses these connections in greater detail, emphasizing how Textitlanecos manage to maintain their ties and commitment to their natal community through their homes and also examines some of the challenges they confront in the process.

THREE

La Casa Vacía

**MEANINGS AND MEMORIES IN ABANDONED
IMMIGRANT HOUSES**

We can go home again, provided it has not been altered
beyond recognition during our absence.

Yi-Fu Tuan, 1980: 470

I arrived in Textitlán for the first time in September 1999; I planned to
rent a house. My family and I would begin what would become one of
many research trips, and I was in need of a modest home that could accommodate us. I was able to find one home, still under construction and
lacking a bathroom. The owner told me not to worry; I could walk across
the street and shower at his house whenever I wanted. I imagined traips-
ing my three year-old twins to my landlord's home every day to bathe
and decided to look elsewhere.

When I returned to my home in Pennsylvania, I began asking my informants in Kennett Square how I should go about looking for a house.
I had worked with these families for several years, and they were enthusiastic about my upcoming trip and the opportunity to know their
hometown. Of the eighteen families whom I knew well, fifteen had

homes that they had left behind in Mexico. Two of those fifteen families had extended family members living in their vacated homes, whereas the others had left their homes empty. Although they acknowledged that these houses were not in use, most of the owners were reluctant to rent them, although it was never clearly stated why that was the case. In the end, I did rent one of these empty homes. My landlord, Mario, seemed happy to let me rent the house, but his wife Ofelia seemed reluctant to let me have the home. At the time, they and their children had lived in the United States for five years and had not once returned to use the home.

When we arrived in Textitlán, I was relieved to learn that Mario and Ofelia's house was fully furnished and had a fully functioning kitchen with a stove, refrigerator, and sink.[1] Our transition was easier because the house was furnished, but it took a while to become accustomed to the peculiarities of the typical Mexican house. The drive to Textitlán from the main airport in Guanajuato took nearly three hours, and when we finally arrived in Textitlán, Ofelia's parents, Doña Elena and her husband Don Pedro, were there to greet us and show us the house, which we had rented sight unseen. The house was a simple two-story structure constructed of reinforced concrete beams and brick; the interior and exterior walls were painted stucco. Doña Elena explained that there was no telephone, as the house had been empty for five years. The gas for the stove and water heater were supplied via portable propane tanks that were located on the back patio. She had purchased a new tank, which she assured me should last for two to three months. To conserve fuel, she recommended that the small hot water heater, which looked more like a toy than a hot water source for an entire household, be turned on only when we were ready to shower.

The household water supply for cleaning and bathing was housed in a large *tinaco* (tank) located on the roof of the house; someone would pass by every morning selling potable water in large plastic jugs. "You'll hear the man in the street calling, '¡*Agua*! ¡*Agua*!,'" Doña Elena explained. "Just go to the door and tell him you want water and he'll bring it to you." The water in the tinaco would be replenished during the night when the *municipio* (county) pumped water through the pipes to individual houses.[2] Water was pumped every day except Tuesday and Friday, she cautioned us, so we would have to be careful to conserve water those days. She casually recommended that we check the tank every morning, however, to confirm how much water was available before taking our showers. "This is a two-story house," Don Pedro warned us. "Sometimes the water pressure won't be strong enough to fill the tinaco." When I asked what we should do when there was no water, Doña Elena patted my hand and said we were welcome to come to her house to shower if need be, and then nimbly led me up a narrow two-story staircase (with no railing) to the roof of the house to show me the tinaco and how to check the water level.

Doña Elena then handed me a ring with four keys, one to the front door and to each door on the first floor. Most Mexican homes are configured in a curious but pleasantly open architectural style. This means much of the "inside" of the house is open air, so that once you step out of a room into the hall you often find yourself standing "outside" in a roofless passageway, as was the case with our house. This architectural style bodes well for the temperate dry climate, and for this reason Mexican homes in Textitlán have no central air conditioning or heating. The openness also can be unpleasantly cold during the nights throughout the winter months when temperatures drop to the high thirties. The open nature of the house design also means that an intruder can enter the house over the garden wall, which is the reason for having a key for each room's sturdy steel door. Doña Elena recommended that I lock the doors to all of the rooms when we left the house, just to be safe.

My memories of our first few days in the house would be a blur were it not for my field diary. There I documented that our most pressing household problem was a lack of water, as it appeared that it was more common for the tinaco to stay empty than to fill. This meant Ken and I spent considerable time packing our toiletries and children in order to head to Doña Elena's house to bathe. I asked my neighbors if there was anything that could be done about the water, and they suggested that I hire a plumber to install a small pump that would provide the additional pressure needed to get the water to the roof. Then a few days later Ken and I woke up to the sound of falling water and assumed it was raining. December is not the rainy season, we later learned, and it was extremely unlikely to get rain at that time of year. The running water was our tinaco overflowing, the result of a broken shut-off valve. I dressed quickly and ran up the street to find Don Pedro to help us fix the problem while the elderly woman who lived next door scolded my husband for wasting water; she did not yet realize that Ken did not speak Spanish and could not understand anything she was saying. Don Pedro arrived a few minutes later, and after talking to our neighbor and assuring her he would fix the problem, he went off to find a plumber. Within an hour we had the valve repaired and from that day forward we had water.

The everyday difficulties we experienced living in a Mexican house were not uncommon. My neighbors commiserated about the water problems and explained that most new houses were built with cisterns under the first floor, thus overriding the gravity problem. They also acknowledged that with our rented house, long unused and also not up to date, we should expect difficulties keeping things running smoothly. As we settled in and became accustomed to the idiosyncrasies of the house, we adjusted, although during some weeks it seemed that every day brought a new peculiarity to which we had to adapt. Our house was located on a main street, which meant that we had to retreat to the back of the house to escape the noise of cars and motos rumbling along the busy street. It was a nuisance to have to constantly monitor the propane tank, but the delivery trucks passed by two or three times a day with their distinctive music booming through the neighborhood to alert everyone that they were on their way. Retrieving a new tank was as simple as standing on one's front stoop and signaling the drivers, who would then stop and connect the gas tank in less than five minutes.

Don Pedro and Doña Elena found my questions about running the house comical and sometimes exasperating. When our gas tank did finally run out unexpectedly at the end of our third week in the house, I went to Don Pedro to inquire how I could buy another, as I had failed to notice the gas trucks in the street that morning. It was midday and my household had ceased to function; our gas stove was useless and although we had water, there was no means to heat it. Don Pedro had bad news, however. The Mexican Republic was in the midst of a propane shortage. "There is no gas," he said simply. It took me a moment to take in his meaning; then my American sensibilities kicked in and I asked, "Who can I talk to? Surely there is some way for us to get a tank of gas." Don Pedro just shook his head and replied, "Débora, when there is gas the trucks come around playing their music and you can call for them to make a delivery. Did you notice there was no music this morning? When there is no music, there is no gas."

As we became accustomed to living in a Mexican home, I was also troubled by another aspect of the house: particularly the fact that the house looked as if someone else were still living there. I was unsettled by the perfect order I encountered in the house when we arrived. The bed was dressed with coordinated bedspread and drapes, there was a white lace tablecloth on the kitchen table, and there were several large live plants on the patio and balcony. The walls were also decorated with family photos, including Mario and Ofelia's wedding portrait and school photos of each of their children.

Why would the house look like this? I wondered. I worried that Mario and Ofelia had planned to return to Mexico for the holidays, and perhaps they changed their plans to accommodate me. In the midst of survey research I began to realize that my rental house was not at all atypical. In fact, I was struck that some 16 percent of the homes in my survey community were casas vacías and, like the home I was renting, most of these failed to bear the marks of an uninhabited house.

It was almost impossible to determine whether or not a house was a casa vacía from the street. This is because the majority of these houses were meticulously maintained. In fact, the only way to positively determine that a house was vacant was to ask a neighbor. During my survey research I could determine the casa vacía from other homes by knocking on the door. Inevitably a neighbor came out and asked me if I was looking for the homeowner. When I replied that I was, the neighbor told me that the owners were living in the United States and almost always referred me to the person responsible for the home, usually extended family members. These caretakers rarely lived in the house but often would visit (sometimes daily, usually weekly) to check on the house, and more important, to maintain the appearance that the house was occupied. Thus began my interest in the casa vacía and my curiosity regarding why Mexican families, who occupy the lower rung of the socioeconomic ladder in the United States, would hold onto their Mexican houses that they rarely, if ever, used.

The casa vacía is often accounted for in survey research; it is used to determine the influence of U.S-Mexico migration in Mexican communities. Yet these structures have never been studied in their own right. Nestled in urban and rural communities, these houses represent more than an economic imperative to work away from home. These houses are homes, albeit empty homes, but nevertheless they play an important role in the lives of Mexicans who use the structures to maintain connections and develop social and familiar ties with their communities on both sides of the border.

Casa vacías take many forms, from rural farm properties to urban mansions. The importance of these houses was not immediately obvious but was obscured by their lack of occupancy. Unlike many other forms of expressive material culture such as clothing, photos, and automobiles, these houses are the centerpiece of premigration family life and memory and hold strong emotional attachments for the men and women who have migrated and settled in the United States. This is why, I later realized, my informants were hesitant to rent their homes to me. These houses are more significant than any other aspect of their material culture and represent the immigrants' place in their natal community. These houses have been left, but casa vacías are much more than abandoned houses. The meanings that are attributed to these houses by migrants and those who have remained in Textitlán further calls into question the understandings of the concept of home, and by extension, the sense of belonging.

HOUSES FAR FROM HOME

Among the places that a person can occupy on a given day, the home carries perhaps the most significant emotional weight. Home is a person's starting point at the beginning of each day and it is the place one returns to at day's end. Many people see their homes as the center of their emotional and familial worlds. But what does it mean when you say you are "at home"? Home is an abstract signifier that calls to mind a wide variety of associations and meanings. Most commonly, home refers to a person's primary place of residence, but it is also used to express the essence of emplaced experience, or belonging. When home is used to reference a house, it is often meant as the key dwelling from which all other places are compared (Manzo 2003). Feelings of "at-homeness" are the "usually unnoticed, taken-for-granted situation of being comfortable in, and familiar with, the everyday world in which one lives and outside of which one is visiting" (Segert 1985: 287, quoted in Manzo 2003: 49). The ideas of home and feeling at home are deeply linked to sentiments of belonging, acceptance, and emplacement.

Drawing from the idea of home as a particular dwelling place, it is also often used to signify feelings of security and comfort. These associations are directly related to the primacy of home as the quintessential place in human experience. In essence, home becomes a landscape that provides the setting for the expression and development of the self. In its most idealized conceptions, home can be the one place where a person can freely express him- or herself without fear of rejection or censure; "being at home" is also commonly defined as being your true or authentic self.

The aforementioned associations among home, the self, security, and comfort centered in a specific structure (or house) often blend together to create an archetypical image of home. This image is often linked to a specific structure; in fact it is rare to think of "home" without referencing a specific house. Although these meanings of home appear fixed and set, in reality home is a rather malleable concept. The ideas and associations of home do not necessarily have anything to do with the actual place in which one resides. Mexicans in Kennett Square have settled and in many cases bought houses in Pennsylvania. Although they are building their lives in Pennsylvania, they often express a limited attachment to their United States houses and lifestyles that are in a sense their "houses far from home" (Rodman 2001).

This is due in part to the culture shock common when settling in Kennett Square, a place that is completely foreign to most Mexicans who settle there. The inconsistent acceptance of the Mexican population by its citizen neighbors also contributes to this. When I asked Mexicans in Kennett Square about the idea of their home or where they felt most at home, often the response was "Mexico."[3] Nations, neighborhoods, and local communities can also reference the idea of "home," but during my fieldwork in Mexico I found that "home" was not just their homeland or pueblo; it also referenced a specific house, albeit a vacant house. "Home" in this instance is not the place where they currently live but where they once lived full-time. This is true of Mexicans who have arrived in Kennett Square recently and those who have lived there for years.[4]

This fact was brought forth time and again during my fieldwork in Mexico. When I was living in Mexico I took my children to visit my friend, Mercedes Gonzales. I had been alone in Mexico with the children for nearly a month, and I desperately wanted to take a day off and spend time with Mercedes. The journey to the neighboring municipio required that we take three different buses and a taxi to the rural farming community el Tigre. We had traveled nearly two hours when we finally arrived at her home. El Tigre is a quiet *rancho* (rural community) where neighbors live in close proximity and the homesteads are surrounded by acres of pastureland and cornfields. It was a warm Sunday afternoon and I remember feeling relieved and happy to see Mercedes and her family. She and I sat out in her garden talking, and she said, "It feels so good to be back in my own home." She smiled and sat back in her chair relishing the beautiful afternoon.

Mercedes' house was spacious and comfortable with what appeared to be a recently renovated kitchen and bathroom. The large, open garden was overtaken with weeds. Mercedes lamented that the garden was unkempt and recalled the many flowers she had once cultivated there. As we visited, I ask her how long it had been since she had been back to Mexico. She said, "This is the first time we've been here since we moved to the United States. I've sent the children back to see their grandparents, but I haven't been here for four years." The house had sat empty during that time but was maintained by her in-laws in her absence. When she returned to the house, it was, with the exception of the garden, just as she left it. It was well maintained and awaiting her presence.

Why does the casa vacía continue to signify "home" for Mercedes and other Mexican men and women who have settled in Kennett Square? The answer to this question is not straightforward, but it lies in the significance that Mexican settlers attribute to their Mexican properties, which is much deeper and lasting than what many Americans would attribute to a domicile. The home provides a private space and refuge for family members; it is a place of safety as the house protects its inhabit- ants from the real or perceived dangers of the outside world. This became apparent as I observed the courtship customs of Mexican youth. In Textitlán, young men and women do not typically "date." When a young man is interested in courting a young woman, he is often required to visit the girl at her home. These visits may take place in the home or on the sidewalk just outside the front door but always within the protective space of the girl's home where parents or other family members can oversee the couple's interaction.[5]

In addition to the idea of protection, the home also represents iden- tity. For most people, the creation and maintenance of personal space is an essential aspect of their identity. Humans exist in the social worlds they create, in the families, friends and communities that are linked through a shared culture. We live our lives some*place*. Humans are also most at ease in the places where their lives are formed and are corre- spondingly malleable to the individual's influence. Home in this sense is an expression of personal power and autonomy. It is true that the "home" of comfort and essential identity may also be a source of dis- satisfaction or disillusionment for some, but most often it is the one place where life feels under the individual's control.[6] In this regard the casa vacía is a signifier of belonging, of being deeply and ineluctably connected to a place.

My experiences with Mercedes and other Mexican families empha- sized an important and seemingly simple lesson for me: our homes are more than the places where we lay our heads at night. They are the pri- mary location of emplacement and belonging for human existence, where we feel most at ease. It is the place where we start off from and it is the place we return to at the end of each day, or in the case of Mexicans in Pennsylvania, it is the place they return as often as they can afford to do so. Home is a "still point in a turning world, an irreplaceable center of human significance and experience" (Porteous and Smith 2001: 34).

In Kennett Square the mushroom farm owners often dread the end of the year when the pull to return home is the strongest. The numbers of workers returning home typically creates a seasonal labor shortage, as retired farm owners Vince Ghione and John Swain recalled. "I was so embarrassed a few years ago," Ghione said. "A guy [told me he] was going back for Christmas, and I was furious. He's a good man. And he . . . I was talking foolish. [The Mexican supervisor was translating] . . . . And I'm going, 'You can't go home for Christmas because everybody's leaving.' Most of them want to go back at the end of the year. And [the Mexican supervisor] gets it translated back to me, he [the mushroom worker] hasn't been back all year and he has five children. I felt about this big" [making gesture of about one inch between his index finger and thumb].[7]

"The dreaded words," Swain added, "I'm going home for Christmas." These words that can anger or dismay farm owners represent the long-awaited reprieve for mushroom pickers. Jesús Juárez came to the United States for the first time in 1972 at the age of eighteen and returned every three years, saying, "I went back for a couple of months each time. I was here alone and wanted to see my family."[8]

Although it is understandable that men who are separated from their families would want to return home, the longing to return home to Mexico is great even when their nuclear families live together in the United States. Narratives of home, exile, and return are common among these settlers, and although they actively build their lives and set down roots in Pennsylvania, it is not uncommon for them to hold onto their idea of home as Textitlán rather than Kennett Square.

This desire to return to Mexico allows settlers to maintain connections to extended family members and to renew their lifelong friendships to which they were accustomed in their natal community. Similarly, given the lack of social activities available to Mexicans in Kennett Square, it makes sense that they wish to return to the place where they find comfort in the company of their families, friends, and extended social lives.

The desire to return to Textitlán, however, accomplishes more than reconnections with loved ones. For migrants and settlers going through the complicated process of finding a place to belong in the United States, the knowledge that they have a home elsewhere is comforting. Textitlanecos engage in a number of narrative practices that recall home and homeland. They recall memories of their times at home, particularly in contrast to the lives they live in Pennsylvania. In the process, these narratives represent an important means of creating a symbolic place to which they can retreat during difficult times in the United States. Holding onto their homes provides a sense of assurance and stability in times of uncertainty. But for this to be an effective retreat, there have to be actual times when they return to Mexico, and when they return, they have to have someplace to go. Herein lies another instance of the meaning of "home," compressed beyond the idea of homeland or hometown: the actual homeplace.

The most surprising aspect of the casas vacías is not their numbers but their significance to the full-time residents of Texitlán. For the typical United States resident, the idea of having several empty or abandoned houses in one neighborhood elicits images of decay and neglect, such as those associated with America's abandoned urban neighborhoods or depopulated rural communities. Houses rarely sit empty in thriving neighborhoods. When their owner-occupants depart, the houses are sold or rented and new occupants join the neighborhood and larger community.

In the streets of Texitlán, the casas vacías are rarely identifiable as uninhabited dwellings; they are no more likely to be in disrepair than any other house on the street, and rarely will neighbors see these empty homes as a problem. Casas vacías are most often described as a natural consequence of migrating and settling in the United States. This trend is reflected in the current research on international migration, which has recently shifted away from thinking of migrant workers or immigrants as people who come to work and then stay and toward thinking of migration as a transnational process that involves a series of journeys between sending and receiving communities.[9] This is particularly true of Textitlanecos who are not so much residents of either Texitlán or Kennett Square but are journeyers who make the passage between Mexico and the United States, never completely forsaking one place or the other. In describing Textitlanecos as transnational settlers, it is not to say that they live their lives provisionally in the United States or Mexico. They are not transients. Indeed, their lives are lived in Pennsylvania as if they were not ever going to move again. Their personal narratives are often permeated with a desire to return to Mexico, but most are in the process of building permanent lives in Pennsylvania and are buying houses, rearing their children, and sometimes becoming citizens. Yet even so, they maintain their houses in Mexico.

Conversely, some Textitlanecos return home with the intention that they will not return to the United States. They settle into different jobs and rejoin life in their hometown. Lilia Ramírez, whose father and brothers all migrated at one time to the United States to work, spoke of her brother Ramón who had recently returned to Mexico and vowed never to return north. "He says he's not going back, that he doesn't like living in el Norte," she recalled, "but when he needs money, or a new car or wants to buy a house, I expect he'll have to go back."[10] He remained in Textitlán for three years, but recently returned to Pennsylvania with his wife (a Mexican-American woman whose parents were born in Textitlán) and newborn son.

At first, the idea of people living in the United States while maintaining homes in Mexico might seem paradoxical, but the casas vacías make life for Mexican migrants in the United States more comfortable.[11] In the process of making their journeys north and back again, they have kept their homes in the center of their existence. Homes are repositories of family experience and therefore memory, but they are also emblematic of the hoped-for future as well as the "accumulation of each past day" (Mackie 1981, quoted in Porteous and Smith 2001: 43). In this case, the hope is tied to a desire to live comfortably in their homeland without financial worries. So what appears to be a provisional commitment to living in the United States is actually a desire to maintain connection to the natal community while building a life in Pennsylvania. It is a way to exist in two places simultaneously and is the way that many of the Kennett Mexicans are most comfortable shaping their lives after settling in the United States.

The home is also a vehicle families commonly use to express their identity through the manipulation of personal space and external appearance. Unlike other aspects of an individual's or family's material culture, the house "reflects how the individual sees himself, how he wishes to see himself, or how he wishes others to see him" (Porteous 1976: 384). The homes of migrants, much like the homes of families in the United States, are a means through which families can demonstrate their economic success and personal taste. It is not uncommon to draw conclusions about a family based on the type of home they own or occupy. Similarly, the Mexican home is the location of family autonomy through the maintenance of household "rules" of interpersonal behavior. Although house rules may be contested, there is comfort in simply knowing how one is expected to act, and this in turn feeds into the security that householders feel when they are "at home."

HOMES AND MEMORIALIZATION

More than a guardian of personal safety, the house is also a repository of memory, through lived experience and the accumulation of experiences and personal objects that are collected over a lifetime. The daily experiences that constitute a life are fleeting, yet humans are compelled to relive and recall the commonplace events through narrative exchanges with others. The stories one shares regarding personal events reconstitute individual experiences for the teller as well as for those who listen. In the process of creating a story of daily life, what was once fleeting gains a measure of durability (Tuan 1980). Similarly, artifacts and personal objects can embody meaningful human experience and become the "objects of memory" (Kirshenblatt-Gimblett 1989). The significance of the personal objects that adorn or clutter a home is that they are used to reconstruct a narrative past. This is because domestic interiors are repositories of objects that have accompanied their owners over the years.

"These *material companions* to a life are valued for their continuity. . . . [Personal artifacts] accumulate meaning and value by sheer dint of their constancy in life" (Kirshenblatt-Gimblett 1989: 330).

Typically, the material objects that one sees as especially significant—family photos, souvenirs, and mementos—are objects that are likely to move with a person when they leave one residence for another. However, in the case of the casas vacias, the personal objects that adorn the home are left intact, as was obvious during my first weeks in Mexico. This practice of leaving one's house as an object of memory was illustrated by my neighbor, Maria. A few days after I arrived in Textitlán, Maria received word that her documents for permanent residency in the United States had arrived, and her husband Ángel returned to escort her and their children to Ciudad Juarez to retrieve their papers. It was an exciting time. She and Ángel had lived apart for eighteen of their twenty years of marriage, and Maria was ready to move north, even though the expense of flying her entire family back to Mexico meant it was uncertain whether she would ever be able to return. I asked Ángel what they planned to do with their house. For the first few months the house would be looked after by his mother-in-law, who was already responsible for Maria's sister's home. This was complicated by the fact that she was also moving north within the year. Still, he had no intention of selling or renting the house. When I asked who would care for these homes after everyone moved to the United States, he sighed and said, "That's a good question Débora. What will become of these [empty] houses?"

Although Ángel and Maria did not have the means to return to Mexico in the near term, they also acknowledged that they did not have a pressing need to return. When Maria's mother left for the United States six months later, all of their extended family members would be living there. Nevertheless, for some Textitlanecos in circumstances similar to Maria and Ángel's, the idea of returning to Mexico "someday" is a recurring theme in their life stories. When pressed to consider when this might be possible, most discuss plans to return permanently in a few years. In Pennsylvania, my friend Sergio Carmona said, "My girls are little now. I want them to grow up in Mexico, to go to Mexican schools. If we wait too long, we'll never be able to go back." Seven years later,

Sergio and his family were still living in Pennsylvania in a new town-house they purchased in 1999, and his daughters entered third and fifth grade in the fall of 2007.

Sergio's desire that his daughters grow up to be "Mexican," as opposed to "American," is a desire common to many families. Others are more pragmatic about their present options and know they cannot afford to live a middle-class life in their natal community. Among these families, their plans are to work in the United States until retirement age, then sell their homes and return to Mexico for good. Economically, this makes sense because United States Social Security and pension benefits stretch further in Mexico (in fact, a substantial number of Americans retire in Mexico for precisely this reason). Nevertheless, for this young working population, retirement is twenty-five to thirty-five years away, and making such a move is complicated in that their children most likely will be staying in the United States with jobs and families of their own. Many families will most likely return to Textitlán at some point for a vacation, and they reason that the house is paid for, so why not keep it for use at some undetermined time in the future? However, keeping a house for thirty years that might be used two or three times might seem shortsighted, especially when the proceeds from the sale of the house could be used to enhance their lives in the United States.

The Textitlanecos who elect to immigrate to the United States understand that from the moment they move north they are no longer able to afford their vision of an "ideal" life, which means earning a middle-class wage while living in their homes in Mexico. Their lives become a series of negotiations that they hope will provide more choices and economic opportunities, while at the same time not completely sacrificing their lives and identities as Mexicans. With these negotiations comes a constant tension between freedom and control, between having the impossible idealized life in Mexico and its associated autonomy versus the pragmatic control over their economic futures and the lives they can build in the United States. The home in this instance is not an economic investment but an emotional one. It is a means to keep their symbolic place in the community while they live elsewhere.

When doing fieldwork on the casa vacía during the summer of 2005, I met a woman who was caring for the house of an old friend who had moved to Pennsylvania two years before. Doña Celia was using her brother-in-law's house temporarily, although she had no immediate plans to move. When I asked her why her sister and brother-in-law had not sold their large house, which also included a small *tortarilla* (luncheonette) in the front, she said, "When we know our family members are moving north, we don't encourage them to sell their homes here. We know they may not be back for many years, but when they come back, we want them to have *their place* here to come home to."[12]

It is a common stereotype that Mexicans are people who live in the moment. Cinematic portrayals and joke cycles frequently play on this idea, emphasizing that Mexicans as a group are not likely to delay gratification. The casa vacía, however, is exemplar of the typical long-deferred fulfillments that are common with Mexicans who live in Kennett Square. Casas vacías are reified life experiences that have been reconstituted orally through family narrative but also structurally. They are emblematic of the desire to preserve permanent ties with their natal community despite the necessity to deter the immediate gratification of experiencing that community on a daily basis. The sacrifices and experiences through migration are transformed through memories of the lives they have left behind and are embodied in the homeplace into the hope that these connections will endure through their years of absence. This durability makes life in the United States possible, and as many Textitlanecos say, *vale la pena* (it's worth the effort). The casas vacías give meaning to years of sacrifice.

Regardless of whether or not it is realistic that they will go home to live, or their visits are brief reprieves, the care in maintaining and improving the empty Textitlán houses serves a purpose in the community and hearts of those who are attached to them. When I delved deeper into the idea of the casa vacía, I found that these houses are repositories of cultural memory. In fact, casas vacías function much like memorials where the home becomes a medium through which family members who stay behind are able to commune with the memories and shared experiences of those who have migrated. By becoming the custodial caretaker of the casa vacía, a bridge is established between distant relations. They cannot interact directly with their family members in the United States, but caring for the home provides an opportunity to do unto the home as they would do to the family member. The home and its contents become "objects of memory" but not as a life review. The houses serve as place markers for absent families who are still considered members of their home communities. Houses "function most effectively as a symbol when [they are] simply not lived in. An empty house is a potent symbol of the past. The house is also a better symbol of the family which once lived there if another family has not taken up residence" (Williams 1991: 130). Casas vacías are not simply symbols of the past, however; they also are symbolic of memories yet to come, the longed-for return and reunion. In this sense, the objects in the home enable recollection and hope to become palpable, more real.

This symbolism is as significant for families living in the United States as it is for those in Mexico. Porteous argues that the home is the "one sure refuge for the individual who is compelled to venture beyond its confines on a regular basis" (1976: 386). Although one may be away for extended periods, it is rare for a person to have more than one true home at any given time. Instead, people who are forced to leave home for any number of reasons often develop a dual sense of emplacement, what I have referred to as multilocal belonging. Porteous (1976) echoes this idea, distinguishing between the "felt home," where loyalties and emotional belonging reside, and the "euphemistic home," which holds no particular emotional attachment but nevertheless is the place where the person must dwell (388). The relocation from the felt home to euphemistic home is often traumatic.

Some Textitlanecos who live in Pennsylvania are still marginalized in their new neighborhoods. Even as homeowners and long-standing residents, these families often acknowledge that their sense of belonging in the United States is tenuous. If they are not homeowners, their situation is complicated by the fact that they must compete for limited rental housing and ultimately substandard housing. Refusing to let go of the house in Mexico then softens the reality of their lives in Pennsylvania. If they feel out of place here, then they can at least hold onto the idea that they have a rightful place elsewhere. The house allows Mexican families to hold onto dreams of returning home, of once again belonging to their natal communities. At the same time, the Mexican house maintains the position of the absent family in the community. They are not physically there to partake in social life, but their presence is not as easily forgotten because the house looms ever present, prompting their memory for those who care for the home and others who live nearby. Keeping the house intact also adds to the immediacy of the family's rightful place and keeps alive their membership in the community. This is evidenced in their self-identification, for although these Mexican families may live away for decades, they always refer to themselves as Textitlanecos in the United States and in Mexico.

The idea of leaving a house empty yet intact is one that is common in other parts of the world experiencing out-migration that is secondary to a depressed economy. In southern Appalachia, houses that were once occupied by families who have moved to other parts of the United States are often abandoned and not reinhabited by other families (Williams 1991). Similarly, in the Canadian province of Newfoundland, the countryside is dotted with the empty houses of Newfoundlanders who have migrated to Toronto and the United States in search of profitable employment. Folklorist Cory Thorne notes that among Newfoundlanders, "There is a constant desire to return to the island; the houses are kept for an undetermined future time when their return will be possible."[13] These examples echo the behavior patterns of Mexicans who have migrated or settled in the United States for employment. The exit from home in this instance is more akin to an exile than a voluntary movement from one place to another. Thus the attachment to the homeplace is understandable. It is a symbol of resistance to the economic imperative to move for viable employment and indicates the immigrants' true desire: to live in their home community.

In my examination of the casa vacía, I found that the family house in Mexico is not simply a dwelling or an economic investment. In fact, the intrinsic value of the house lies more in the broader community and the migrant families' attachments to that community, as evidenced by the fact that Mexican families maintain their homes regardless of the cost. Don Julio, a former migrant and octogenarian, cares for his brothers' homes. As we sat talking on his patio one morning, he looked out across his street and pointed out three different vacant houses that are owned by families who now live in the United States. He said, "I go to the houses every evening to check everything. Sometimes my brother rents the house but never the entire house. He may rent the first floor, but he always keeps the second floor locked and his family's things (furniture, clothing, electronic equipment, photos) upstairs. The house has all services, electricity, telephone, water, cable [television]. It costs about 800 pesos a month (approximately $80 U.S.) to keep the services, but when he comes back, the house is ready for him. He doesn't have to ask one of his brothers, 'Can I stay with you?' He has his own home to come back to."[14]

Around the corner, Don Victoriano took a break from running his small textile factory. He owns and operates a large machine that knits delicate crochet fabrics that he then sews into sweaters that are sold in Mexico and the United States. As we sat outside his door, he pointed to four houses on his street that are currently empty. Like other Textitlanecos, he not only knows the history of the empty houses on his street, but he also knows who the homes' caretakers are and the frequency with which they visit the home, where the absent families live in the United States, and how often the families who own the homes return to Textitlán. In one case, Don Victoriano attempted to purchase a large, well-appointed house located across the street from his own. He recalled, "That family, they haven't been back in eleven years. I asked his [the owner's] sister if I could purchase the house, they haven't been here in so long . . . but she told me no, they wanted to keep the house."[15]

Don Victoriano's account of the homes was similar to Don Julio's, in that the houses are meticulously maintained by their caretakers, but he also added, "These houses are the migrants' real homes (hogares). They don't just keep them as they left them when they went pa'Norte (to the North). They return with new pictures of their families and hang them on the walls. They bring new things to decorate the homes and improve them, like televisions and stereos. Then they go back to the United States to work, but this is always their home."[16]

Improving the home for their respites in Textitlán, regardless of how brief, is common. Doña Elena, who had been the caretaker for her daughter Ofelia's home when I rented it in 1999–2000, at first minimized her daughter's family's attachment to their first home. "No," she said, "they [Ofelia's family] don't have much left in the house right now." Yet, in the next breath she recalled, "Ofelia built a new bathroom in the house—did you know that?—two years ago, when they were here for a visit." I found this statement puzzling, especially because Ofelia's house already had a large, functioning bathroom. When I asked why they built a bathroom, she replied, "Well, you know that the stairs to the second floor are very steep, and the bathroom is on the first floor. Ofelia didn't want the children walking up and down the stairs at night, so she and Mario built a new bathroom upstairs."[17] When I inquired further about the new bathroom, Ofelia's niece Adela explained that the bathroom construction was started several months before the family arrived on vacation, which lasted a month. Mario and Ofelia's behavior here is significant. Although they have a home in Pennsylvania, they thought nothing of investing several thousand dollars building a bathroom in their former home, even though they have only used it three times since they moved their family to Pennsylvania.

MULTILOCAL BELONGING

The casa vacía also constructs a distinct sense of belonging. Typically, the connection of people to places is conceptualized as solitary: one person feels a sense of belonging in one particular place. In contrast, Textitlanecos belong to multiple places, although their connections to each place can vary from person to person. For many of these settlers there are two homelands. The felt home of Textitlán may always be the emotional home for these settlers, but rarely can one survive anywhere without some place attachment. Living in the United States requires the production of multiple attachments to at least two places: one that is work and place oriented, one that is emotional and people oriented. This "polygamy of place" (Beck 2000) constructs a dialect of place that transcends national borders and challenges the notion of the home country and host society as an either-or dichotomy for winning immigrants' affection and loyalty.

The sacrifice of living in the United States, of leaving family, friends and all that is familiar and comfortable with their homeland, is acceptable because it provides a means to an end: access to the middle class or at least a more affluent lifestyle and a future that is more economically secure for their families. Given the choice, however, most settlers in Kennett Square maintain that they would prefer to live in Mexico, but nevertheless do not want to give up the economic benefits of working in the United States. The displacement associated with settlement is destabilizing. As a means of mitigating this instability, immigrants reconstruct their lives in the United States through narratives as a temporary inconvenience that they believe will someday end. Keeping their homes in Mexico is tangible evidence that they will return.

The house also symbolizes economic and personal accomplishment to other Textitlanecos. Mexicans who have moved their families north must have the means to support them. Samuel Fernández told me that he made his first trip to Pennsylvania to save money to build his house. Starting with one room and then adding on until his family had a comfortable four-bedroom, two-bath home in El Bordo that was near the center of Textitlán, the Fernández home is a substantial life achievement. The bricks and cement correspond to his family's economic success and are testament to the fact that the years in the North paid off. Samuel's family now lives in another four-bedroom home that they purchased in Oxford, Pennsylvania. Nevertheless, he has no intention of selling his Mexican house, which his daughter Adela, living away while in dental school, occasionally uses on the weekends. Keeping the house is a luxury that Pedro can afford, which further demonstrates his economic success.

The connection that the Fernández family members have to their home was underscored in April of 2003 when Samuel and Lucia's oldest son, José (Joe), was killed in a car crash. His death was, understandably, a devastating loss. He was the first Fernández to die in the United States, and he had survived a near-fatal crash just three years before. Joe had returned to the United States in 2000 and worked for a while in Chicago, then returned to Kennett Square two years later. The other members of his family became legal permanent residents and moved to the United States in 2002, but Joe had been not been as fortunate. Samuel had started the legalization procedures eight years earlier, but Joe had turned twenty-one before the family's papers were processed.

Joe had a rebellious streak; his sisters told me that he had settled down since he returned from Chicago. He was dating a nice young woman and was driving home from her house when his car swerved unexpectedly off the road and hit a building. It was a single-car crash not far from his family's home; there were no witnesses to the accident.

The morning after Joe died, his cousin Celia called to give me the sad news and to let me know that the family was planning funeral services for him in Pennsylvania. She also mentioned that there was some discussion about whether they should return his body to Mexico, as the cost to transport his body would be considerable.[18] Despite the cost, the family decided to return Joe's body to Textitlán. It was a difficult decision, because they all knew that in taking his body back, they would have fewer opportunities to visit his burial place, but in the end they concluded that this was what he would have wanted.

As is the custom, a family member in Mexico placed a black ribbon over the front door of the Fernández home in Textitlán as a sign of *luto*, or mourning. My family and I traveled to Pennsylvania for the services, but I was unable to attend his rite of Christian burial in Mexico. I returned to Textitlán approximately four months later. The black ribbon was still hanging, in tatters, above the door. Inside, the house was much the same as when the family left it the year before. Joe's childhood toys were still displayed in his room, just as they had been when he left three years earlier.

Visiting Joe's grave with his sister Adela that summer, I was struck by the inscription on his tomb:

This tomb preserves your body
God preserves your soul
and we preserve your memory.

The Fernández casa vacía, like others in the family's pueblo, serves an almost identical purpose: to preserve the memory of a family and life in a material form that is immovable and indestructible. Mexican families who have settled in Pennsylvania in many ways have also passed from one realm to another. They are gone but also present in the narratives and memories that are elicited when their family and friends see their houses. With their passage remains the chance of return and reunification, a hope that is maintained within the intact homes that are left behind. In this regard, the casa vacía is probably a misnomer. These are not empty houses but homes full of memory and meaning.

FOUR In the Shadows and Out

MEXICAN KENNETT SQUARE

It is a cloudless fall day in Kennett Square. I find myself with unexpected free time before an interview I have scheduled later this morning. Although the trees are shedding leaves, the wind is warm and whipping through the streets. A steady stream of foot and automobile traffic moves along State Street as local residents come into town to work, meet friends for coffee or lunch, or shop in one of the locally owned boutiques. Kennett Square is a small, prosperous community of some five thousand residents in one of Pennsylvania's wealthiest counties and reminiscent of those depicted in Norman Rockwell paintings. The sky is clear blue and the streets are lined with small comfortable houses. Most are sturdy frame houses with airy porches and small gardens. I've parked on the east end of town today where the houses are larger, many made of brick and stone with large manicured lawns and impressive flowerbeds.

But as I walk down the street, my senses are bathed in an unpleasant smell. A foul odor, something like rotting compost or stable leavings, permeates the warm autumn air. Within a few days I would discover that the smell is the perceptible presence of the local mushroom industry, which is one of the defining characteristics of Kennett Square. Somewhere near town a farm is "changing out" the mushroom soil, a mixture of manure and mulch, hay, stable waste, and ground corncobs. The town is known as the "mushroom capital of the world," and Kennett residents are proud of their farming heritage and the success of this local agribusiness. Although residents sometimes complain about the smell, it is generally tolerated as a necessary inconvenience.

I decide to stop by Harrington's Coffee shop. It is a large coffee and sandwich bar, locally owned, and this morning it is bustling with customers. Harrington's is housed in what appears to have been an old retail shop—there are floor-to-ceiling windows across the front of the café, revealing the ancient polished wood floors and a bowed glass counter filled with pastries. As the door swings open, the air is rich with the smell of freshly roasted coffee and baked goods. Several young mothers push strollers toward a large seating area in the back of the cafe, and a group of what I presume to be local merchants exits a meeting room behind the counter, shaking hands and swapping farewells. The men, dressed in dark suits and ties, are accompanied by a single woman wearing a red "power suit." I order coffee and a bagel and find a seat at a table near a large window that faces State Street as I settle in to watch the people walking by. The Barnard Taylor Library, just a block away, seems to have steady stream of patrons this morning; I would later learn that there was a storybook reading for children and that the library is a well-used and important part of Kennett Square's communal identity. I review my field notes from the previous day, and I begin to jot down my observations from my vantage point at Harrington's. Kennett is a busy place, and the downtown is active and lively.

As I sit in Harrington's and take in the street scene, I realize how comfortable and at home I feel sitting among some of Kennett's hometown residents. Although I do not know anyone in the coffee shop, it doesn't seem to matter. It is as if everyone there assumes that I am one of them and that I belong here. We are not "known" to one another, but it could easily be assumed that I am a Kennett neighbor: I am white, educated, and middle class, which is the way many of Kennett's long-term residents would describe their community. I also note that from my vantage point in Harrington's, the one notable absence from this street scene is the local Mexican population. An essential part of the local economy and the ubiquitous mushroom industry, when I began my work here Mexicans were essentially hidden in Kennett Square.

This chapter examines the process of incorporation and the evolution of the sense of belonging from the perspective of Mexican settlers. It examines the transformation of the Mexican community in Kennett Square and the social context that for many years rendered them largely invisible, which then slowly became more welcoming. Based on interviews and observations, I argue that Mexican belonging in Kennett Square was a process contingent largely on three factors: migrant social networks, the attitudes and actions of the receiving community, and access to public space (Probyn 1996; Leach 2002; Buonfino 2007; Mulgan 2007, 2009).

Based on narratives collected over a ten-year period, I document the transition of Kennett Square's Mexican population from once occupying the shadows of town life to becoming a visible presence and contributors to the local sense of place. Most often I found that the practices that Mexican settlers employed to situate themselves were recalled through place-based narratives that articulated their understanding of their situation in Kennett Square (de Certeau 1984).[1] These narratives offer insights into migrant perceptions of emplacement and belonging, as well as their interpretations of local acts of displacement and ostracism through their accounts of exclusion. Although settlers often linked place-based narratives to their new home in Kennett Square, they also recalled emplacement through narrative reconstitution of their past residences. The role of place-based narrative is central to understanding the experience of Mexican settlers; although overt indications of a Mexican presence and open displays of cultural practices were rare in the early years of settlement, Mexicans nonetheless worked to create a sense of belonging in private venues that often went unnoticed by the majority population.[2]

Although they were essential to the ongoing operation of the mushroom industry, when I began this project in 1995, Mexicans were seldom acknowledged as part of the community. At that time, Mexicans constituted nearly a third of Kennett Square's population and some eight thousand Mexicans lived in the surrounding county, yet their proximity was overshadowed by a discourse of exclusion that defined identity and belonging in Kennett Square.[3] It was this paradox, of an affluent community that identified with its mushroom industry and had clearly prospered because of it and the perpetually absent Mexican laborers who harvested mushrooms and made their prosperity possible, that drew me to study migration, settlement, and adaptation in Kennett Square.

I begin by describing the daily life of Mexican families in the mid-1990s during my first months working in the field and then analyzing the discursive and spatial practices of the long-term residents that limited the ability of Mexicans to feel like they belonged to the community. As the Mexican population grew and became more engaged in life in Kennett Square, Mexican narratives shifted to demonstrate a gradual transition toward emplacement and belonging. What is significant here is not so much the demographic shift in Kennett Square's population, but the process by which Mexicans in Kennett Square came to see themselves as part of the local community. This transition changed their social relationships with longer-term neighbors in Kennett Square and allowed them to establish themselves as rightful members of the community.

SITUATING LOCAL IDENTITY: BELONGING IN KENNETT SQUARE

The importance of belonging has become an emerging interest for scholars and policy makers alike (La Grange and Ming 2001; Alleyne 2002; Wiborg 2004; Savage, Bagnall, and Longhurst 2005; Buonfino and Thompson 2007; Chow 2007; Johnson 2007; Striffler 2007).[4] Only one of many factors that influence immigrant experiences, belonging is closely associated with other salient aspects of immigrant life, including the development of social networks, the accumulation of social and cultural capital, and involvement with local political organizations. In communities where populations have been relatively stable, the idea of belonging is often interpreted as straightforward: if you've spent most of your life in one place, you belong to it. But in periods of instability or rapid social change, such as in times when migration and settlement transform what were once familiar neighborhoods into new destinations of immigrant settlement, people are more likely to feel that they do not belong (Dench, Gavron, and Young 2006; Mulgan 2009). Feelings of displacement can also occur for longtime residents when they see their neighborhoods transformed around them and perceive their hometown as changed and unfamiliar.[5]

Indeed, the message that settlers do not belong may be expressed through explicit or implicit messages that they receive from landlords and neighbors, the labor market, and public authorities (Mulgan 2009). In this regard, the sense of belonging is also a fundamental aspect of the sense of place (Harvey 1996; Morgan 2000; Savage, Bagnall, and Longhurst 2005).[6] In common usage, when one speaks of a sense of belonging it is often to reference an existential context, such as a long-term attachment to one's hometown or neighborhood. It can also reference a sense of ownership of or deep incorporation in a place or mutual understandings between people who reside in a common location (Leach 2002). Belonging is also characterized as a fundamental human need; it influences most aspects of human experience including health, a personal sense of satisfaction, and life choices (Baumeister and Leary 1995). Similarly, belonging is viewed as necessary for human survival, because it is vital to know whether the place and people in the environment can offer the necessary support systems for day-to-day existence, such as adequate work, shelter, and safety (Mulgan 1998, 2007, 2009; Buonfino and Thompson 2007).

Migration scholars typically characterize the sense of belonging in one of three ways: as an expression of legal rights, such as citizenship or legal status to reside in a nation-state (Karst 1989; Castles and Davidson 2000); as an aspect of individual or group identity (Lovell 1996; Nast and Pile 1998; Savage, Bagnall, and Longhurst 2005); or as a feature in the development of the sense of place (Leach 2002; Cresswell 2004; Massey 2005). Although the emphases of these studies vary, it is clear that each of these aspects of the sense of belonging is intimately interconnected. Using the concept of citizenship as an example, it becomes clear that these characteristics of belonging are not distinct: citizenship in modern democratic societies, for instance, involves both rights and responsibilities. It assumes that the individual citizen "belongs" to the nation-state and as such has the right, through participation, to influence and shape the nation and local communities (i.e., the expression of legal rights). The citizen's identity is similarly shaped through his or her residence, interactions, and understandings of the nation-state, and citizenship assumes a de facto territoriality by locating the citizen as a resident of the nation-state. Thus, by exercising rights and responsibilities as a citizen, individuals shape their local communities and the larger society (i.e., the sense of place), while at the same time one's identity is influenced through understandings of what it means to be a citizen (Gupta and Ferguson 1997; Castles and Davidson 2000).[7]

In everyday experience, the importance of belonging extends beyond discussions of migration, globalization, and the role of the state. Although the legal rights that accompany citizenship and legal permanent residency are important determinants of the immigrant experience, for many the responses and reactions of local residents and officials within the places where they reside most directly affect their day-to-day lives. In Kennett Square, it was the changing responses of the majority population that facilitated Mexican responses to their new home; as the longer-term residents became more welcoming, Mexican narratives reflected these changes and expressed a sense of connection to Kennett Square that was not common in the early years of settlement.[8] Indeed, often it is the local exchanges between newcomers and longtime residents that determine the ability of settlers to develop a sense of belonging in new destinations.[9] Belonging is not limited to a tangible or localized (territorially bound) experience but is also achieved in virtual or imagined social spaces (Gupta and Ferguson 1992; Probyn 1996; Bell 1999; Fortier 1999).[10]

To reconstitute the process of belonging for Mexicans who settled in Kennett Square in the late 1980s and early 1990s, I have identified three periods of Mexican incorporation: Early Settlement and the Evolution of the New Destination, which took place largely between 1994 and 1998; Being and Belonging, primarily the years 1999 and 2000; and Adaptation and Incorporation, 2001 through 2005. I have established these periods based upon events that many people in Kennett Square (Mexicans and American) identified as transformative. The events I document here demonstrate the process through which the sense of place and belonging develop and highlights how Mexican social networks in Kennett Square emerged. I identify these events within distinct time periods as a way to illustrate transitions in the broader Mexican community and Kennett Square but not to suggest that every Kennett Square resident experienced these periods in exactly the same way or as definitive.[11]

I begin with an overview of Kennett Square as I found it in 1995 and examine the discursive practices that were in play that effectively erased the Mexicans' presence and their contributions to the community. Drawing upon this context, I then discuss each of the periods of Mexican incorporation in turn, drawing upon my direct observations, oral history interviews with Mexican settlers from 1995 to 2001, and a series of oral histories that I collected after 2001.

MEXICANS, MIGRATION, AND MUSHROOMS

Kennett Square's mushroom houses, small clusters of single-story white cinder block buildings, are found throughout the community and in the surrounding county. It is easy to overlook the nondescript mushroom houses, but the mushroom is an iconic symbol in Kennett Square. Mushrooms are sold in all local markets and gourmet shops. The town hosts an annual mushroom festival and parade. For many years there was a mushroom museum.[12] Mushrooms appear in art, advertisements, and children's books. The elementary school curriculum includes instruction about mushroom production, and it is a local custom to embellish floral arrangements with portabellas. Here homeowners and businesses display mushroom topiary and lawn sculptures. Local businesses, whether or not they are associated with the industry, include mushrooms in their logos. Certainly, the local identity and economy is rooted in the mushroom industry, and local residents acknowledge that this is what sets Kennett apart from other neighboring farming villages.

Promotion of the mushroom is viewed simultaneously as a means of civic boosterism, which in turn contributes to local interpretations of the community. The image that the local English-speaking residents have of themselves and their town is that of a hard-working, family-oriented community. When asked about their community, Kennett Square's longer-term residents cited the town's legacy as a historic Quaker settlement and described themselves as inclusive and peaceful. This, they explained, was apparent in the local political system: the first African American principal of Kennett High School was appointed in the early 1970s, and the mayor throughout the 1990s and his predecessor were both African American.[13] Similarly, the mushroom industry was described as a product of solid American values; the cohort of owners and growers consisted primarily of the descendants of Italian immigrants who picked mushrooms at the turn of the century. These men and women described themselves as the quintessential expression of the American Dream: honest, hard working, and dedicated to their community. What they had, they worked to earn. They described maintaining their family farms as a constant struggle. Mushroom growers were sometimes invited to community meetings to talk about the industry, which growers often described as being threatened by competition from the global agricultural market, particularly the proliferation of imported mushrooms.[14] Local residents were responsive to growers' concerns, and as longtime community health nurse Joan Holliday told me, "The mushroom industry is so vital to the Kennett community and what we're about. I can't imagine Kennett without this industry."[15]

Yet despite the talk about mushrooms and the pervasiveness of it as a symbol of local identity, few acknowledged the Mexicans who picked them. This was evident in all the promotional literature on mushrooming, from the publications of the American Mushroom Institute and the Mushroom Museum to locally produced Web sites, produced to educate local and national audiences on the industry and its heritage. The Kennett Square Mushroom Museum, which was locally owned and operated by a farm owner, offered an impressive professional exhibit of the industry's history and the process of growing mushrooms. The one-room exhibit included model mushroom houses, photographs, and video displays that provided a glimpse into a commercial farm. Yet there was no mention of the industry's labor, particularly that the labor force has always been drawn from newly arrived immigrants. Instead, the tiny harvesters at work in the model mushroom house were all Caucasians, allowing the visitor to imagine that mushroom laborers are part of the white working class rather than Mexican nationals and other laborers of color who have dominated the population of mushroom workers in Kennett.[16]

Similarly, a locally produced Web site, MushroomLovers.com, offered a virtual tour of a Kennett mushroom farm. These photographs were devoid of human subjects, with the exception of the edges of gloved hands that are busy picking mushrooms. As is typical in the discourse of mushrooming, the spawning, harvesting, and packing are described in the passive voice: "Mushrooms are harvested at the peak of freshness and shipped to the packing house."[17] The children's book Let's Go to a Pennsylvania Mushroom Farm (Yocum 2000) was written by a local elementary school teacher and details the stages of mushroom production in a comparable manner.[18] There is no mention of the actual people who work in (and are thus vital to sustaining) the industry. Rather, the author describes the industry as an essential aspect of local heritage.

It is not surprising that the mushroom growers, like most producers of consumer products, strategically marketed mushrooms to prospective consumers so that their production was apparently ideologically neutral and independent of the social, economic, and political circumstances that facilitated production and profit. These examples were exceptional because they were intended for the local community of schoolchildren, residents, and consumers. The local discourse about Kennett Square's mushroom industry effectively divorced the industry from Mexican labor, fostering the impression that the industry, and as a consequence Kennett Square, functioned independently of Mexican labor.

When Mexican workers were occasionally mentioned in relation to the industry, it typically involved labor problems. This was evident on the rare occasions when the Immigration and Naturalization Service (INS) conducted raids at farms and packing plants (Bustos 1994a,b). For example, when growers spoke about Mexicans, they often complained that immigration laws threatened the industry by producing labor shortages.[19] Although these occasional statements reflected the fundamental role that Mexican labor played in this industry, rarely were the contributions of Mexicans acknowledged, let alone commemorated, in the industry or community.

Thus the predominant discourse of the mushroom industry worked to enhance the industry in the eyes of locals while simultaneously minimizing the role that Mexicans contributed to the industry, and by extension, the broader community. The balance between acceptance of the industry and the Mexican laborers who work there seemed to require persistent effort. This is because the citizen townsfolk, who are outside the bounds of the industry and its promoters, could not as effectively erase Mexican presence and the local changes that result from widespread Mexican settlement. By 1995 the Mexican population had grown to the point that it could no longer be confined to the margins of the community, and Mexicans steadily began moving into the community.

EARLY SETTLEMENT AND THE EVOLUTION OF THE NEW DESTINATION

When families began to be reunited in the early 1990s, many began to purchase homes in established neighborhoods that were previously home only to English-speaking residents. Peggy Harris,[20] the director of the local migrant health clinic, described the situation: "[T]his is what the [English-speaking] community is objecting to . . . Mexican families moving into, buying housing or renting low-income family housing for the kids and for their wives to raise in a nice community and to be part of the community. And now it's not being accepted. It's being stereotyped, as you know, 'a [Mexican] family moves into my community I'm going to have drugs and alcohol and all that garbage and all that stuff that I see down at Center Street [an apartment complex where many Mexicans live in Kennett Square].' "[21]

This opposition culminated in a "yellow ribbon campaign," when English-speaking residents tied ribbons to the front of their houses in protest of Mexican families moving into their neighborhoods.[22] Although there was no abrupt "white flight," houses once owned by whites were typically purchased by Mexicans. Yet despite the fact that Mexicans were buying homes and raising families in Kennett Square, thus returning to Mexico less frequently, many English-speaking residents continued to conceptualize their Mexican neighbors as transients who would eventually return to Mexico.

The idea that Mexican settlers were transients who lacked a desire to make their home in Kennett Square was not entirely an invention of Kennett Square English-speaking citizens. Rather, several narrative versions of this idea were transmitted from the Mexicans themselves, via their social service or health-care providers (who constituted the majority of bilinguals in the community), to the English-speaking population. The common thread in these stories is the belief that although Mexican families are living settled lives here now, at some point in the future they will return to Mexico. The "evidence" that supports this idea is the continued close relations that this population maintains with families and communities in Mexico. This should hardly seem surprising when one considers the parents, grandparents, siblings, and other extended family members who remain in Mexico. Regardless of whether the goal of returning to Mexico will ever be realized, the English-speaking majority in Kennett Square seized upon this idea as a means of explaining why local Mexicans who are settled, and by conventional indications permanently settled, nevertheless are not considered part of the community.

The attitudes of Kennett Square's English-speaking population about Mexican commitment to the community during this time cannot be underestimated. Belonging is governed as much by the social environment as by the individual's willingness to become part of the community (Dench, Gavon, and Young 2006; Buonfino and Thompson 2007; Mulgan 2009). As a shared social process, belonging cannot be effectively realized unless newcomers and long-established residents can subscribe to a common, or at least complementary, vision of their community (Pred 1984; Mulgan 2009). In order to be incorporated as a member of the community, a person or group must fit into the *idea* of the community, which requires the tacit or overt acceptance of the established residents (Chavez 1991; Anderson 1994). Acceptance by the long-established residents does not mean that community members have to know all of their fellow citizens; in many instances they never meet them nor hear of them. However, incorporation into the broader social imaginary, that is, the ways in which people imagine their social existence, particularly how they fit in with others and expect a commonly held understanding of social arrangements, is essential (Taylor 2002). This incorporation ensures that in day-to-day activities and long-term community planning, new residents are not only considered but also included in decision-making processes. When Kennett Square's established residents refused to imagine Mexican settlers as part of the existing community, Mexicans were not included in long-term community planning, nor were they part of community events.[23]

One might expect undocumented residents to experience exclusion; however, Mexicans who were legal permanent residents were no more readily incorporated into the Kennett Square social imaginary in these early years of settlement. Many Mexicans told me that although their status as legal permanent residents provided access to economic privileges, such as improved employment mobility, they felt no more at home or part of the local community than their undocumented counterparts. This social context did eventually shift, but during the early years of settlement the overt and implicit opposition to Mexican settlement made belonging in Kennett Square difficult.

When I began my work in Kennett Square, I spent many days at Project Salud, a migrant health clinic. I selected Project Salud as an initial field site for two reasons: it was the one place that most Mexican families access during their first weeks in the Kennett Square and it served as the Kennett Square Mexican population's only community center. During the first weeks, I would sit in the waiting room and strike up conversations with the clients as they waited for their appointments. After a few weeks, however, I decided that sitting out front was not necessarily the most productive use of my time: my exchanges were cut short as people were called for their exams, many seemed nervous, possibly about seeking medical care, thus making conversation difficult. When I mentioned this to the clinic director, Peggy Harris (a registered nurse and certified nurse practitioner), she suggested that I volunteer as clinic nurse. Her reasoning was that it would make me a familiar face to the Mexican population, and it would be a help to the clinic staff, as their increased patient population strained limited resources. During the next five months, I worked in the clinic two to three days per week. I spent most of my time as a clinic nurse: vaccinating children, providing health education to patients with chronic illness, and translating for the physicians. It was through these initial interactions that I became acquainted with many settling families and was able to commence fieldwork on a regular basis.

Project Salud was then housed in an office building on Birch Street. It was a unique health clinic for its time because it was a nurse-managed clinic. There were two part-time physicians who worked a combined total of twenty hours per week and were responsible for co-signing orders that were outside the scope of practice for a nurse practitioner in the Commonwealth of Pennsylvania. The day-to-day operations of clinic were managed by Peggy Harris and her nursing staff. Harris was responsible for managing most of the client cases in the clinic, which saw about four thousand clients per year.[24] Although the clinic was open to anyone, the majority of the clients were newly arrived Mexican families and more established Mexican settlers who did not have health insurance.[25]

Like so many aspects of the Mexican community in Kennett Square, Project Salud was largely invisible to the casual observer, as it was tucked away behind the offices of a propane company and a twelve-foot chain-link fence. The main office was a large open waiting room, sparsely furnished with hard plastic chairs and a few tables. In the corner was a play area filled with toys for toddlers and small children. The main desk sat prominently in the center of the room and was staffed by a receptionist. There were large colorful Spanish-language posters promoting healthy lifestyle behaviors and information about various chronic illnesses, such as diabetes and high blood pressure. Although there were no books or magazines, the small side tables offered a variety of pamphlets providing information on topics ranging from how to use an infant car seat to proper nutrition.

Although the clinic staff was exceptionally friendly and welcoming, the clinic space itself often felt vacuous and cold. During the winter months the waiting area was drafty, as the clinic itself seemed to sit in a natural wind tunnel; gusts of freezing air often slammed the clinic door against the outside wall. The examination area, which was often warm to the point of discomfort, consisted of two treatment rooms and a small lab that doubled as a nurses' station, all accessed through a narrow hallway. The small exam rooms each housed an exam table, a rolling chair (for the physicians and nurses) and one hard chair for patients and family members. In the corner of each room was an office desk. The desk allowed exam rooms to double as the physicians' and nurses' offices, an arrangement that Peggy Harris frequently lamented was less than ideal. The clinic space often felt cramped and there was always another person waiting to be seen by a practitioner.

From the main waiting room area, there was another long hallway that led to the offices of La Comunidad Hispana (LCH), a social services organization.[26] The clinic and LCH were run by the same executive director but funded by different grants from state, county, and private sources. This arrangement worked well for LCH and Project Salud clients, who often required services of both agencies. The clinic and LCH functioned as a type of community center for Mexican families in Kennett Square and the surrounding county: it was a place where Mexican settlers knew they could go for information, social support, and health care. While I was working in Kennett Square, there was no other agency, cultural center, or clinic for newly arrived Mexican settlers, which points to the limited social support available and an essential lack of recreational and cultural activities for families. In the mid-1990s, Mexicans relied on Project Salud and LCH to learn how to negotiate life in Kennett Square and often mentioned the agencies as important aspects of adapting to their new home. The agencies filled an important source of social support in the absence of other social networks within the Mexican community.

Mexican settlers in Kennett Square could count on a warm welcome at the clinic and LCH, but in the broader community their participation and inclusion—the visible expressions of belonging—were slow in coming. The first Mexicans in Kennett Square were men who came to pick mushrooms. They followed a long line of low-skilled workers who had cycled out of the industry as better opportunities became available. Many of the men who brought their families to settle in Kennett Square in the early 1990s had lived in area for years on a seasonal basis. For the most part, these were single men who lived on farms and were rarely seen in town. Their lives were austere; it was common for as many as eight to ten men to live together in a two-bedroom apartment. They slept in shifts and had little time for recreation because they worked long hours. These Mexican men were in the United States to work and send money back to their families; they were not necessarily interested in spending extra money on their accommodations or recreation. Nor were they interested in putting down roots. For them, Mexico was home.

Often the men migrated with friends or family members from Mexico and established friendships through work, but they rarely saw their time in the United States as a means of developing a social life. Alfonzo Ramírez recalled his work life in the early 1970s: "I had a brother in Pennsylvania picking mushrooms. They had a lot of work in the mushrooms because the owners didn't give us a day to rest. We would start picking every day at four, or sometimes two in the morning, and we would pick until night, sometimes eleven o'clock at night. We slept for two hours, sometimes more, sometimes less, and then we went back to picking."[27] While relating this story, Mr. Ramírez made it clear that he was not unhappy working for 18-20 hours a day. As he said, "I would work seven days a week, and I didn't want to take a day off. I was bored at home (in the apartment), so I worked.[28]

Most of these early settlers reported that they received amnesty under the Seasonal Agricultural Worker provision of the Immigration Reform and Control Act (IRCA), and were eligible to bring their families to Pennsylvania. I met others who had obtained legal residency status through other means, such as marriage to an American citizen, but this was rare. Although they had legal status, men still had to wait between four and eight years to receive permanent residency for their families. In some cases, women and children came to Pennsylvania immediately, as undocumented immigrants, while they waited for their applications to be ratified through the slow and tedious immigration process; but the majority of families I spoke to elected to wait in Mexico until they could be legally reunited.

During my first months in Kennett Square, there appeared to be two distinct groups of residents living in the same place but occupying distinct social realms: Mexicans and English-speaking American citizens, the majority of whom were of Anglo-European descent and spoke English. Mexican families did, in many respects, live as a community apart from their English-speaking neighbors. At times, however, the two communities came face to face. Mexican men often worked for American farm owners or company managers, and Mexican children attended Kennett Square schools alongside their American peers. Mexicans and longer-term residents also encountered one another in local businesses, as English speakers owned all but a handful of local grocery stores, restaurants, and other businesses. The majority of the doctors, teachers, and social service providers were also English-speaking, so Mexican families seeking these services encountered Americans in these contexts as well.

These opportunities for contact between Mexicans and longer-term residents were, on the whole, superficial encounters. Mexicans occupied a distinct social space in the community. The contrast between the homes of Mexicans and other Kennett Square residents is one example of this. Most of the homes in the Kennett Square borough were built in the late nineteenth through the mid-twentieth centuries. Although there are a number of large stately homes on Kennett Square's west side, overall the houses in town are small by contemporary standards, typically three bedrooms with one or two baths.[29] In the late 1990s, some farmland surrounding Kennett Square was sold to developers and transformed into suburban neighborhoods, many featuring large houses of three thousand to five thousand square feet. As the preference for larger homes increased among suburban residents, the smaller houses in Kennett Square were less often purchased by the town's longer-term residents. More often, these homes were either starter homes for newly married couples or small families or simply not the preference of middle- and upper-class residents, who were choosing larger houses on expansive properties in the surrounding county. As English-speaking residents moved out of Kennett Square for larger suburban developments, Mexican families began to move into the modest neighborhoods in town. This was a slow transformation; by the time I completed fieldwork in Kennett Square, the majority of Mexican families continued to live in one of Kennett Square's apartment complexes.

The Center Street and the Lafayette Street Apartments had long been Mexican-only residences. Local residents considered these complexes a "problem." During my first months in the field, I was often warned to never enter either complex alone and that many of the apartments were believed to be drug dens and frequented by prostitutes. My first visit to the Lafayette Street Apartments was enlightening. Walking into the brick three-story garden apartment complex, I was overwhelmed by the smell of mold. The hallways were cold and dank and painted a garish institutional green. The floors were covered with a sticky industrial carpet worn down from years of use. Once I had been inside several apartments, it was obvious that there was more diversity in the living situations of the residents than was communicated in the local oral tradition, and I learned to expect anything.

The exteriors of Lafayette and Center Street complexes suffered from years of neglect. There was no attempt to landscape the grounds, and in many places the grass was either high or barren to the point that there was nothing left but compressed dirt. The complexes did have common space outside, and often men congregated after work in the afternoons and socialized on balconies or in the lawn with friends. Although children lived in the Lafayette complex, I never saw them playing outside. In another complex just outside of town in Toughkenamon, there was a large treed grove just behind the apartment's parking area where residents placed old chairs. Most sunny afternoons after work the young men of the complex would gather in the grove for hours to hang out.

Some apartments, despite being in disrepair, were fashioned into cozy homes for families. Decorated with secondhand furniture and other items, these apartments were often too small for most families, but they were clean and well maintained. They were arranged with care to demonstrate the family's efforts to make the modest apartments homelike. Other apartments housed single men who bunked together to cut down on expenses. These apartments might house eight or twelve men, and the conditions signaled that this was not "home" but a place to sleep or, in some cases, nothing more than a temporary shelter during the working months. These apartments were often poorly maintained by landlords, untidy, and outfitted with a mishmash of cast-off furnishings with sheets, rather than curtains, hanging in windows. Rarely would single men attempt to personalize the space, beyond a calendar, a holiday gift from a local Mexican restaurant, or perhaps a Mexican flag. Overall, the apartments inhabited by single men were dark and drafty but sufficient for a brief work stay in the United States.

One day while visiting Juan, the father of a woman I met in Textitlán, my then three-year-old son, John, asked to use the bathroom. When I told him John's request, Juan hesitated. As always when we came to call, he greeted us in the apartment foyer where we would chat for fifteen minutes or so, sharing the news of Textitlán and his family. He never invited us in, and it was clear that he did not want us to see the apartment. In this case, the alternative of John relieving himself outside prompted Juan to invite us in to use the apartment bathroom. We passed through his small living room/dining room and found eight men huddled together on two large sofas and several chairs. They were watching television and there was no light on in the room, so it was dark and cool. "Mommy, there are so many men in here," my son commented on the compact space that surprisingly accommodated such a large group. There was hardly room in the bathroom for both of us, but it was clean. The linoleum was buckled and worn to the point that I could not tell what color it had been, and although the paint was not pealing, it bubbled, giving the walls a wavy appearance. The mirror over the sink was cracked, the silver worn away leaving dark blotches, and there was a steady drip from the faucet. When John sat down, the toilet wobbled from side to side; it was clearly not bolted to the floor. Juan's apartment was not the worst example of immigrant housing in and around Kennett that I saw, but it also was not atypical of the apartment complexes that were reserved for Mexican workers and their families.

Although there were a variety of domestic situations for Mexicans living in Kennett's apartments, it was also true that most Mexican men

and women living in Kennett Square with their families used the Lafayette and Center Street apartments as temporary housing. Several women
told me that their apartments were always in disrepair, and that although their rents were expensive for the community (approximately
$600–$700 per month in 1995), the absentee landlords were rarely available or willing to fix problems or renovate the common spaces.[30] When
better living quarters became available, families moved out and into
large houses that had been subdivided into apartments or into one of
several trailer parks that were located just outside Kennett Square.[31]

As a rule, in the mid-1990s, Mexicans did not participate in local events
sponsored by the citizen population. Many times men told me that they
were instructed by their bosses to stay away from community events.
Some of the men I talked to did not see their exclusion as a problem
per se, because they were planning to go home in a few months and they
spent most of their time working. As more families settled in Kennett
Square, however, the lack of entertainment and the boredom associated
with living in the United States became a common complaint. The design of Kennett Square's small community was also not conducive to the
informal social interactions that were common in Mexico, and the area
had no public transportation.[32] Women who did not have jobs outside
the home were left alone in their small apartments with children for
ten to twelve hours a day while their husbands were working or alone
when their children started school. In Textitlán, women rarely needed to
learn to drive; most of their daily activities were located within walking
distance of their homes, and the extensive public transportation system in
the village was available for trips out of their neighborhoods. Once in
Kennett Square, however, women often described feeling trapped in their
apartments until their husbands returned from work in the evenings.

Even with access to transportation, Mexican families often complained
that there was little to do during their leisure time. There were no movie
theaters within ten miles of Kennett Square, and those featured only
English-language films. It was even less likely to see social and cultural events that commemorated or even acknowledged a Mexican presence, such as celebrations of Mexican cultural heritage or the observance
of Mexican national holidays.[33] There were several Mexican-owned

businesses, mainly restaurants and small grocery stores, but almost no Mexican representation on local governing boards. Although they were unlikely to participate in community events, the degree to which Mexican families were actively excluded from community events was nevertheless difficult to measure. What was clear is that in most cases, they were not considered in the planning and implementation of local events. In the case of the Mushroom Festival, by far the largest and grandest event of the year, Mexican men told me that their bosses at the mushroom farms told them they should not attend the festival. Although the men were not offered a reason as to why they would be unwelcome, by 1998 Mexican workers were incorporated into the event as part of mushroom picking demonstrations, and one year there was a mushroom picking contest. In other cases, Mexican women told me that they did not take their families to Kennett Square's community events because they simply felt unwelcome.[34]

For this reason, I was not surprised that many Mexicans complained of feeling alienated and isolated from the local English-speaking population. However, many also felt little connection to their fellow *paisanos* (countrymen), even those who had lived and worked in Kennett for many years. One afternoon I was talking to Vicente Zavala, a local restaurateur, about living in Pennsylvania. Vicente crossed the border for the first time when he was fourteen years old, and though there were other migrants who had spent more time in Kennett Square, he was the most prosperous Mexican I met. He spoke English comfortably, owned two restaurants, and had purchased a home in an exclusive neighborhood just outside of town, although he admitted that he and his family had not made friends with other families in his neighborhood.

During our conversation, Vicente began to describe his impression of the Mexican community. "You know," he recalled, "so many people don't respect our customs here." I had thought he was talking about Americans, but I was mistaken. When I asked for clarification, he went on to explain, "And when they [a Mexican couple who were getting married] ask us [Vicente and his wife] to be, you know, in the wedding. They used to a come to the house like three, four times a week. But they got married and never . . . never . . . never again. They never came [to visit].

Yeah. See that's when I think they try to . . . how you say that . . . I think they try to use you. Cómo se dice? Use? . . . Like when I was padrino (godfather) for a little girl. And the parents . . . they didn't tell me but, someone [another friend] told me that they expected me to pay for that [the baptismal party]. . . . It wasn't a little, it was a big party. They had two pigs, a live band. And I found out they wanted me to pay. I say why? I mean I bought the baby all the clothes you know, in Mexico. The tradition is, you buy the clothes. You buy them a present. . . . it's what we used to do [in Mexico]. But since then, I don't see them for years, and I don't know why. Because I'm always here [in the restaurant]."

Vicente's expectations were based on his understanding of Mexican customs of patronage and fictive kinship as they were practiced in Textitlán.[35] Although he was disappointed with the responses of these families, it was not that he was unwilling or unhappy to be part of their lives or even to help pay for their celebrations. But he was disillusioned when people he helped did not fulfill their social obligations in return by maintaining their friendships.

Many of the settlers' responses to living in Kennett Square were consistent with what one would expect after moving to a new community, especially because coming to Pennsylvania entailed adapting to life in a foreign country.[36] Mexican reactions to living in Kennett Square were also indicative of another issue: the sense of belonging is a process influenced by everyone living in the community (Mulgan 2009). It was not uncommon in Kennett Square for longer-term English-speaking residents to create distinctions between residents who they considered local, or "people who belong," and those who were nonlocal, or outsiders (Urry 1987, 1995).[37] These distinctions worked to segregate the Mexican population and were reproduced through a variety of cultural practices such as differential access to public space or services, exclusion from the cultural life of the community, and overt racial or ethnic discrimination. These distinctions point to the fact that Mexican residents did not have equal access to the community's resources. For Mexicans who had recently arrived, this exclusion from community life inhibited their ability to feel like they belonged in Kennett Square, making their adjustment to life in the United States more difficult.

In most respects, reuniting families was a positive decision for Mexican families. I knew several men in Kennett Square who had recently received legal residency papers for their wives and children. They were delighted to have their families join them, knowing that living together as a family would mean they could see their children grow up and their wives would be available to help manage their households and take care of them.[38] Some men also had to adjust to living with their families again.

One afternoon I stopped by the Fernández home to visit and found my friend Julia loading several baskets of dirty laundry into her husband's 1985 Buick Regal. Julia and I had met in Mexico before she moved to join her husband Enrique, and I often stopped by to visit during their first year in Pennsylvania. It was a cold, rainy day and Julia was directing her two teenage daughters to help. "I'm sorry we can't visit today, Débora," she called as she walked back into the trailer to fetch another basket of clothes. "Enrique just returned from work and we have to get to the laundromat before dinner." The Fernández family lived just outside Kennett Square in an aging trailer that was to be their temporary home until they could find something more suitable. The trailer was a doublewide that sat awkwardly on a steep lot with three others. It provided adequate space for the couple and their four children, but it was old and drafty, the floorboards squeaking mercilessly whenever anyone walked from room to room. When the family moved in during the summer, the trailer was sweltering, the lone window air conditioner clearly inadequate to cool the space. With the approach of winter, cold air whistled through the flimsy windows. The trailer had no washer or dryer, making laundry day a several-hour ordeal. While Julia and her daughters carried overflowing baskets of dirty clothes to the car, Enrique stood outside, watching. He leaned against the vehicle as I approached to say hello. He greeted me but seemed rather glum. When I asked, "What's up?" he replied, "I just got home from work, and now I have to go out again to drive them to do laundry. We'll be there for hours, and I'm tired. I worked twelve hours today, and I haven't even had time to take a shower." I knew it was typical after a long shift in the mushroom houses for men to go home, shower, and rest for a few hours because they were exhausted and anxious to wash away the smell of mushroom soil that permeated not only their clothes but also their skin and hair.

Julia heard Enrique's last remark and recognizing his reluctance said in a teasing tone, "Oh enough! You want clean clothes and we can't drive. The clothes don't wash themselves." She looked at me and shook her head as if to say "what does he expect?" as she closed the trunk and started to get in the car. "I'm sorry we can't stay and visit, but come back another time, Débora," she said as she and her children piled into the car. Enrique reluctantly followed, then he started the car and they drove away, leaving me standing in the muddy gravel driveway, amused by this unexpected stumbling block of family reunification: relearning how to balance individual needs with those of the reunited family.

Moving to the United States also caused the unforeseen consequence of isolation and alienation for women and older children. When women and children began arriving in the mid-1980s, the community changed dramatically. Whereas Mexican men generally found living with their families extremely satisfying, women and children were not always so pleased with their new homes. Women were likely to be housewives, especially those with small children, as they had been in Mexico. Women expressed feelings of isolation and often mentioned that these feelings surprised them. While living in Mexico, they had long dreamed of re-uniting their families in the United States. Isolation was clearly not part of their experience in Mexico. Separated from their extended families and longtime friends, women found their situation extremely frustrating. Having spent their entire lives in one small community where they had long-standing and strong social connections, many of the women who arrived in Kennett Square felt out of place. Alma Bedolla was a housewife and mother who had lived in Kennett Square six months when I met her.

My visits with Alma often took place during the late morning, while her six-month-old baby boy took his morning nap. Alma lived on the first floor of a once stately home two blocks from the center of town. From the street the house looked large, but the first floor apartment seemed too small for a family of four. It consisted of three rooms and a kitchen that looked as if had once been a walk-in pantry. Each of the rooms was over-flowing with children's clothing, baby gear, and toys, including two car seats, a stroller, and a high chair. Like many old houses, this one appeared to have limited storage space.

Walking through a long foyer, the first room we entered was the children's bedroom. It was large and airy, painted white with high ceilings and expansive bay windows. Alma had painted the baseboards and window frames bright blue. Judging from the windows and style of the woodwork, the children's room was most likely the main living room when the house was a single-family home. We crept quietly through the children's room, as the baby was asleep, and entered a rather dark, cramped dining room. This room had a modest wood table with four chairs and a large wooden cupboard where Alma kept dishes, pots, and pans. Beyond the dining room was a small square kitchen. This room included a small refrigerator. On the adjoining wall was a small sink, and directly across from the refrigerator was a narrow apartment-size stove. There was only room for one person in the kitchen.

During many of my visits, Alma spent most of her time in her closet-sized kitchen. Adept at maneuvering the small space, Alma could stand in one spot and pivot from the stove to the refrigerator to the sink as she prepared meals for her family. On a typical day, Alma was awake by 6 a.m. to prepare breakfast for her husband. The family customarily ate a hearty meal of eggs, beans, and sausage with tortillas. After her husband departed for work, Alma would wake her daughter and help her get ready for school. Alma walked with her daughter to the elementary school, just a few blocks from her apartment, taking her infant son along in the stroller. Her husband left for his morning job by 7 a.m. and returned at 2 p.m. for *comida*, the main meal of the day. Comida was the only time her family was together on workdays, and then only for a few hours.

Alma's family situation was unusual in that they were able to maintain the mealtimes that were customary in Mexico. Her husband, Miguel, worked two jobs to support the family. During the day he worked at a mushroom farm, cleaning out spent mushroom soil and replacing it with fresh soil. He returned for a few hours in the afternoon, then left in the early evening to join a cleaning crew that provided janitorial services for office buildings in a nearby city, sometimes not returning until after midnight.

While she was alone during the day, Alma tried to busy herself by getting out of the house. She did not know how to drive, so she had to rely on friends or acquaintances for transportation out of town. When the weather was warm she would stroll around town with the baby while her daughter was in school, but when winter arrived Alma spent most of her days and evenings in the apartment alone. She would cook, clean, and take care of her children, and she spent most of her time without contact with other adults. The family had a small television set but could not afford cable, so the only stations available broadcast in English. The short, cold winter days also bothered Alma, and she said, made adjusting to her life in Kennett Square more difficult. "I hate the cold," she often said, "and the sky is so dark here."

Alma said of the people she had met since arriving to Kennett: "I've met a lot of people at my church, and they've all treated me well. But I don't really have friends here, just acquaintances. It's very hard to meet someone here who you can really trust."[39] Developing trust (*confianza*) is a major obstacle to belonging for Mexican settlers in Kennett Square. Mexican narrative accounts of adjusting to life are riddled with stories of misunderstandings and disappointments.[40] Lack of trust was not limited to Mexican and American interactions. Mexicans often described their friendships with one another as distant and disconnected. When Alma mentioned her disappointment that she had no friends in Pennsylvania, I recalled a previous conversation and asked about her relationship with a woman named Leticia who often drove her and her children to the grocery store and to the pediatrician's office. She said, "Leticia is not my friend (*amiga*); she's an acquaintance (*conocida*)." She continued, "I have many acquaintances here, but it is difficult to find someone I really trust. I feel sad about that. . . . My husband says that I should be content that we have a good life here, that he is a good husband, not a drunk (*borracho*), not a womanizer (*mujeriego*). It's true, but I still can't feel happy here."[41]

The lack of trust that Alma described was not a reflection on Leticia's character so much as it was that the two had only met one another recently. In Mexico, families typically live in neighborhoods and with the same people for a lifetime. These long-term relationships are often based

upon interactions between families that span generations. When a Mexican says, "I have confidence in that person," it is a much weightier statement than it would be for the typical American. The confidence expressed
by Mexicans about their friends and neighbors means not only that they
trust the individual but also that the person comes from a family of
good people (*gente decente*). Alma continued, saying, "Sometimes it feels
impossible to meet a person of confianza here, because all of the [Mexi-
can] people are new. . . . It's difficult to make new friends here."[42]

The situation was similarly difficult for older children, even though
they were attending school with other Mexican students and were enrolled in programs to assist them. Students who arrived to Kennett Square
were eligible to enroll in the Migrant Education Program for three years.
Migrant Education assists students with homework and provides social
support for children and their families as they transition into life in
the United States. Loretta Perna,[43] a Migrant Education Student Support
Specialist, commented that recently arrived students "are the students
who are not doing well—most of them. I mean it's very rare when I meet
someone who says, 'Yes, I was excited about coming; I'm doing great.'
Most of them, the first year, they hate it. They do not like being here.
They do not want to go to school. They want to go back."[44]

It is not uncommon for women and children to want to go back to
Mexico during their first year in Kennett Square, and even some who
had lived in Kennett for several years continued to have difficulty adjusting. What was noteworthy about Mexican women's narratives of
adjustment was how they went about reconstituting their lives in the
United States. In the early years of settlement, women often related stories of profound homesickness. They were sad about their lives in Kennett Square, particularly when compared with the lives they left behind.
When asked about their lives in Kennett Square, most women talked
about the lives they had left behind and thus focused on a past sense of
belonging rather than their present displacement. For example, Maria
Elena Gutiérrez, a mother of three who arrived in Kennett Square in
1996, recalled her life in Mexico when asked about adapting to life in the
United States: "The life I had in Mexico was much more family centered.
It was family centered because my family is so big; we had a social life

but always with the family. Together as a family we would go out to parties, we would go out to the plaza and now we don't go to parties too often, there is no plaza . . . . The only thing is that in Mexico we could have a better social life, much more full, because there we could have this [social interaction] every day, going to the plaza, and there would always be people to talk to. Here the first few years, living in a trailer with few neighbors, it was difficult."[45]

Maria Elena's emphasis on public space ("there is no plaza") and the family relationships highlight the two central aspects of Mexican life that are often the most difficult to reconstitute in the United States: long-term relationships and a claim to public space. In the most ideal case, migration from Mexico brings a nuclear family together. Because work is what drives most of the Kennett Square Mexicans north, the extensive family networks of grandparents, parents, cousins, and lifelong friends are often left behind. Even in circumstances like those in Kennett Square, where many families are from the same village in Mexico, I witnessed situations of extreme isolation because settlers did not necessarily live near old friends who had also moved to Kennett Square, and even when known friends lived within close proximity, work schedules often limited social time. In addition, like many small towns across the United States, Kennett Square had no spatial equivalent to the Mexican central plaza where people congregate and socialize. In fact, in the instances where Mexicans would congregate and claim a public space, it inevitably caused problems for their English-speaking neighbors who saw this simply as loitering.

One afternoon in 1998, I witnessed an encounter in front of the Kennett Square public library. I had been working in Harrington's and left to walk toward my car, which was parked nearby. En route, I noticed three Mexican men standing on the sidewalk in front of the library. I made note of this instance later that day, simply because I had never seen Mexican men congregate there before. I had heard a few longer-term residents mention Mexicans who "hang out" there and heard that some women in the community had complained of being afraid to enter the library when the men were standing around outside.[46] The men were young, appearing to be in their early twenties, and were wearing baggy jeans, oversized

T-shirts, and baseball caps. They seemed to be talking amiably to one another, gesturing and smiling as they interacted, although I could not hear their conversation. As I walked, I noticed two women walking alone and another woman with two small boys walking toward the library. As they approached the men, I noticed that the womens' gates shifted and they walked more quickly and purposefully toward their destination. The men continued to talk, but became silent as the women passed by. The first two women averted their gaze down and away from the men. The third woman, whom I assumed to be a mother accompanying her children, had been looking down and talking to the children, so she did not notice the men right away. When she was some twenty feet away from the men, she looked up, and then took each boy by the hand, guiding them past the men. She did not appear to greet the men, but she held her head up, posture erect, as she walked past. The men nodded in an apparent acknowledgement or greeting as the woman walked past, but she did not respond. The boys were young, probably preschool aged. They had to pick up their pace to keep up with their mother but continued to stare openly at the men and watched them with interest as they walked. The taller of the two children craned his neck to continue looking at the men even as his mother urged him along, finally through the library door. As the woman and children passed, the men looked toward the door and said nothing, then returned to their conversation.

I returned to my car, thinking about what I had witnessed and the possible interpretations of this event. One could assume that this was a group of ne'er-do-well immigrants, lazing away a warm day, and that the women, by avoiding a possible interaction with the men, were expressing racial intolerance. It could also be that the women felt awkward approaching the men simply because they were unknown to one another. Although these interpretations are plausible, after speaking to a number of Mexicans and longer-term residents in Kennett Square I recognized these, and other similar instances of encounters in public spaces, as competing interpretations of the use of public space. The Mexican men, by virtue of their presence, were making a claim to the space in front of the library as a rendezvous point. As they passed by, the first two women were signaling discomfort, or possibly disapproval, as they encountered the men. Finally, the third woman, while not averting her gaze, simply ignored the men and their nonverbal acknowledgment whereas her children gawked openly. Each of these behaviors suggests that by taking up their positions on the street, the men are not only worthy of their attention, they are unusual or unexpected in this location or out of place.

Although I never heard of direct confrontations or police calls in response to Mexicans "hanging out" in public spaces, from time to time Mexican men told me they were asked to leave public places where they were standing around, for example by owners of convenience stores. Most Mexicans that I spoke to recognized that their Kennett Square neighbors were not happy about having people socializing on the street. Perhaps in response to this, it became customary for Mexicans to socialize inside their homes or apartments or, in fair weather, on their front stoops and in their yards or—as I mentioned above—behind their apartment buildings. As a result, their lives and activities were largely out of sight.

What I found striking about many of the narrative accounts of Mexicans during this time was how their experiences differed from studies of newly arrived Mexicans who settled in the gateway states of California, Texas, and Illinois.[47] Whereas all new arrivals typically express feelings of displacement, gateway communities offer migrants established social support networks that typically include a thriving immigrant community, recreational events such as festivals honoring the patron saint of the hometown, and family celebrations of holidays, birthdays, and weddings. These networks and events that help ease the transition to life in the United States are not available in the first years of settlement in a new destination. The Mexicans who settled in Kennett Square were pioneers, creating a permanent Mexican community without the benefit of established support networks. Although a large and growing Mexican population was developing in Kennett Square, the migrants had not yet established a Mexican cultural center and there were few Mexican-sponsored recreational or social events. When Mexicans did attempt to establish recreational spaces, these were met with resistance and objection.[48] Likewise, there were few family celebrations, such as baptisms or weddings, because families typically returned to Mexico for these events or simply did not celebrate them.

Perhaps because they were so new to the community, in the mid 1990s most Mexican women structured their spatial worlds within their homes in Kennett Square, even when those homes were cramped and claustrophobic. These apartments and trailers were not comfortable living spaces, but they were places completely within their control and therefore allowed them to feel at ease if not at home. The judgments the Mexicans made in assessing their state of belonging during early settlement were based on the interactions that they had with longer-term residents and the broader community through work and everyday activities. These encounters helped to shape their understanding of their place in the community and similarly influenced their interpretations of how much freedom they might have to establish themselves within the community. Not surprisingly, as Mexican families started to purchase homes and became a more permanent presence in the Kennett Square, this interiorly focused aspect of the Mexican community started to change perceptibly.

BEING AND BELONGING

Belonging is understood as an emotional response, a feeling of being accepted as a member or part of a community or group. Mulgan (2009) identifies belonging "feedback circuits," or communicative responses to newcomers that are indicative of whether or not a group is accepted in its new environment.[49] These range from the very intimate, such as the ties that newcomers have to families and friends and associations with local organizations and groups, to interpretations of macro structures, such as whether local economic conditions and employment options provide adequate opportunities and the implementation of the political system, particularly whether it empowers or disenfranchises residents. Much of what determines a person's sense of belonging develops from responses to what are essentially spatial practices, the daily routines that people engage in, allowing them to "mark" or "inscribe" spaces with meaning (de Certeau 1984). When a community expresses support for new groups and their cultural practices, this can reinforce belonging for all residents of a community (Mulgan 2007, 2009).

Determining what cultural expressions are displayed and where and under what circumstances the displays take place can send powerful messages to all members of the community. Whether public cultural expression is limited to nominal expressions, such as the use of bilingual signage, or is displayed through formalized celebrations of cultural practices, including festivals, public observations of holidays or family events, and the implementation of formal ritual practices, the freedom to express oneself culturally is of vital importance in the development of belonging. It is through these practices that newcomers express their ownership of their new home, and through their participation with longer-term residents that they create a shared community. In the spring of 1999, about six months after Buena Vista townhouse community was completed, Kennett Square seemed to transform into a more welcoming place for its Mexican residents. This was largely because Buena Vista was the first distinctly Mexican place in the community, and it was built with the support of the longer-term residents of Kennett Square.[50]

Buena Vista townhomes are located right outside the city limits of Kennett Square.[51] Built by the Alliance for Better Housing (ABH), an independent nonprofit organization created to develop new housing for low-income families in Chester County,[52] the townhomes sit atop a hill overlooking U.S. Route 1 and offer a view of the surrounding countryside. There are twenty-four houses in the development; they are arranged in a circle facing a central grassy knoll with a large wooden gazebo at its center. The gazebo is used for community picnics and cookouts. A large circular drive surrounds the knoll, and there are parking spaces in front of each row of townhomes. Tucked in the far corner of the property is a large play gym, the same quality as those common to elementary school playgrounds.

At the entrance to the subdivision is a one-story townhouse that is a combination office and community center for the ABH. The basement area is used as a community center and includes a large meeting room, a fully stocked kitchen, and a smaller meeting room. Though the community center is free and open to all residents of Buena Vista, residents are asked to sign up to use the room for communal or private events.

The homes are standard frame townhouses with small decks. When the floor plans were being discussed before the community was built,

Howard Porter,[53] the executive director of ABH, asked prospective buyers what features they wanted. Like many small townhouses, these consist of an unfinished full basement and two finished floors of living space. Each has a small foyer and stairs leading to the second floor to one side. The original plans included a large living-dining area, powder room, and a large eat-in kitchen with a sliding glass door leading to the deck. Porter changed this floor plan, transforming the first floor powder room into a full bath with a shower stall. Porter explained that many of the Mexican families wanted this change: men came home dirty from mushroom farms or construction and wanted to bathe immediately without walking through the house.

Within a few months of opening, this otherwise standard suburban community of uniform, beige vinyl-sided townhomes blossomed into a distinctly Mexican community. Shortly after settling in, new homeowners began tending their small front yards so that by the time spring arrived, their gardens were a riot of color, with flowerbeds overflowing with geraniums, impatiens, and petunias. The warmer weather also transformed the community's common areas into centers of activity. Children played on the sidewalk or along the drive, and people visited house to house as neighbors got to know one another. On temperate evenings families who were not working an evening shift pulled their chairs out onto their small porches and sidewalks to visit with neighbors, recreating the street scene common in Textitlán.

Once Buena Vista opened, the English-speaking population seemed to soften to the idea of Mexican settlement, and there was a palpable change in local attitudes toward Kennett Square's Mexican population. These changes were most noticeable for the families who lived in the new townhomes. But Kennett Square's longer-term residents also seemed more ready to embrace the idea that Mexican families could be part of Kennett Square's local identity. Buena Vista was featured in a number of positive stories in the *Kennett Paper,* and word spread through town that the Mexican residents were not merely maintaining their new homes, but also they had created a beautiful neighborhood that exceeded the expectations of their English-speaking neighbors. In the months that followed, more Mexican families purchased homes in town, and the Alliance for Better

Housing purchased property close to Kennett Square's town center and planned another small townhouse community. In years past, ABH's attempt to develop property in town stirred considerable controversy for some of Kennett Square's longer-term residents who were afraid that ABH would rent their properties to large groups of Mexican men.[54] After the success of Buena Vista, ABH found that their plans for subsequent new development were met with more even-tempered responses.

I spent many fieldwork hours in Buena Vista documenting the transitions of Mexican families and the events that took place in the community center. During the first year, Porter worked to bring the small community together. As the director of ABH, he was aware that some of the residents had known each other prior to moving to Buena Vista, and in one case, two families living in the same townhouse row had been neighbors on the same street in Textitlán. For the most part, however, neighbors were unfamiliar with each other and had to get to know one another. Shortly after families moved in, Porter and his staff hosted a pot-luck party to celebrate, inviting all of the Buena Vista families as well as friends and supporters from the local community. The small community center was overflowing with partygoers, but Porter later mentioned that the pot-luck idea caused confusion for several residents who were clearly unfamiliar with the concept. Instead of bringing food and staying for the party, which was arranged on their behalf, a few families thought they were being asked to bring food for Porter's party to celebrate ABH's achievement. Porter noted that these women prepared elaborate dishes, brought the food to the party, then left.

This type of miscommunication was soon resolved as regular community gatherings became more common. As part of my research, I went from door to door to meet residents of Buena Vista and talk to them about their experiences as new homeowners. I learned that the women wanted to get to know one another, and they were interested in activities to facilitate social interaction. As an experiment, I organized weekly meetings that we referred to as *charlas* (chats) in the community center, where women could drop in, eat, and talk. For the first few weeks, I brought snacks and drinks; thereafter this role was assumed by women in the community.

These meetings were revealing in that they gave the women a forum where they could discuss their everyday experiences and problems and get to know one another more intimately. Older women sometimes talked about the difficulty of raising teenagers in Pennsylvania and their surprise at the differences in child-rearing practices. Younger women often brought their infants and young children with them. In July, Magdalena Rodríguez brought her newborn son José with her to the charla. Her presence prompted her neighbors Gloria and Zulema, both in their early forties with children ranging from sixteen to twenty years old, to reminisce about their days as young mothers in Mexico when life seemed much more straightforward. Gloria recalled, "Ah, I remember living alone in Textitlán with three small ones while my husband worked here. I was always busy, but I had my mother with me every day." Like Magdalena, the other mothers of small children would also find support from their older, more experienced neighbors. These mothers, many of whom had children born in the United States, would also talk about raising their children in Pennsylvania. Maria Elena Gutiérrez, a mother of two young daughters said, "It worries me that my girls aren't going to know their uncles and aunts and cousins." It was difficult to be so far from their extended families and home, and most of the women expressed fears that their children would not think of themselves as Mexicans.

In the months after Buena Vista was completed, the women of Buena Vista not only became acquainted with one another but also invited friends who lived outside the community to visit. Buena Vista became an important part of everyday experience for Mexicans in Kennett Square. The townhouse community gave these Mexican families decent homes and a social center that they had never had in Kennett Square. The fact that the long-term Kennett Square population responded positively also facilitated the process of belonging, allowing Mexicans to "read" their physical and social environment in a new way. Following what I would come to term the "Buena Vista social network," I realized that the construction of this community served as an anchor for one segment of the Mexican population in Kennett Square. Buena Vista's residents became the start of a functioning social network that established a sense of belonging for those who were associated with Buena Vista and, to a lesser degree, Mexicans who did not live there.[55] This transition was followed by a period when the narratives told by Mexicans in Kennett Square and the activities that they engaged in shifted. For the first time, I began to witness events and hear stories that reflected Mexican understandings of their legitimate place in the community.

INCORPORATION AND ADAPTATION

Within a year of Buena Vista's opening there were other notable changes in Mexican Kennett Square: Mexicans began claiming public spaces through direct interactions with the Americans (particularly when Mexicans were fluent in English) and Mexican families began holding celebrations locally that had previously been observed almost exclusively in Mexico. It was not uncommon in Kennett Square to overhear Americans commenting upon their Mexican neighbors in public. From time to time I would overhear commentary and critiques about the Mexican population while on the street and in grocery stores. These statements would lament the changes taking place in Kennett Square or describe the perceived failings of new Mexican neighbors. On one occasion, Manuel López-Peña, a Buena Vista homeowner and a foreman in a nearby manufacturing plant, recalled an encounter with an English-speaking woman in a grocery store. He said, "I was in the [grocery] store, and this lady, she was talking to another American woman. She was saying how Mexicans are lazy and other mean things. She was standing right next to me, but, you know, she didn't know that I speak English. So I said something to her. I said, 'Excuse me, but I can understand what you just said.' She looked surprised, and she said she was real sorry. She was real apologetic. . . . I said, 'You know, you gotta be careful. You really never know who speaks your language.'"[56] Manuel's decision to speak out was surprising, as many of the encounters that Mexicans have with the long-term Kennett Square residents were more guarded than this. This incident suggests that Manuel felt comfortable enough in his position in the community to correct the woman. He could have feigned unawareness of what the woman said and remained in the shadows of the woman's experience; instead he challenged her brazen and unfair characterization of him and his group. His assessment, "you gotta be careful," also censured her behavior and communicated that he also has a legitimate place in the community.[57]

Other instances of emplacement and belonging evidenced by Mexicans were less confrontational and simply expressed recognition of Kennett Square as their home. Throughout my fieldwork, Mexican families occasionally celebrated baptisms and quinceñeras in Kennett Square, but for the most part, they returned to Textitlán to mark special occasions.[58] In Textitlán it was customary for families to rent one of the many large *salones de fiestas*, or party rooms, for occasions such as a child's first birthday party or baptismal celebration. Hosting such an event in Textitlán would cost a fraction of the expenses one would incur in Kennett Square, and because many Mexican families were anxious to celebrate these events with their extended families and friends, returning to Mexico for these celebrations was a logical choice. There were also only a few places in Kennett Square that could accommodate large groups of forty or more people, such as the fire hall, but the cost of renting these places for many families was prohibitive. In addition, facilities offered limited food choices, as local caterers could not provide the standard Mexican offerings that were commonly offered in Textitlán.[59]

The celebration of family events indicated an important turning point for Mexican families because these events indicated that Mexicans felt connected to the area. A family celebration in their new community, particularly time-sensitive events such as a baby's baptism or a child's birthday, is often assumed to be a natural consequence of living in a new place. In Textitlán, infants are usually baptized within the first few months of life. Yet in the early and mid-1990s, I observed that it was not unusual for families to postpone baptisms and similar celebrations until they returned to Textitlán. Thus babies were sometimes baptized as late as two or three years of age, and other events, such as weddings, were celebrated in Mexico exclusively. When families decided to begin celebrating these occasions in Kennett Square, it signaled a new level of incorporation and a shift in Mexican attitudes about family life and belonging. Families celebrated these events locally because they had friends and family members to invite to them. They also had access to and felt comfortable using local spaces for these events.

Buena Vista's community center provided a space for families in the neighborhood to hold events. I was invited to several celebrations at the center. One Saturday evening in May 2000, my husband Ken, our children Helen and John, and I were driving to Buena Vista for a birthday party. It was a special night because it was the first party my friends Luís and Maria Elena would host at their new home: a fifth birthday party for their daughter Patricia. I met Luís and Maria Elena during my first weeks in Kennett Square. Maria Elena became pregnant with their first child just three months before I found out we were expecting twins. Our families were close; of all of my Mexican friends in Pennsylvania, only Luís and Maria Elena had actually visited us at our home.[60]

As we drove to Buena Vista, I asked Ken what he thought the birthday party would be like. "That's simple," he replied. "I think it will be just like the parties we attended in Mexico." When we arrived, we realized Ken's speculation was correct. The party was nearly identical to a standard Mexican family celebration. The community room in Buena Vista was arranged to accommodate forty people. Long tables were placed end to end and covered with white paper tablecloths and pink paper placemats. The ceilings were decorated with pink and white balloons and pink streamers. At the center of each table were several small bowls of jalapeño peppers and a small stack of napkins. In the corners of the room there were coolers of cold beer and soda. In the center of the room was a small table with Patricia's birthday cake. It was a large white sheet cake with pink roses embossed with "Feliz Cumpleaños Patricia."

When we arrived, Luís and Maria Elena were there to greet us and escort us to our seats. They asked us what we wanted to drink and then went to fetch the sodas and beer. We were among the first guests to arrive. Helen and John soon became restless waiting for the party to begin, so Ken and I walked them around the room and eventually outside. Once everyone was seated, Maria Elena, Luís, and several of their neighbors began bringing plates of food to each guest. Much like the party events up to that point, the food was exactly what we would have enjoyed in Mexico: carnitas, rice, brown beans, and tortillas.[61] When all of the guests had been served, Luís and Maria Elena finally sat down to eat.

As we finished eating, Patricia began to open her gifts. In Mexico it was not uncommon to have a professional photographer on hand to document the party and opening of gifts. Here, one of Luís's neighbors served as the official photographer. When all of the gifts were opened, Patricia was serenaded with "Happy Birthday to You," translated into Spanish, and the cake was cut and distributed to the guests. At this point, the party format departed from those I had attended in Mexico. Typically, after the cake is eaten, children go outside for play and piñatas. When we went outside, I was surprised that there would be no piñatas. "It's too dangerous," Luís explained. "We're afraid that the kids might hit each other with the stick." I told Luís I was surprised, as piñatas are a common activity in many American birthday parties. "Aren't you being a bit too cautious?" I asked him.

"Well, maybe," Luís responded. "We had a community meeting after we all moved in, and decided that we would not use piñatas here in the community center. I think Howard [Porter] mentioned it would be a liability if someone got hurt, so we agreed it was for the best."[62] Instead, the candies that would have been placed in the piñatas were distributed among the children. Shortly afterward, the party began to break and everyone departed for home.

In the final months before we moved to Virginia, my family and I were invited to baptisms and parties for children's first communions, and each came to follow a familiar routine that was similar to those I had witnessed in Mexico with minor adaptations such as the ones mentioned above. In some cases, we were the only American family attending. By the time I finished weekly fieldwork in Kennett Square in 2001, other American families, most often friends who Mexicans met through their work, were also attending these celebrations.

The celebrations were not the only indication of belonging and emplacement. Men and women both remarked that living in a decent home, particularly in proximity to other Mexican families, was a major influence in allowing Kennett Square to feel like home. Maria Elena Gutiérrez said of moving into her new home: "Now [since moving from a trailer to Buena Vista] I don't miss our social lives in Mexico as I once did; I have a new life here and it is very social. We live with Mexican neighbors and Patricia has friends to play with here. . . . Truthfully, I am more connected here now than I once was."

Mexicans were also laying claim to the public space of Kennett Square, and in some instances, were held up as model members of the community.[63] Celia Espinosa was one of those model immigrants. She was extremely bright, learned to speak English quickly, and worked as a waitress in Mexican restaurant on the weekends. In many ways Celia was a fortunate young woman. Her father had received documentation through the amnesty in 1986, and she and her family were able to obtain legal residency fairly quickly. She was also fortunate to have studied beyond elementary school during the years her father worked in the United States when she and the rest of her family remained in Mexico. While many Americans in town knew of her and her accomplishments, few were aware that her background in Mexico helped to ensure her academic successes in the United States. Nor were many aware that when she joined her family in Pennsylvania, she had a difficult and traumatic transition and that she had been diagnosed with anorexia nervosa and suffered an extreme weight loss during her first year in Kennett Square. Celia and I met when I worked in the clinic, and I became a close friend of her extended family.

When Celia graduated from high school, she invited me to attend her ceremony. "You have to come," she said, "but I'm not sure my mom and dad will be there." I knew Celia was joking about her parents, Mario and Ofelia, although the humor here was related to the fact that she knew her parents were ambivalent about taking time away from their jobs, even for the event of her high school graduation. This was a significant change from what Celia would have expected in Textitlán. There her graduation would have been celebrated with a huge party for her family and friends.

Mario and Ofelia were very proud of Celia's academic accomplishments and often said so. She graduated near the top of her class and planned to attend Penn State University at the main campus, which was no small achievement.[64] Despite their own financial successes, Mario and Ofelia often made comments that indicated they believed that their prosperity was tenuous. A day away from work meant a day without pay, and thus they were extremely uncomfortable taking time off even for her graduation.[65]

Kennett High School's graduation was held outside in the large lawn in front of the school on a warm evening in June. There was a large crowd when Ken and I arrived with our children, and we were relieved to find Ofelia and Mario without much difficulty. They were sitting alone with their younger children toward the back of the many long rows of chairs. The graduation ceremony started promptly. From our seats we could barely see the podium when a local Protestant minister stood to offer a blessing for the ceremony. Offering the prayer in English, he was accompanied by a translator who echoed his benediction in Spanish for the benefit of the Mexican parents and family members in the audience. I was delighted that the school administrators had made the effort to do this but disappointed when I realized it was the only part of the ceremony that would be translated.

As the graduates doffed their caps, the crowd began to disperse. Mario leaned over and asked me if we would join his family for dinner at the nearby Mexican restaurant; we agreed to meet them there as soon as possible, knowing that the graduation traffic would likely delay our arrival. When we arrived at the restaurant, Mario and Ofelia were waiting for us at a large table. There was room for both of our families, and Mario mentioned the extra chairs were for Celia and a few of her friends. "I don't know who will come with her, but we have chairs for her friends if they join us," he told me. We waited for a while for her, but when it became obvious that Celia was not going to join us, we ordered our food. While we waited, Mario attempted a conversation with Ken but was only moderately successful. Mario and Ofelia were very sweet people and were always politely attempting to include Ken in their conversations, despite the fact that they knew he spoke little Spanish. Mario spoke and understood some English and would often speak in a hybrid Spanglish so that Ken would not feel left out.

Although I thought it unusual that Celia did not join us for dinner, her absence was not completely unexpected. She, more than most of the young women I had met, often lamented the changes that she and her family had experienced since the family moved to Pennsylvania, and her parents did not seem upset that she did not show even though it was clear they hoped she would.

"In Mexico," Celia once told me, "we always knew what to expect. I always felt confident about how to act with my friends, my parents, and my teachers. Here, I sometimes feel lost. I'm never quite sure I'm doing or saying the right thing, and that makes me nervous." Later, when Celia called me to thank us for attending her graduation and for the gift we gave her, she also thanked me for having dinner with her parents. "They were happy you came," she said. "I'm sorry I wasn't there." Because her family did not plan a graduation party or dinner for the family at her house, Celia did not realize that her parents planned to go to dinner after the ceremony. "I thought they would go home after the ceremony, so I went to a graduation party with some of my friends," she said.

The following August, I accompanied Mario and Celia to Penn State. Mario asked me to drive his truck most of the way, as he was unfamiliar with the route to the university. When we arrived, we visited a few offices on campus to submit Celia's health forms and other necessary paperwork. Then we located her dorm, unloaded her belongings, and found a resident assistant who would help her navigate the orientation process and her introduction to the university. Celia was nervous but also quite excited about the start of school. Neither she nor Mario wept as they said good-bye.

Mario and I left campus that evening, driving for many hours in silence. For a time I thought he was asleep, but then he shifted and started rummaging around for something under his seat. I heard the familiar "pop" of a drink can opening, and looked around. "Want a beer?" he asked as he started in on his own. Mario was not a heavy drinker, but I knew from visiting the family that he did usually have a beer in the afternoon when he returned from work. I smiled and declined his offer, making a mental note that at some point I should fill him in on Pennsylvania's open container laws.[66] I drove along carefully and well within the posted speed limit until we returned to Kennett Square. It was nearly midnight.

A week later, I got a call from Celia, who was crying. When I asked what was wrong, she said, "I want you to come get me."

"What?" I responded, baffled. Celia was clearly distressed but couldn't find the words to express herself. "Has something happened?" I continued. When she still could not find the words, I finally said, "Dime en español" (tell me in Spanish). Slowly she explained, "I don't like it here and I want to go home. Nothing has happened, but I'm starting to feel like I did when I first came to Pennsylvania. I don't have anyone to talk to and I don't want to eat. I know I'm losing weight already."

I started to feel dizzy. Who to call? As I questioned Celia further, I discovered that I was the first person she had called. She had not spoken to her parents since she arrived on campus. I took Celia's call for help seriously, also bearing in mind that many college students have trouble adjusting during their first semester. Finally, I decided to call Migrant Education, knowing that they had on-campus support staff who could probably help Celia immediately. "Celia, it's late. I can't come get you today, and I have to work tomorrow. In the meantime, I'm going to make some calls to Migrant Ed to see if someone can come over and talk to you." We agreed that if she still wanted to come home this desperately in a few days, I would make arrangements to come to State College.

The Migrant Education staff put me in contact with a mentor assigned to Mexican and other recently arrived immigrant students. Celia received a visit that evening, and she remained in contact with her mentor throughout her first semester. When we talked a few days later, she was feeling better. She wanted to come home, she said, but once classes started she was also wary of falling behind. She returned home for Labor Day weekend and continued to call regularly, but by the end of the semester, her calls were much less frequent.

The following spring, Celia and I met for lunch shortly after she returned from college. We talked about what happened the previous fall. She said, "It was so strange, I couldn't believe how unhappy I was at first. But it got easier. The people at the college—the professors, students, and everyone really made me feel welcome, like they wanted me to stay." Over the next four years I would see Celia more often in Textitlán than in Pennsylania as my fieldwork began to focus on her hometown. The last time I saw her, she still talked about moving back to Mexico, but she also spoke fondly of her friends in State College and Kennett Square.[67]

Although Celia's experiences of displacement were extreme, her adaptation to life in Pennsylvania and eventual sense of belonging were in many ways characteristic of other Mexicans living in Kennett Square. The interactions that she had with longer-term residents and the broader community through school, participation in organizations, social activities, and other events helped to shape her place attachment. Based upon her experiences, she was able to interpret Kennett Square and State College as her new home, and eventually she determined that she belonged to these places.

CONCLUSIONS

The degree of incorporation experienced by Mexican families in Kennett Square shifted noticeably between 1995 and 2000. This transition was in part the result of a typical adjustment to living in a new community. At the same time, the experiences of Mexicans in Kennett Square also point to some of the distinct difficulties migrants might encounter in new destinations. The lack of a group of experienced settlers who are available to provide a support network for new arrivals is particularly significant. Mexicans who have lived in their settlement community the longest are more likely to know how to negotiate life in the new destination, and they can share that knowledge with other new arrivals. In Kennett Square, Mexicans often made their way to La Comunidad Hispana, the migrant social services office, but the lack of a cultural or recreational center coupled with the initial opposition from the majority population when Mexicans claimed places for social activities were key obstacles to belonging. Once they were able to determine that the majority population began to have a place for them, that they could be incorporated into the community rather than ostracized and rejected, things began to change (Mulgan 2009). This was particularly true for the earliest arrivals.

Many Mexicans did eventually develop a sense of belonging, but it would be a mistake to assume that all Mexicans felt like they belonged in Kennett Square or experienced the process of belonging in the same ways. I also met Mexicans who said they simply could not adapt to Kennett Square and eventually moved on to other places, or they simply returned to Textitlán, vowing they would never return to el Norte. This account has documented the story of a group of early settlers. I also met a number of newcomers who began arriving between 1999 and 2000. Many of these men and women experienced a similar homesickness, but they found a growing Mexican population within a larger community that was becoming more accepting of their presence. Loretta Perna, a student support specialist for Migrant Education noted in 2002 that "there are some . . . like I'm working with about ten girls right now who have only been here for one year or less and they're doing well. It's amazing. And they're in the honors program. And what I mean by that is yes they're taking ESL classes, but . . . they're doing great. They're making their As. They do their homework. They're motivated."[68] As we talked, it was clear that the students who were most successful had stronger ties in Kennett Square: extended family, friends, and their families had more long-standing and extensive social networks. These connections helped the students adapt to their new lives by offering support when they needed assistance negotiating life in Pennsylvania.

The overall social context in Kennett Square had also changed. In the early years of settlement, Mexicans either were not welcomed or welcomed with ambivalence.[69] As the English-speaking majority came to see Mexicans as part of the community, it further allowed settlers to feel like they belonged in Kennett Square. The success of Buena Vista was a major influence here. Many in the long-term population were skeptical that a low-income housing development like Buena Vista could become a thriving, well-maintained community. Buena Vista's success was a powerful rebuttal of these low expectations.

Perceptions of belonging shaped the broader Mexican understanding of Mexicans' place in Kennett Square's community and similarly influenced their interpretations of how much freedom they had to express themselves. Such interpretations are important because they shape the ways in which Mexicans were able to manage their lives and level of engagement with others in the new destination. By the time my fieldwork ended, I had witnessed a remarkable shift in the sense of belonging among Mexicans in Kennett Square. They were not alone in making this transition, however. In the chapter that follows, I explore the responses of the majority population as this once largely invisible population emerged from the shadows and established itself as a part of the larger social context of Kennett Square.

FIVE Bridging the Community

NATIVISM, ACTIVISM, AND
THE POLITICS OF BELONGING

To say "migration changes things" is to make a statement that is at once a truism and yet vastly understated. At the turn of the century, estimates suggested that approximately 2.3 percent of the world's population consisted of labor migrants (Andreas and Snyder 2000: 7), a number so small that it was statistically insignificant, yet the influence these mobile laborers had on their natal and settlement communities was remarkable. The reciprocal influence that settlers from western Mexico have had on Kennett Square and that Kennett Square has had on its Mexican settlers is immediately obvious. Migration has afforded a relatively underprivileged group of laborers substantial class mobility, and in return these women and men have transformed the culture and sense of place in Kennett Square. For many years, Mexicans living on the periphery of this prosperous farming community were scarcely noticeable. By the mid-1990s,

Mexicans were not only visible in the community, but also they had become one of the defining characteristics associated with Kennett Square identity. They transformed the local social and political structure in multiple ways for everyone who calls Kennett Square home. This chapter focuses on the English-speaking majority's response to changes in what they perceived as "their community" as Mexican settlement and visibility became more conspicuous. The result was the formation of Bridging the Community, a community-based movement created with the purpose of facilitating the integration of Mexican families into the fabric of daily life in Kennett Square. Using Bridging the Community as the social context through which Kennett Square approached integration, I explore the sense of belonging by examining the connections between human emotion, social action, and the sense of place. More specifically, this chapter explores how anti-immigrant sentiment can find its voice through social agency.

NEGOTIATING SETTLEMENT: NEW DESTINATIONS, NEW STRATEGIES

One of America's greatest ironies is that although it is a nation of immigrants, the country also has a long-standing history of ambivalence about its newest arrivals. American fear of immigrants and foreigners finds its clearest expression in the form of nativist movements and a tendency to scapegoat immigrants for undesirable changes in the society. Opposition to the new era of immigration that precipitated the emergence of new destination settlements also coincided with an upsurge in nativist movements and discourse nationwide, most notably in California with passage of Proposition 187 in 1994 and the publication of books such as Peter Brimelow's *Alien Nation* (1995); together these actions gave voice to the growing fear that immigration was likely to "transform—and ultimately, perhaps, even to destroy . . . the American nation" (Brimelow 1995: xv). Aside from the legislative changes and shift in public discourse about immigration, nativist responses to new destination settlements have also grown since the mid-1990s. Most recently, the responses to immigrant settlement have included the formation of organized social movements, such as the Minuteman Project, many of which embody the characteristics of sanctioned vigilantes.[1]

I use the term "nativism" to encompass the range of emotions that are discernable as intense opposition or hostility toward an internal minority group based on its foreign or "un-American" heritage or connections. It is closely tied to feelings of nationalism and national identity. Nativism draws upon broad "cultural antipathies and ethnocentric judgments" and translates them into actions against those who live in the United States but are perceived as "enemies of a distinctly American way of life" (Higham 1974: 4; see also Sánchez 1997). Nativism has further been described as emanating from a deep "cultural anxiety" from a citizen population that "worried that middle-class values would be inundated by rural, peasant hordes" (Graham and Koed 1993: 29). Cultural anxiety, as it is referred to in the literature on the various responses to immigrant settlement, is the prevalent fear held in common by certain members of the citizen population and often accompanies immigrant settlement in new and diverse places.[2]

The response to cultural anxiety about the growth of immigrant populations has varied with each era of immigration. During the last major influx of immigrants in the late nineteenth and early twentieth centuries, citizens alleviated their concerns about immigration through organized social action. Broadly referred to as "Americanization" movements, these organizations shared a common vision to assimilate immigrants into the perceived "mainstream" culture of American society.[3] Americanization movements have a long and complex history in the United States. They first emerged during the classic era of immigration, from the early 1880s through the late 1920s. Although some groups called for immigration restrictions (Walker 1896), the primary work of Americanization movements was to transform the immigrant population and help new immigrants succeed in their new homeland. Americanization movements were never a single enterprise but flourished in diverse structures under many sponsors, such as churches, settlement houses, state governments, and varied volunteer associations, and fell into one of two broad categories (Graham and Koed 1993). The first category was liberal; it emphasized "immigrant gifts" and worked to create a sense of national welcome. Groups in this category valued the immigrants' foreign cultural inheritance and offered support in order to hasten the transition toward accepting American cultural norms. The second category of the Americanization movement was more coercive and reactionary and emphasized assimilation through learning English and shedding prior cultural traditions and practices. These "100 per cent Americanism" groups reflected the nativism that was common in the United States in the early twentieth century. Despite the fact that Americanization movements came in many varieties, and many were led by immigrant leaders, the legacy of the full assimilation movements, coupled with a reinterpretation of American cultural identity as multicultural as opposed to monolithic, worked to effectively discredit the Americanization movements of the early twentieth century (Higham 1974: 204).

One of the central issues addressed by Americanization movements of the early twentieth century, particularly those that sought to fully assimilate immigrants, was to protect the position of the majority native-born population vis-à-vis the newly arrived immigrants. Throughout the 1990s, the expressions of nativism resonated with prior periods of anti-immigrant sentiment, but there have been distinct differences between what has been termed the "new nativism" (Perea 1997) and the nativism of earlier periods. Most notably, the new nativism tends to focus on the documentation status of immigrants, claiming that adherents have no issues with legal immigrants but oppose only illegal aliens, who are characterized as criminals capable of any number of criminal offenses (Nevins 2002). Because the new nativism is likely to characterize undocumented immigrants as criminals, their presence is seen as a distinct threat to local communities as well as the future of American society.[4] Late twentieth- and early twenty-first-century nativist movements are also more likely to focus on distinct group characteristics, such as immigrants' inability to speak English (Tatalovich 1995; Sánchez 1997).

As the Mexican population in Kennett Square emerged so too did the nativist responses toward Mexicans. The chief complaint was that Mexicans would transform the local community. In Kennett Square, hostility toward Mexican settlement has fundamentally been a reaction against local social and cultural change. Although I characterize the events in Kennett Square as an example of nativism, it is important to distinguish benevolent groups that seek to welcome and assimilate immigrants from hostile groups that wish to restrict immigration, limit the rights of immigrant residents, characterize immigrants as criminals, and, in some cases, promote hate against a group of people based on their ethnicity, language, religion, or immigration status. Kennett Square's longer-term population never endorsed the idea that Mexicans residing in their community were criminals simply because some were undocumented. In fact, I never once heard a long-term Kennett resident make distinctions between local Mexicans who acquired legal documentation and those who had not. Instead, the instances of nativism were reactions to the perceived fear that the longer-term population might lose their place as the community experiences rapid demographic transformation, and the primary focus was toward assimilation of Mexicans living in Kennett Square.

Before Mexicans began settling in Kennett Square in the late 1980s, the borough had been a largely white, upper-middle-class small town, the residents of which prided themselves in their socially progressive community. As Mexican families began setting down roots and purchasing homes in the early 1990s, however, the limits of their progressive ideals and community tolerance were tested. What initially transpired in Kennett Square is not surprising; there was a series of community protests directed against Mexican settlement that exposed local nativist sentiment.

The protests themselves soon became a point of contention in the community, but not between English speakers and Mexicans. Instead, a marked division emerged within the English-speaking community. This division, characterized by active public debate, was prompted by a widespread fear that, in opposing Mexican settlement, the town ran the risk of being labeled a racist community. Ultimately, the discussions that ensued worked to persuade community members to work toward a social contract of inclusion, one that some in the community believed was more consistent with the local residents' image of themselves and their community.

As events unfolded, local actors moved from the nativist responses toward organized social actions that were reminiscent of the American-

ization movements of a century earlier. The initial protests to discourage
Mexican settlement, such as the Yellow Ribbon Campaign, are described
in detail later in this examination. These actions were met with charges
of racism, and the charges of racism facilitated activities to rehabilitate
the town's image and manifested in a new social movement called Bridging the Community. Kennett Square's efforts to incorporate immigrants,
however, took a new form with the arrival of the new destination, one
that was not immediately identifiable as an Americanization movement.
There were no overt efforts to transform immigrants into "mainstream"
Americans; instead, Bridging began to redefine what it meant to be a
Kennett Square resident, through a reaffirmation of American political
ideals. Bridging promoted the idea that Kennett Square should include
Mexican families as part of the "melting pot." It encouraged assimilation
and worked to minimize the cultural differences between Mexicans and
the longer-term citizen population, thus created an agenda for Mexican
inclusion that nevertheless required immigrant transformation to join
the local community.

The events surrounding the formation of the Bridging movement are
noteworthy because they provide a clear illustration of how collective
emotional responses of anxiety and fear work to foment social action in
an effort to reaffirm local identity. Mexican settlement incited a palpable
anxiety because of the changes it brought about for many in the English-
speaking population, but the consequences of resisting those changes
also brought the threat of a damaged community image. These changes
worked together to compel Kennett Square's English-speaking community to reconfigure the previously hostile response to Mexican settlement and subsequent expressions of Mexican autonomy.

The result was a broad-based move toward local social action through
the auspices of a social movement that was characterized as an emblematic expression of Kennett Square values; it was inclusive, progressive,
and supportive of Mexican settlement. The Bridging movement coalesced
around a pervasive concern to maintain (or reestablish) Kennett's socially
progressive image and communicated that Kennett Square's English-
speaking majority had apparently reached a consensus and elected to
welcome Mexican settlement. As a product of the organizers' particular

worldview, Bridging the Community underscored the limitations of the social movement as a tool for community change and the difficulties new destination communities face as they adapt to Mexican settlement.

FROM YELLOW RIBBONS TO BRIDGING THE COMMUNITY: THE TRANSFORMATION OF COMMUNITY OPINION

Bridging the Community was initiated in the spring of 1997 at the height of conflict in response to Mexican settlement and encroachment into neighborhoods and communal spaces that were once exclusively the domain of the English-speaking community. These changes were inevitable given the increased number of Mexicans living in the Kennett Square Borough since 1990. The 1990 United States Census figures indicated that of the 662 Hispanics/Latinos living in Kennett Square, only 374 were of Mexican origin.[5] Before 1980, there had been a small group of Latinos, mainly Puerto Ricans, living in the area since the 1960s. By 2000, the total number of Hispanics/Latinos had increased to 1,470, of which 1,154 were Mexican (U.S. Census Bureau 2000). This once invisible workforce became a conspicuous attribute of the area by the early 1990s. More problematic was not simply the overall number of Mexican settlers but the additional numbers of women and children who accompanied their husbands and fathers to Pennsylvania from Textitlán.

As families were reunited, local public school enrollments bulged with Spanish-speaking students in need of English-language instruction and educational assistance. In 1980, for instance, there were only 192 Hispanic students in the Kennett Consolidated School District (KCSD). This number increased to 299 by 1990, and by the start of the 2000–2001 academic year, the total number of Hispanic students enrolled in KCSD reached 890, raising the percentage of Hispanic students in the district from 8.2 percent to 24.5 percent in only two decades (Pennsylvania Department of Education Statistics 1980, 2000-2001). Similarly, the numbers of Mexican families seeking affordable, adequate housing found it difficult or impossible to locate residences. The number of women seeking prenatal and well-woman health care doubled, and adults who wished to enroll in English as a second language (ESL) and high school equivalency courses (GED) were turned away or placed on waiting lists. In short, the need for educational and social services for families began to outpace the community's ability to provide them.

While their numbers were increasing, Mexicans and their advocates also initiated efforts to improve the working and living conditions for Mexican workers and their families. This was most evident when workers walked out on strike on April 1, 1993, at Kaolin Mushroom Farms, one of the largest mushroom producers in the area. With this action, Kennett residents quickly became aware that things were changing and that, at a minimum, Mexicans were no longer the compliant workforce that they had once been (Corchado 1999). Local social services providers and advocates, who in the early 1990s began to take steps to challenge the status quo, only enhanced this visibility. This was most apparent with the development of the nonprofit organization Alliance for Better Housing (ABH) in 1993.

Affordable housing had long been scarce in Kennett Square. Sheila Druily, then the executive director of the local Latino social service organization, La Comunidad Hispana (LCH) founded ABH to address housing needs for Mexican and other low-income residents in the area. Druily knew that there was a need for these services. Tenants in the Center Street Apartments and Scarlet Manor Apartments, both situated on the southern edge of town, had long complained that they were being overcharged for the run-down two-bedroom units they were renting for $600 or more per month, but they also recognized that they had few other options.[6] Guillermo Rivera of ABH confirmed this, saying, "Everyone knows that if a family moves out of one of those apartments, there are probably three more families waiting to move in."[7]

In 1994 ABH, now under the leadership of executive director Howard Porter, initiated efforts to develop low-income housing in Kennett Square and the surrounding area but met strong resistance. The first project that ABH initiated was the purchase and renovation of 420–422 Broad Street, an abandoned duplex situated three blocks from the center of town. The homes were to be rented to two families, clients of LCH. When local residents got word of the planned renovation, several organized a flyer distribution and blanketed cars in town with notices that ABH had plans to house eight to twelve single men in each home.[8] The Kennett Square Borough Council meeting in which Porter was scheduled to appear was flooded with local residents who had attended to protest ABH's plans. The council passed a number of ordinances aimed to close down ABH. According to Porter, this included one ordinance that read, "The Borough will attempt to determine who is funding Howard Porter and to halt that funding."[9] Many of the ordinances passed that evening were illegal and immediately revoked at the following Kennett Square Borough Council meeting. The response of the citizenry was a visceral reaction to false information (ABH had never intended to rent their units to single men), yet the incident is telling in that it indicates the level of anxiety related to Mexicans moving into town and reflects the nativist sentiment in response to changes in the community, particularly the fear that the English-speaking population had of sharing its community with Mexican nationals.[10]

The community changes that took place between 1994 and 1997 prompted a variety of rancorous community disputes and debates regarding Mexican settlement. As a process that brought a number of unpredictable consequences for the community, Mexican settlement was the cause of considerable anxiety for Kennett Square's citizen population. Recall that the socioeconomic differences between the English-speaking citizens and Mexican settlers were significant. Nestled in Chester County, Kennett Square is a prosperous, highly educated upper-middle-class community.[11] The Mexican settlers in comparison were low-wage workers and most adults had not completed elementary school. The coexistence of these disparate populations in the same small town (Kennett Square is exactly one square mile) created circumstances fraught with uncertainty and anxiety.

Although anxiety is often assumed to be an individual emotion and derived internally, it is inherently relational and exists as a phenomenon between a person or persons and their environment(s) (Spielberger 1972). In the case of Kennett Square, anxiety can be understood as an individual's or group's affective response to a specific social situation; it is initiated from contexts involving personal and social relations in which systems of shared meaning, or expectations of shared meaning, fail (Perin 1988). As Mexican families moved into neighborhoods throughout Kennett, it was clear that the English-speaking residents could no longer rely on the assumption that the family living next door would speak their language, share their aesthetic preferences, or hold the same cultural values. Although in many cases the divide between Mexicans and Anglo-Europeans was not nearly as wide as that perceived, the presence of Mexican families meant that neighborhood life was no longer familiar or predictable. The changeable nature of community life that was initiated by rapid Mexican settlement produced communal anxiety, which was expressed through resistance to Mexican settlement and access to communal space.

The initial reaction from Kennett Square's English-speaking population is not atypical for a community undergoing a rapid population transformation. Under normal circumstances, people are most at ease and actually derive comfort from social settings that are familiar and commonplace, and they will work to maintain distinct boundaries between what is known and unknown. Although such boundaries are never rigid and fixed, people tend to be most comfortable when they perceive that they are in control of their circumstances. When one seeks new experiences to break the routine of daily life, there are thresholds beyond which the novelty associated with discovery or curiosity can lead to feelings of anxiety or fear (Perin 1988). It is a mistake to assume that Kennett Square's long-term residents were resistant to all local change; in fact, the town was actively engaged in revitalization of the downtown and neighborhoods throughout the course of my fieldwork. Kennett Square residents are as likely to seek novelty and new experiences as anyone, but they are also likely to prefer to do so on their own terms.

Mexican settlement in the late 1980s was not overly problematic for most Kennett residents, nor was it a public issue. Settlement began slowly, and then it took off throughout the early 1990s. By the time the Mexican population grew to a third of the overall population, the threshold of tolerance was breached, and English-speaking residents perceived there was too much Mexican settlement. The distorted responses to ABH's proposed refurbishment of an old house are emblematic of the anxiety that many in the English-speaking community were expressing at that time. Mexican families moving into neighborhoods were perceived not as new neighbors but as a threat to the community.

By framing my analysis around fear and anxiety, I engage contemporary social scientific discourse that frames the motivation to act collectively, whether the action is peaceful or violent, as a collective emotional response. There has been considerable examination of the role that anxiety and fear play in the production of social action in response to perceptible transformations in the social structure. In this regard, emotion is important not only in "culturally produced and mediated experience, but in social and bodily agency as conceived in terms of its foundations in social structure" (Tudor 2003: 243). Although social scientists have only recently begun to explore the function of emotion in social life, there has been a long tradition of using emotional response as a means to explain social action. Notable examples include Smelser's (1962) analysis of social movements that frames collective action through notions of love-hate relationships and Melucci's (1996) discussion of the function of identity and collective emotional response in social movements. Similarly, Massey and Denton (1993) describe white flight from inner city neighborhoods as prompted by fear of African Americans moving into previously all-white communities. More recently, Glassner (1999) and Furedi (1997) published book-length expositions on the "culture of fear"; both texts examine fear as an individual as well as a group emotion, and argue that in many social contexts in late modern society, fear "influences [social] action in general" (Furedi 1997: 2).[12]

Anxiety is a common response when a person or group perceives that their environment is threatened, regardless of whether or not it actually is. The context of the individual's or group's appraisal of a particular situation influences their reaction to it (Spielberger 1966, 1972; May 1977). Like other emotions, anxiety is not merely felt, but also it invariably produces action on the part of the person experiencing it (Perin 1988; Gray and McNaughton 2000). Constance Perin (1988) argues that one can identify more or less anticipated patterns of behavior from groups that are subjected to ambiguity in social contexts. She links uncertainty with the biologic responses of anxiety or fear, so that what is physiologically the urge toward freeze, flight, or fight "results in paralysis, avoidance, [or] attack" (Perin 1988: 9).

This phenomenon is the focus of Perin's study of established suburban residents' responses to newcomers (who share the same racial and class status of the established residents) moving into their neighborhoods. She notes, "Intolerance for ambiguity' is not merely a personal trait . . . . When shared systems of meaning become unreliable, how to act becomes uncertain. With those meanings, we define our social expectations. Whatever is believed to dismantle meaning and thereby disable action evokes both curiosity and fear; whatever calls certainty into question comes under the heading of novelty, incongruity, confusion, sheer difference and discrepancy. On the one hand, humans socialize curiosity and arousal as learning and development and, on the other hand . . . humans socialize fear responses of freezing, flight and fighting as *social discrimination, stigmatization, and withdrawal*" (Perin 1988: 9, emphasis added). Social discrimination and withdrawal can take place regardless of whether actual differences exist between established residents and newcomers. When the differences are marked, the social milieu is less predictable, and this type of social anxiety is more likely (May 1977; Perin 1988).

As the population of Mexican women and children in Kennett Square increased, there was a concomitant fear that English speakers were losing their place and possibly their advantage in the community. These perceptions resulted in anxiety, which further led to protests against Mexican settlement and overt limitations on their use of public space. This was particularly true of recreational or social spaces that were designated "Mexican" and became another observable flash point in the community. The dinner theater The Big Apple, located just outside of town, evolved into a Mexican dance club that regularly featured Mexican and Latin music and live bands and was a regular source of controversy. The club was a popular recreational spot for Mexican families for several years in the early 1990s. Although a profitable business, in November of 1995 the owner decided to close the club, citing complaints from the English-speaking residents and ongoing disputes about zoning. Complaints centered on the club's alleged associations with drug dealers and commercial sex workers and brawls among patrons. The demise of The Big Apple came several months after a stabbing that resulted in a death near the club. Although the club owners (local Anglos) denied that the event took place on their property, they closed the club in response to the pressure of the township and local residents (Benson 1995).

Similarly, as Mexican families have been reunited, many have begun to purchase homes in established neighborhoods, prompting complaints and small-scale protests from English-speaking residents who feared their new neighbors would devalue their properties. In the spring of 1997, the residents of Stenning Hills, the majority of whom were American citizens, began to notice that Mexican families were purchasing homes in their neighborhood. Most of these Mexican families were large, typically with three to five children. Also common was the presence of other adults living in the home. Most often these adults were men who were members of the extended family, others were close family friends, and still others were acquaintances renting space from the homeowners.

With these adult males there came additional vehicles, and in some cases homes had as many as five cars or trucks parked in driveways and on the street. It was the presence of these adult men and their cars that first prompted anxiety in the residents of Stenning Hills. Several of the citizen neighbors began complaining to the Kennett Square Borough Council that their Mexican neighbors were violating zoning ordinances, which prohibited more than two unrelated adults living in one household. Although acknowledged by the Borough Council, no action was taken in response to the complaints. By mid-summer, several residents began organizing a peaceful protest with their fellow citizen neighbors, attaching yellow ribbons to their mailboxes and front doors in what they described as a protest against overcrowding in their neighborhood (Hutchins 1997a). The ribbons were nearly unnoticed until a reporter for the *Kennett Paper* ran an article and suggested that the yellow ribbon campaign was racially motivated (Hutchins 1997b).[13] The citizen neighbors responded quickly and viscerally, clearly resenting the idea that their protest had been interpreted as an act of racism. "I was so upset when I saw the charges of racism," one anonymous organizer reported. "Racism is not the issue. Overcrowding is" (quoted in Hutchins 1997b). To date, many of the organizers recall these events bitterly, believing their actions were wrongly interpreted (Corchado 1999).

This protest is problematic in that the symbol of expression, the yellow ribbon, has long been a symbol employed as a symbol of hope and homecoming, most recently by families of military personnel during times of active combat. Yellow ribbons have adorned the homes of families of military personnel and by parents of missing and abducted children and others who have lost contact with a loved one yet not lost hope for their survival and return. In these instances, the ribbons are signs that those who wear them are incomplete without their loved ones (Santino 1992).

Yellow ribbons, however, have been used to express a variety of issues since their use was popularized as a symbol of support for, and later to welcome home, American hostages who had been held in Iran (Parsons 1981, 1991).[14] During the 1991 war with Iraq, yellow ribbons were used to symbolize support for the troops but not necessarily the war itself. During the first Gulf War, Pershing and Yocom (1996) note that yellow ribbons were employed as "a medium for the expression of bigotry, as was the case when people used yellow ribbons to convey anti-Arab or anti-Muslim sentiment" (56). Furthermore, the ribbon concept was employed in a peaceful protest during the antinuclear movement (Pershing 1996; see also Westerman 1995). Yellow ribbons do not represent a single ideological position but have been used to symbolize a variety of social and political perspectives.

What is striking about the use of yellow ribbons in Kennett Square is the way that the organizers interpreted their actions, which they explained was to protest the violation of zoning ordinances by Mexican families. By placing the ribbons, the organizers said they hoped they would get the attention of local officials who would start to enforce the zoning laws. However, I argue that the selection of yellow ribbons as a symbol of protest in 1997, just six years after the Gulf War (the most recent widespread use of yellow ribbons nationwide before the Kennett Square incident) cannot be considered either a random choice by the organizers or one that can be neatly divorced from the aforementioned associations.[15]

As a recognized American symbol, yellow ribbons are most often associated with nationalism and national unity.[16] They have also been associated with "utopian longing for traditional constructions of the family and nation" (Mariscal 1991: 99). In Kennett Square, the yellow ribbon organizers were making a clear statement that they believed their community was threatened economically—zoning ordinances are almost always instituted to protect property values (Perin 1988). However, this protest was also against a distinct way of life that involved sharing a single-family home with any number of extended family members or friends. Because this was a specific complaint, it suggests that the yellow ribbons were an expression of the organizers' desire to "take back" the community, which I have previously argued they were fearful of losing. Like others who have employed yellow ribbons, these ribbons were used as a sign of hope that the Kennett Square Borough Council would enforce the ordinance and limit the number of people Mexican families could invite to live in their homes. In addition, these ribbons can also be interpreted as a visible means of discouraging other Mexicans from moving into the neighborhood (Hutchins 1997b; Corchado 1999). Yellow ribbons were an expression of exclusion and the anticipation that the English-speaking residents would be able to take back their neighborhood; they were a material demonstration of an already present cognitive boundary that English-speaking residents perceived was breached when Mexican families moved into the Stenning Hills neighborhood. In this instance, yellow ribbons were used as an attempt to re-territorialize and to protect the local community from the perceived cultural threat of a growing population of Mexican families.

It is clear that, as Mexican families began moving into Kennett Square in greater numbers, the population shift galvanized a reconsideration of the English-speaking population's understanding of what it meant to be a member of the community. What became an issue and what continued to resonate later as an issue in the Bridging movement was changing community identity, which most English speakers fiercely resisted. In a letter to the editor of the *Kennett Paper*, Kenneth Roberts, then the Kennett Square Borough Council president, commenting on the state of Scarlet Manor apartments (apartment complex occupied primarily by

Mexicans) wrote, "It is a shame that billions of dollars are being spent for housing and an equal amount hasn't been spent on educating the people on how to live in *our culture* and lead full and productive lives" (quoted in Hutchins 1994, emphasis added).

I frequently heard statements on the streets from Kennett's English-speaking residents that the community was changing too quickly and not for the better. With few exceptions, it was clear that their expectations were that Mexicans were to adapt to life in the United States by adopting American cultural values, which were always assumed to be superior.[17] One concerned citizen, similarly distressed about the poorly maintained condition of Scarlet Manor Apartments and the changes he observed in Kennett, said, "I was raised in Kennett Square, and this is not Kennett Square" (Patrick Donohoe, quoted in Hutchins 1994). The fear of community change emerged from the realization that the taken-for-granted expectations of "normal" everyday life or the "natural" state of affairs in the community was utterly contingent. The neighborhoods and streets that long-term Kennett Square residents had inhabited for their entire lives were suddenly becoming different, and perhaps they would one day be unrecognizable (Subramaniam 1999).

It is a mistake to consider the English-speaking community as a unified collective opposed to Mexican settlement or that the changes in the community were universally seen as threatening. Editorials and letters to the editor printed in the *Kennett Paper* reflect the opinions of a number of citizens who openly dissented to the aforementioned actions, in some cases characterizing their neighbors' protests as acts of racism. "When so much of life seems random and unpredictable," wrote one local resident, "there are still some constants that we count on. Like stupidity and prejudice, for example. Kennett Square's borough council has once again demonstrated that bigotry is alive and well in Kennett Square. What else can one assume but massive brain damage and monumental small-mindedness from a group of people who would choose a boarded-up eyesore (420–422 South Broad St.) over a rehabbed dwelling that would cost the taxpayers nothing" (Ernst 1995). These vocal opponents clearly influenced some local reactions and seemed to have tempered much of the overt anti-Mexican sentiment that was once common in Kennett Square.

Subtle changes in opinion regarding Mexican settlement were echoed in a number of venues. In addition to Mrs. Ernst's letter to the editor in the *Kennett Paper*, in an interview with the *Dallas Morning News*, Jane Perrone, one of the "yellow ribbon" organizers, expressed remorse about the campaign, but she emphatically denied that her actions were in any way racist, insisting instead that she and her neighbors were opposing overcrowding and violations of the zoning laws. To demonstrate that she was repentant of her prior action, when Mexican families began moving into their new houses in the Buena Vista Townhome complex, Ms. Perrone and other members of the Four Seasons Garden club presented the families with gardening equipment as a gesture of welcome and good will (Corchado 1999). Other Kennett Square residents similarly spoke openly to me about the yellow ribbons and some of the aforementioned incidents, with one of several explanations for these events. Some insisted that racism was not involved with the protests and that the incidents were misinterpreted. Others suggested that although there may have been members of the community who opposed Mexican settlement, those people were not representative of the larger community. Finally, others suggested that although there were problems associated with Mexican settlement in the past, community sentiment had changed.[18] The significance of these multiple interpretations of community opinion and action is that there was a decided shift away from openly discouraging Mexican settlement. More important, this shift took place after insensitive actions toward Mexicans were publicly criticized by other members of the community and transmitted in the local press.[19]

The events in Kennett Square between 1994 and 1998 emphasize a discernable relationship between human emotion and behavior that is common in complex societies, one that can be employed as a means of social control. One powerful basis of social control rests in the relationship between emotion (the impetus to action) and behavior (the bodily expression of the emotional pull). The maintenance of behavioral norms and complex cultural values can be accomplished when the consequences of stepping outside those norms provoke feelings of embarrassment or shame. To avoid these emotions and the negative associations they inspire, individuals are motivated to restrain their behavior and maintain social norms. In short, the avoidance of shame can be a powerful motivation to act appropriately (Elias 1982: 138).[20]

I propose that organized social action that is prompted by the fear and anxiety of unfamiliar social contexts, such as a significant increase in Mexican settlement in a small English-speaking community, can also incite action that is organized and peaceful and ultimately seeks a political objective. Such action can reestablish the familiar comfort zone within the social context by securing one's position within the community hierarchy. This type of social action serves the dual purpose of affirming the identity of the social actors as a collective and also achieving a political objective through group solidarity. Commonly referred to as new social movements (NSMs), these group actions offer a means of reestablishing control and asserting identity in what might otherwise be perceived as an uncontrollable situation.

Historically, social movements have offered a means for people with common interests to join together to work toward shared goals and to assert political power. Academic examinations of social movement organizations generally group these movements into two broad categories: "old" or "ideology based" social movements, where social action coalesces around shared grievances or perceptions of social injustice. Trade unions are the most salient example of these movements. Often members united around a common ideology, which determined the course of action for the movement. Ideology based social movements were common in the United States until the early 1960s, when social scientists began to identify a perceptible shift in the basis of social movement membership. These movements, termed "new social movements," were similarly directed toward improvement of the social milieu; however, the basis of membership was no longer predicated on a shared ideological framework. NSMs were based on less objective elements, such as "identity, status, humanism and spirituality, and as such the link between mobilization and grievances became less compelling" (Laraña, Johnston, and Gusfield 1994: 8; Johnston and Klandermans 1995; Della Porta and Diani 1999). This is not to say that contemporary mobilization factors deny the fact that shared grievances continue to be a factor in group cohesion; however, in many cases grievances are fundamentally linked to issues of identity. This is evident in movements where feminist, gender, or sexual issues are central. In these cases, the grievances and political objectives of group members are inextricably centered on notions of identity for the activists. Still, the overwhelming emphasis in these groups and what holds them together are their shared experiences and common identity (Laraña, Johnston, and Gusfield 1994: 21). Like their ideology-based counterparts, NSMs can be seen as a means of achieving or maintaining political power through collective action that can challenge or reaffirm the status quo.

In new destination communities, anxiety and fear are precipitated by the unknown and are a consequence of rapid community change. Unlike Mexican settlement sites in the historic gateways of Mexican migration (Singer 2004), the new destination community is likely to be a place where Mexican settlement is a recent phenomenon, thus the receiving community is generally less prepared to adjust to the sometimes rapid changes afforded with large-scale Mexican settlement. In such cases, a large shift in the ethnic composition of a settlement area radically alters the local identity of the community and produces a situation where fear of the changes taking place, and the associated unknown consequences of these changes, could lead locals to develop a systematic social action consistent with a NSM to reassert their identity and political power. The founding of Bridging the Community in Kennett Square offers an example of this process.

The accusations of racism and general disapproval from within the community coincided with a shift away from protest and toward community development, from a focus on the "problems" associated with Mexican settlement and toward one emphasizing the "potential" benefits that these newcomers could contribute to the community.[21] The move away from Mexican settlement as a problem to a community asset is, at least in part, a response to dissenting Kennett Square residents who were unhappy with the community action against settlement. Moreover, no one in the community was satisfied with the racist label they had acquired after the yellow ribbon campaign of 1997.

Within a period of five years, these changes forced longer-term Kennett Square residents to take stock of their community: they could not continue to ignore their Mexican neighbors or the changes that they were producing. Those who continued to be unsatisfied with Mexican settlement were compelled to express displeasure in a manner more socially acceptable to the broader community and to possible outside observers (such as journalists and ethnographers).[22] In fact, in some cases this did indeed happen. For example, the key opponents to the ABH renovation of 420–422 Broad Street sought positions in the next Kennett Square Borough Council election and were successful. Similarly, there were others who were not involved with the aforementioned protests but nevertheless wanted to actively direct the course of social relations in Kennett Square in a way they believed would be positive and socially inclusive. Many of these Kennett Square residents found their place in Bridging the Community, a new social movement that was intended to foster mutual aid and ethnic integration but simultaneously minimized Mexican influence in the community.

BRIDGING THE COMMUNITY: A PLACE FOR "EACH AND ALL"

The racial and ethnic tension that centered on housing and recreation issues was a response to the growing visibility of the Mexican population that some local residents saw as a threat to their community. The anxiety prompted from these changes in Kennett Square, along with the disorganized, often rancorous protests exemplified in the yellow ribbon campaign and the ABH protests, prompted activist and community health nurse Joan Holliday to initiate community-based conversations that she hoped would heal the growing divide in Kennett Square.[23] In the spring of 1997, a group of Kennett Square area citizens, under Holliday's leadership, began meetings to discuss "the Kennett community." These meetings were designed to strategically unite a cross-section of the population, looking for a means to increase local participation in community events and services.

When Holliday called Kennett Square residents together in 1997 to reflect on their community, it was commonly acknowledged that the town was not known for strong communal participation, particularly across racial and class lines. This did not deter Holliday, a Chester County Health Department nurse, from trying to transform this reality. Ever since Holliday began working in Kennett Square in 1982, she had been a discerning observer of the social relations in the area. She arranged these early meetings to initiate dialogue around the idea of community development, working specifically to create a process by which community members from all parts of the area could come together. Through her position in the county health department, Holliday was intimately familiar with the cultural and economic diversity present in Kennett Square and surrounding communities. Writing of her observations, Holliday noted that during her home health visits she became aware of the marked divides in this small community. She wrote that she was "struck by the lively spirit of the struggling poor as well as by the comfort of the other segments of the community. Although this community is small, the varied 'worlds' seem to know very little about each other" (Holliday n.d.). The fact that Kennett Square residents from different racial, social, and economic groups were not interacting in any meaningful way seemed both unfortunate and unacceptable. She writes that the Kennett Square community "holds a diverse representation of life. . . . I sadly experience a lack of unity and crossing over of the different cultures, economic groups and age groups. In essence, I see that the community has no way to meet in the middle—where human spirit and potential become significant and differences drop away" (Holliday 2001a.).

Drawing on her extensive social network and a firm conviction that community participation could overcome the differences that plagued the community, these early conversations that Holliday initiated grew into Community Bridging Generations, later renamed Bridging the Community.[24] The concept behind Bridging the Community was simple: to create a community-based forum to facilitate volunteer efforts in Kennett Square, provide networking opportunities for local activists, and in turn integrate all members of the community.

The importance of the Bridging movement in the understanding of social life in Kennett Square is fundamental in that the timing of the initiation of the movement corresponds with the eruption of communal anxiety and the associated fear that the English-speaking community was losing control of the town. In this sense, the Bridging goals of minimizing the differences associated with race, class, age, and ethnicity were fundamental to the long-term success of the movement, because these perceptions of difference ignited the protests, which, by 1997, most Kennett residents agreed were divisive and counterproductive.[25] Part of the Bridging focus was a decided shift away from divisive rhetoric to community-based conversations that emphasized the benefits of a diverse population. Those who might have been stigmatized for any number of reasons (teenage mothers, for example) were reconceptualized as nevertheless vital to the overall functioning of the community. In its most idealistic moments, Bridging endeavored to facilitate a sense of belonging in that the goal of the movement was to find a place for those residents who would not otherwise fit into the ideal vision of Kennett Square.

Although initially conceived as a modest community effort to minimize differences and increase volunteerism in Kennett Square, Bridging the Community quickly transformed into a structured social movement that was unique in its organization and implementation. Bridging was conceived entirely as a local effort. Its leadership refused to establish its position in the community through a bureaucratic structure, and therefore it did not conform to the conventions of standard nonprofit or public service organizations. Rather, the activities of the group were based on a short list of guiding principles that endeavored to keep the movement perpetually in process. For example, there were no bylaws, board of directors, and elected officers. The group had no official home or office space, but met bimonthly in rotating locations around the area, such as the public library, churches, and community centers. Bridging the Community organizers also refused to accept funding from sources outside the community, insisting that outside money could be a direct path to outside influence. Participants were also exhorted to "come from the heart," and to avoid participating in activities and projects they did not have a strong commitment to seeing through. The group strongly advocated that Bridging projects be implemented by and for the Kennett Square residents and supported locally through volunteer efforts or by local financial support. The organizers were quick to point out that

Bridging was not simply a community improvement club or social organization but rather an association that they see as a vehicle to regenerate and subsequently transform the community.

The intention of this "structure-free" framework was meant to illustrate, by example, that the organization was an outgrowth of the broader community (as opposed to the interests or desires of a small percentage) and was designed to evolve with community. Despite this goal, the meetings consistently followed a standardized format and lacked neither form nor organization. Regardless of a stated commitment to fluid and evolving processes, the objectives and superficial workings of the organization belied the fact that there were both a distinct structure and leadership to this organization. For instance, although there were no elected officers or board of directors, Holliday was the initiator and main overseer of the group, and her efforts ensured that the process moved forward.[26] She was responsible for making the logistical arrangements for each meeting, such as finding a meeting space, making announcements in local papers, and recruiting new participants to attend. Holliday also prepared a list of volunteer opportunities and contact information that was distributed at each meeting. In addition to a group of ten to fifteen people who regularly attended most meetings, there was also a steady stream of newcomers who came to enlist volunteers for their projects or who were there to expand their social networks. During the time of this study, Bridging meetings were well attended, with some forty to sixty participants whose ethnic and racial composition that was consistent with the English-speaking population of the area, with approximately 80–85 percent of the participants Caucasian, 15–20 percent of the participants African American, and no Mexicans.

The community projects that have been undertaken by Bridging participants have been striking considering the modest resources of the organization. Bridging accomplishments include a mentoring program for elementary students, a tutoring and homework assistance program organized through local churches, and an after-school program for middle schoolers. The organization has been praised for its youth outreach programs, all of which have attracted the attention of Kennett Square residents and neighboring communities. The chief of the Kennett Square police attributed the significant decrease in juvenile crime in the first three years of the Bridging movement as the result of its youth programs, and organizers from the neighboring city of West Chester have considered replicating the Bridging process. In all, the English-speaking community considered Bridging the Community an unqualified success and a reflection of the Bridging motto that Kennett Square is "every day a better place to grow up and grow old" (Holliday 1998).

PHILOSOPHICAL FOUNDATIONS: ENVISIONING KENNETT AS A UNIFIED PLACE

These community-based efforts were significant in that in a relatively short period, Bridging had developed a program of sustained community volunteerism. At the same time, however, the group's successes were diminished by the fact that in first five years of the organization it did not effectively recruit Mexicans or Latinos into the organization. When asked about this, Holliday acknowledged that this was not so much a deficiency in the group itself but a reflection that Bridging is a process. She contended that as the group demonstrates itself as a positive force for community change, more people will want to become involved, and in time this will encompass all members of the community. Moreover, Holliday also insisted that advocates of Mexican or Latino interests (such as social workers and health-care professionals) are valid representatives of Mexican or Latino interests in the movement, although they themselves are not Mexican or Latino (Holliday 2001b).[27]

The reasons why Bridging was more appealing to the English-speaking community than to Mexicans and Latinos is clear by examining the foundational principles of the group, which were embedded in a structured philosophical process that was not readily apparent from the open community gatherings. The guiding principles of the movement were developed and elaborated in regular meetings of a smaller core group of eight to ten participants that was identified as the Each and All group.

The Each and All group convened bimonthly to conduct in-depth intellectual discussions regarding the fundamental principles of the Bridging organization. The membership of this group stood out from the general Bridging participants in a number of ways. For instance, participants in these meetings had to be identified as members of the Kennett Square community, a stipulation that was interpreted broadly, as a number of key members, including Holliday and her co-organizers, did not live in Kennett Square. The other members of Each and All included distinguished citizens who lived or worked full-time in Kennett Square and were thus considered community members. They included schoolteachers, a dentist, the then-current executive director of LCH, a mushroom farm owner, housewives, and employees of the Kennett Square Borough, among others. Notably, members of this group were all highly educated, white, and middle or upper class.

The principles developed by the Each and All group were rooted in a shared belief system reminiscent of contemporary New Age and Judeo-Christian philosophies, although the group was careful to distance itself from any formal religious affiliation and members uniformly dismiss associations with New Age thinking. Central to this belief system was the notion that, to be effective, group members had to be willing to set aside their personal agendas and come together to participate in "reflective dialogue," a process in which the group worked toward a new model or vision of the community. The group insisted that the basis of discovering the untapped community potential is found through a thoughtful consideration of Kennett as a unique place.

Drawing on local history and legend, the Each and All meetings emphasized that the land occupied by Kennett Square historically had been home to peaceful inhabitants: the Algonquin Indians, the Society of Friends (Quakers), and now a larger, more diverse population that is nonetheless peace loving. Based on this history and reflective thought, the group determined that this history was an expression of the "socio-ecosystem" within which the community is located. Socio-ecosystems of different places and regions exhibit different core processes and distinct ways of life. In much the same manner that different ways of life evolve differently in distinct regions of the United States in relation to the local

THE PROBLEMATIC "US": EMBODYING
COMMUNITY PROCESS

Despite their noble goals to unite the community, the Bridging leaders trusted their own abilities to fairly and equitably envision the "whole" of the Kennett Square community without the participation of a substantial portion of that community. This meant that the movement was founded on its particular worldview, and subsequently it did little to integrate the community. The limited visionary framework of the community was the central focus of the movement and prevented the Bridging leadership and participants from considering worldviews that were different from their own or more importantly reimagining the community as someplace completely distinct from the Kennett Square they had always known. Although Bridging promoted the idea of unity in the community, communal inclusion was predicated on a marked degree of assimilation to the values and expectations of the English-speaking majority. This was obvious in the meeting formats. All meetings were conducted in English and emphasized positive New Age philosophies that strongly opposed anyone criticizing events or people in the community and encouraged the membership to be prepared to give something back to the community through volunteer work or financial support. Bridging leaders presumed that all community members had a similar ability to engage and participate in community events. As a result, the group attracted well-established residents who had the time and resources to dedicate to community projects.

Limiting the development of the philosophical work of Each and All to designated "intellectuals," whether or not they lived in Kennett, essentially guaranteed that the majority of the Mexicans living in Kennett Square (who did not speak English) would not participate in the Each and All process. When I raised this issue with Each and All members, they maintained that their membership must have the ability to read the same books, write about the community, and engage in deep intellectual discussions that follow the aforementioned philosophy of the organization. This reasoning does not explain why other area Latinos who fit the criteria, such as Puerto Ricans and Mexicans who live in Kennett Square, speak English fluently and have degrees in higher education, have not participated in the early development of the organization.

So although the group had some remarkable accomplishments and seemed well intentioned on many fronts, it was also clear that the organization perpetuated the cultural and political status quo. The Bridging movement offered a vehicle for the English-speaking community to "make a difference" through good works programs that reflected the values and priorities of the English-speaking population. This is not to suggest that Mexican families had distinct or opposing cultural or moral values. Rather, by not taking active steps to recruit Mexican or Latino participation, Bridging developed into a social movement that effectively excludes anyone who is not already part of the historic "mainstream" of this community.

In Kennett Square the transformation from unorganized, insensitive protests to an organized social movement is suggestive of a concerted attempt to restructure the community and find a place for all members, recent and long-term. The fact that the Bridging organizers have fallen short of this mark is not to say that the movement is ineffective but suggests that there are many obstacles on the path toward incorporation, and even well-meaning social actors can have significant difficulty as they become accustomed to local change.

When examined as a form of nativism, the purpose of a movement such as Bridging the Community is very much in line with the Americanization movements of a generation ago. The purpose of the movement can be viewed twofold: to promote a change in community discourse about Mexican settlement and to define what it means to be a community member in Kennett Square. Bridging offers an opportunity for local actors to influence the community in a manner beyond their actual numbers. With a relatively small group of participants (even the largest estimates of around 100–150 members represent only 2–3 percent of the town's population), the group has succeeded in making a substantial change in volunteer efforts and community services. Similarly, the group has also done much to promote its vision of local history and identity and in doing so has linked volunteerism, community participation, and maintaining a general positive attitude as natural by-products of the Kennett Square

socio-ecosystem and, by extension, Kennett Square identity. Thus, by nat-
uralizing an interdependent alliance between "the Kennett Square community" and the land through the concept of the socio-ecosystem, the
group has in effect defined what it means to be a community member.
Those who do not come into line with the notion of "peaceful progressive
inclusion" are simply not living in harmony with the true nature of the
community, and because the group is convinced of its own ability to visu-
alize the true potential of the community, those who fail to fall into line
with this accepted vision of the community risk becoming perennial
outcasts.

One could similarly interpret the activities of the Bridging movement
as an effort to permanently stall Mexican integration. Looking closely
at the movement's emphasis on community "potential," it is clear that
although there is unlimited possibility for momentous achievement, this
philosophy similarly enables the group's membership to interpret its out-
comes as a success even if nothing is ever accomplished. The movement
has helped regain, or perhaps has even exceeded, the community's reputation as a progressive place, and in the process it has created a much
more hospitable community for Mexicans. This is the major positive con-
tribution of the movement. At the same time, Bridging also has allowed
its participants to maintain their central role in leading the community
despite their diminishing numbers as Mexican families move into town,
in essence allowing the English-speaking population to "take back"
their community while maintaining their reputation as a civil, tolerant
community. Like many of the Americanization movements of the twentieth century, the Bridging movement is well intentioned. However, Bridging the Community has fallen short of its goal of incorporating Mexican
settlers, making further integration and mutual understanding in Kennett Square unlikely.

six There and Back Again

THE PILGRIMAGE OF RETURN MIGRATION

It was three o'clock in the morning on January 23, 2003. Felipe Ortega, my friend and research assistant, was driving me to the airport in León, Guanajuato. We were in a hurry to arrive when the airport opened at five. The previous evening my husband had called to tell me my father was gravely ill and was scheduled to undergo cardiac surgery the following morning. With a nonrefundable ticket in hand, we were headed to the airport so I could plead my case with the ticket agent, hoping that I could find a seat on the first plane out to the United States. The streets were completely empty and dark.

On my lap I held a small reproduction of the black Christ, Esquipulitas. About twelve inches tall, this resin image was a rough approximation of the one that hangs in Textitlán's magnificent church. On our way out of town, Felipe and I had stopped by the home of René Guzmán, a friend with whom I had scheduled an interview later in the week. I wanted him to know I was leaving and that I wasn't certain when I would be back. We spoke briefly with René in the courtyard outside his home, and when I told him of my father, he went back into his house and brought out the image of Esquipulitas and handed him to me. "Tell your father," René had said, "this is our patron and that the pueblo of Textitlán is with him. Tell him about the miracles of Esquipulitas and that he [Esquipulitas] will be with him." I gratefully accepted the gift, and we bid our farewells.

A few hours later we were trying to find our way through one of the many small towns that line the country roads away from Textitlán. I had never driven this route at night before, and Felipe had never driven it ever, so it was up to me to guide him through each of the small towns that led from Textitlán to León. When we finally reached the two-lane highway I gave a sigh of relief, knowing the roads were well marked from this point forward. There were only a few vehicles on the road, mainly large freight trucks. Just outside the pueblo of Valle de Santiago, Felipe slowed suddenly. "What's wrong?" I asked.

"Nothing," he replied. "We're coming to a railroad crossing. Can you look to the right to see if a train is coming?"

"You're joking. Isn't there a warning bell and gate at the railroad crossing when a train is approaching?" I had never noticed this before, in all my trips to and from the airport.

"No, no signal or lights. It's rare to have a warning signal, so we have to look," he said. "Is it clear?"

"Yes, it's clear, but honestly Felipe, how do Mexicans live like this, with so much risk?"

He smiled as we drove over the tracks and said, "By miracles."

A RITUAL OF MARGINALITY: FIESTAS
AND THE RECONSTITUTION OF PLACE

Each January, the streets of Textitlán, Guanajuato, swell with cars bearing license plates from the United States. Young men wearing athletic clothing with American sports team logos hang out on street corners in large numbers, and a palpable excitement pervades the otherwise quiet routines of daily life in this industrial pueblo. Mexican migrants to the United States are more likely to return home between November and January than in any other months (Massey et al. 1987), due in part to holiday celebrations; in Textitlán, January is set aside in order to honor of *El Señor de Esquipulitas*, the black Christ. In Textitlán the *Feria de Esquipulitas* (Festival of Equipulitas) is the event that lures Textitlán natives back to their homeland each year.

It would be incomplete to write an account of the transnational cultural practices that emerge from Textitlán without exploring the spiritual lives of the people who reside there. At the center of this discussion is Textitlán's patron, Esquipulitas, and the annual *feria* (festival) in his honor.[1] The feria is a complex spectacle that reinforces local identity and sense of place through religious and secular festivities. When Textitlanecos return to their natal community, they do so at a time that allows them to engage in folk religious practices that reaffirm their right to belong to their community as they are welcomed as *hijos ausentes* (absent sons and daughters) who are part of Textitlán but no longer live there year-round. This is accomplished through participation in the feria, particularly the *peregrinación* (pilgrimage) that draws all Textitlanecos together through a common devotion to Esquipulitas and reconstitutes their identity as local actors who contribute to the spiritual and social life of the community.

Shortly after my family and I settled in to our home in Textitlán, my neighbors began to tell me about Esquipulitas and stories about the miraculous journey that had brought him to the pueblo. From these stories I sensed an implicit connection between Esquipulitas and return migration, but the nature of that connection was unclear. Although Textitlán was not always a migrant town, the feria is often referred to, both historically and today, as a potent emblem of local identity for Textitlanecos. The nature of what the feria represents, however, changed as the pueblo became the home of a substantial number of migrants who also live in the United States.

The first men to travel to the United States for work were recruited in the 1940s as part of the Bracero Accord. Textitlán's men continued to seasonally migrate as the need arose, so that by the early 1980s seasonal migration had become a way of life for many families in the pueblo. In the late 1980s, when women and entire families began to move north, the custom of returning specifically for the feria became commonplace. Nearly all of the migrants that I met spoke of the importance of their return journeys, but their return was not simply a visit back home either to reconnect with family members or to seek respite from a year or more of hard work. That could be accomplished any time during the year. Instead, it was important that their return coincide with the feria in January because it marked them as Textitlanecos. "The feria is who we are," observed Francisco Castillo. "It's our custom."[2]

The feria is not merely an expression of collective identity; it is a complex public spectacle, which in the context of international migration to the United States becomes a tool of political legitimization and identity construction. Most of the year, Textitlán is a quiet industrial pueblo governed by a small population of *comerciantes* (merchants) and educated professionals. These residents are wealthy and influential, and they distinguish themselves from other well-to-do residents in that they have not migrated to the United States for work.[3] These year-round residents are by far the wealthiest members of the community; their children are likely to leave the pueblo to be educated in one of the state's major universities or perhaps even the prestigious national universities in Mexico. They own the major garment manufacturing businesses, and they are also the pool from which local elected officials are selected. Unlike the many Textitlán families who live on both sides of the border, these elite year-round residents constitute the local political and business leadership; they are also the residents who organize and run the feria in January.

Textitlanecos who reside in the United States also visit the pueblo at other times during the year, such as over the summer holidays. These visits have much less significance for returning migrants as well as year-round residents. Returns at other times of the year are sporadic and involve fewer people; they are also less likely to be noticed or cause upheavals in the community. When families return during the feria season, their presence permeates nearly every aspect of day-to-day life. They are a grudging reminder of the pueblo's transnational connections, a fact that

Once they depart, migrating Textitlanecos who return for the feria are often called *los ausentes,* the absent. The journeys undertaken between Textitlán and Kennett Square not only take ausentes to a place; the journeys are also occasions to engage in the social life of their natal community, to re-emplace.[6] The journey home, then, is seen by most Textitlanecos as a necessary aspect of living in the United States. Just as many young men view migration as a rite of passage en route to full manhood, returning to Textitlán is a journey to reaffirm identity as members of the natal community. Although Textitlán and Kennett Square are linked through these ongoing journeys, Textitlanecos who also live in the United States do not conceptualize their natal community as an extension of its counterpart in Kennett Square. Textitlán, rather, is an open site of cultural reproduction. It is at once integrated with its sister community, Kennett Square, through a shared population and experiences, yet it is also a distinct place that is reshaped and reinterpreted in response to the movement of its residents. A devotion to Esquipulitas is the bond that joins the two together.

FERIA AND BELONGING

When ausentes return to Textitlán in January, they arrive in the midst of a community celebration that draws them in, reaffirms their identity as local subjects, and re-emplaces them as Textitlanecos. The events that make up festivals are particularly well suited to cultivate emplacement and allow returning migrants and others who might be considered outsiders to integrate into the community. In many Mexican communities, festival participants frequently interpret these events as an expression of communal identity and a dramatization of cultural heritage that prescribes the essence of what it means to belong to a particular place (Nájera-Ramírez 1997).

In January, the pueblo is frenetic with events and entertainments, which further serves as a distraction from the influx of people from the United States. "Everyone is happy during the feria," Emilio Guzmán once remarked on a particular raucous January afternoon as a car full of young men drove down the street in front of his home, stereos blasting. At other times of the year, the extra noise, crowded streets, and general inconveniences caused by returning ausentes typically would be annoying. But the normal state of affairs is suspended for the festival, and returning Textitlanecos are less obviously disruptive to the life of the community.

The feria does more than mitigate conflicts between ausentes and year-round residents, however. The state of flux that is common during festivals makes the renegotiation of local identity and cultural norms more likely. Textitlanecos engage the feria and, in the process, one another. This engagement through local festivities makes it possible for people with competing interests to reinterpret the boundaries of the community and its identity vis-à-vis the outside world as well as to reconsider the place of ausentes in local affairs. In some cases, the feria creates a temporary inversion in social relations, so that returning ausentes "belong" in the same way that any newcomer is welcomed during the feria season.[7] In other cases, participation in ritual events such as the pilgrimage honoring Esquipulitas is set apart. Such ritual events are seen as the foundation of community identity, and by engaging in these sacred practices ausentes are re-emplaced so that some of the divisions created by international migration are lessened. Thus the feria becomes a vehicle for belonging and re-emplacement.

Festivals are also cultural performances that reflect the sociopolitical context in which they take place. They mark a change from everyday life, a "time out of time" (Falassi 1987) that is bounded by clearly framed events that allow a breach in normal social relations (Turner 1969, 1978). The distinction between festival time and everyday activities has long been acknowledged as an instrument of social control that is employed by those in power to maintain the status quo (Paz 1961; Brandes 1988; Beezley, Martin, and French 1994). In this respect, festivals are diversions from the daily routines and hardships of life. Octavio Paz likens the Mexican fiesta to an institutionalized "revolt . . . . By means of the fiesta society frees itself from the norms it has it has established" (Paz 1961: 51). The release Paz describes functions as a social safety valve where citizens are permitted to engage in open, raucous behavior that is culturally sanctioned, which in turn helps them to work through their frustrations with daily life. As the fiesta draws to a close, Paz argues, participants are able to return to life as they have known it. The community may be more content than before, but no significant social change takes place as a result.

Festivals are more than a means of social control. They are tools to produce meaning and to renegotiate identity and relationships (García Canclini 1995; Guss 2000). There has been a general trend in festival scholarship to overlook how festive events constitute differential power relations beyond the bounds of the community. More often, festivals are characterized as cultural performances enacted within a small, isolated locale, often with little influence beyond their boundaries.[8] It is not that these studies preclude the possibility that local festivals are influenced by the outside world, but festival scholars have been slow to shift focus away from face-to-face communities as the subjects of festival scholarship (Brandes 1988; Harris 2000, 2003).

Festive events that occur in transnational communities create distinct meanings and interpretations. Like nearly all festivals, they allow opposing groups to focus attention away from their differences and toward a common identity and heritage, but this common heritage is unlikely to be representative of everyone. In fact, it is not always clear whose identity is represented, because the festival can work to obscure power differentials and transnational influence at the same time it appears to reunite opposing groups. In their attempt to rejoin their hometown, returning ausentes disrupt the community through their presence and participation in the festival, because they are both strangers and insiders. Migrant communities are often ambivalent toward migration and its effects (Goldring 1988); residents are powerless to change the economic, political, and social realities that fuel labor migration and subsequently divide their town. Through festive commemoration, however, they can evoke memories of the community's past, typically the past before their residents began migrating and then settling in the United States. Looking back to an imaged past transforms festivals such as the Feria de Esquipulitas into a type of "compensatory practice"; if the community cannot stop immigration and return, they can celebrate their common heritage from the past, the time before migration (García Canclini 1995: 113).

In the context of international migration, festivals can be expressions of traditionalism, which "often appear as a resource for enduring the contradictions of contemporary life. In this epoch in which we doubt the benefits of modernity, temptations mount for a return to some past that we imagine to be more tolerable" (García Canclini 1995: 113). Traditionalism (*tradicionalismo*) is the practice of creating traditions that are symbolically or actually linked to the past so as to create a common bond. It is likely to arise in contexts where there is an acknowledgement that the effects of modernity, here manifest most clearly in international migration, weaken local culture and communal ties and eventually lead to social disintegration. Traditionalism takes shape in a variety of contexts; it can manifest itself in an organized movement to promote nationalism or, as in the case of Textitlán, it can emerge as an informal ideology of the cultural performances that constitute the feria.[9] In either case, traditionalism is a popular movement that is interpreted and transmitted by the cultural or intellectual elite to the general population. Although they are not the architects of traditionalism, the members of the community are essential to its implementation. For traditionalism to function successfully, ordinary people must be integrated into the ideology or movement and accept not only the traditionalist practices but also their roles within them (Lessa 1979; García Canclini 1995; Olvin 2000).

Traditionalism in the Feria de Esquipulitas creates, as well as covers, distinctions between ausentes and year-round residents. Like other festivals, the feria moves Textitlanecos through a number of ritual practices that produce symbolic transformations in its participants, most notably re-emplacing ausentes. This process also masks an essential effect of the festival: participation distinguishes the insider from the ausente not only by virtue of who participates but also by who has access to the most significant aspects of the feria. Shifting attention away from the examination of how the feria creates a collective identity and toward the boundaries it creates within the group exposes not only the ways through which different groups in the community are formalized but also how those distinctions are rendered legitimate (Bourdieu 1992).

Festivals are conceived of as collective endeavors, but they are managed by a controlling interest, a group of people who are authorized to shape the event. In Textitlán, the non-migrating elites manage the festival, and they are the ones who partake in the key festive rituals and events. The social practices that create these distinctions are what Bourdieu named "rites of institution" because they lead to the "consecration and legitimation of an arbitrary boundary," the boundary that keeps ausentes in a subordinate position, even when their wealth and accomplishments in the United States would suggest that they should ascend the social hierarchy in the pueblo. The traditionalist ritual practices in the feria "establish a fundamental division in the social order," so that on the surface what appears to be a communal reunification is actually the means by which the group is constituted and defined, thereby instituting the distinction between "ausente" and "Textitlaneco" (Bordieu 1992: 80–81).

AUTONOMY, SPIRITUALITY, AND LIVES FULL OF RISK

The reliance on Esquipulitas or a divine being is not isolated to those Textitlanecos who have migrated; western Mexico is known as an area of intense religious devotion, particularly to the practices of the Roman Catholic Church. God (as expressed through the Christian Trinity) and the saints are often called upon for assistance in everyday situations, whether extreme or mundane. Often believers rely on the assistance of a particular image of Christ, such as Esquipulitas, or a saint, such as Saint Michael the archangel, the Virgin of Guadalupe, or the Virgin of San Juan de los Lagos, to help them through difficult times. The Textitlanecos I spoke with said that they had a special devotion to Esquipulitas and the Virgin of Guadalupe.

Most often, it is clear that Textitlanecos see Esquipulitas or other iconic images as symbolic representations of the Christian God, and their reliance on divine assistance is evident in everyday interactions. When they discuss their plans for the future, most Textitlanecos say, *"Primer Dios,"* indicating that they put God first, and if their plans are in accordance with the will of God, they will come to pass. Similarly, good fortune is also attributed to divine intervention, greeted with the expression *"qué milagro*" (what a miracle). These statements represent an everyday spiritual devotion in which human action is not viewed as independent from the realm of the spiritual. Individuals are expected to behave responsibly, and if they do not, they are held accountable for their actions. But it is also extremely uncommon to hear a person attribute their good fortune to individual effort. Some Textitlanecos make *promesas* (vows) to an image of Christ or a saint when they have an important request. For example, my landlady Doña Elena once made a promesa to travel to the shrine of the Lord of Mercy (*el Señor de la Misericordia*) in Tepatitlán, Jalisco. She asked that the Lord of Mercy grant her request for a safe return for one of her grandsons, an undocumented laborer in the United States.

Conversely, some Textitlanecos express a distinct devotion to Esquipulitas as the grantor of blessings. In these instances it is not clear whether supplicants consider the image of Esquipulitas a symbol of Christ, or if the image itself is presumed to be divine and therefore an agent capable of granting requests. Esquipulitas is most often referred to as an image (*la imagen*), however, suggesting that it is understood that he is symbolic of Christ and not a god in his own right.

Most basically, Esquipulitas is Textitlán's Christ. As the Father Jesús Elena de los Reyes,[10] Textitlán's parish priest noted, "For many people of Textitlán, he [the image of Esquipulitas] represents the protection of Christ. Since the first instant that I arrived in Textitlán he [Christ through Esquipulitas] has been protecting the work of every Textitlaneco."[11] Esquipulitas belongs to the pueblo; he watches over the people as a protector and is believed to intercede on their behalf. Esquipulitas also represents local identity and being a Textitlaneco. Esquipulitas's arrival two hundred years ago coincided with the founding of Textitlán as a distinct community, and as a result, he has become integral to the identity of Textitlanecos, regardless of where they reside.

Transmigrants are not alone in their devotion and reliance on divine assistance in everyday circumstances, but their lives are replete with risk and for this reason they are seen as having distinct spiritual needs. This is evident in prayer books and devotional readings for migrants that are produced by the Roman Catholic Church in western Mexico. These pocket-sized texts are written by bishops and priests and contain prayers for assistance with the most common migratory dilemmas. These include prayers to recite before leaving home, starting the journey north, crossing the border without documents, losing a job, being deported or arrested, and looking for work. The prayer for those who would cross the border without documents reads,

> Jesus, eternal Lord, at this moment I am in the borderlands, and have decided to cross although I know it is against the law. You know well that I do not want to challenge the laws of this nation. But my economic reality makes me desperate to find work and a better future for my family, thus making my crossing without documents necessary. I feel that I am a citizen of the world and of a Church that knows no borders. I ask You, Lord, to give me passage to my destination without difficulty or obstacles. You know well that I want only peace and tranquility for all. Guide my passage and give me the strength that I need to face the challenges that await me, and that Your will be done. Amen. (Ruiz-Velazco 1997; my translation)

Consistent with the official church doctrine, such prayers communicate the fear that all migrants, documented and undocumented alike, face as they make their journey away from their homeland. Their need for divine assistance is great; it is the only support they can be certain of as they make their way north.[12]

The risks of going to the United States to work extend beyond those found in the desert frontier. Once safely on the other side, tasks such as finding a job and a place to live can also pose significant difficulties. For family members who stay behind, there is the chance that a husband may abandon his family for another woman. I have met many widows in Textitlán who have lost their husbands to accidents or injury. Elena Guzmán's husband migrated seasonally in the early 1960s when their children were infants. He was murdered in Los Angeles, but she never learned the exact circumstances of his death. What is more, I heard many stories of *los perdidos* (the lost), those who migrated and simply vanished, never to be heard from again. During the course of completing a survey questionnaire, a female respondent in Textitlán explained, "Seven years ago my brother left for the United States. He said he was planning to go to Pennsylvania, but we don't know what happened to him. He has never written or called."[13]

The decision to work in the United States means that the individual and his or her family must give up significant control of their lives. Although going north is often assumed to be a sure way to make more money and advance one's economic situation, migration is in many respects a leap of faith. Many men and women thrive when they arrive to work in the United States, but I have met many men who shared stories of their failed attempts to find work after they crossed the border. Having no one to rely on while they were in the United States, they often swore they would never endure the arduous and costly trip north again. "I went to the United States two times," one man from Textitlán explained, "and I never found a job. Never. It cost me $500 for the coyote and it was all for nothing." When Textitlanecos who were once undocumented recount their experiences and the uncertainties they endured, they make it clear that apart from divine assistance these men and women were truly alone. It seems fitting that they consider surviving these experiences miraculous and that they hold a special allegiance to their local guardian, Esquipulitas.

Esquipulitas watches over the ausentes at home as well as abroad. Although homecoming is not a straightforward event, it is much easier than making the trip north. For ausentes, the journeys from Mexico to the United States and back again are repeated often, sometimes annually or biannually, and are always emotionally charged. One day while I was having coffee with my neighbor Lucia, she told me that her husband never tells her exactly when he is planning to return to Pennsylvania, as it casts a deep sadness over his last few days at home. "He doesn't tell me because he doesn't want to see me cry," she recalled. There is more at stake when the immigration is undocumented; many simply refuse to discuss their experiences en route, especially crossing the border. Recalling these experiences, especially when one is planning to revisit them within a month or two, is simply too painful. Ramón Ramírez told me, "I suffer when I cross *pa'Norte*.[14] I don't want to talk about it, to recall it."[15]

Coming home, however, is a different experience altogether. Historically, immigration authorities in the United States have not pursued those who leave the country, regardless of whether or not they entered legally. Thus returning to Mexico is as easy for an undocumented immigrant as it is for any American citizen: set your date, buy a ticket, and head home. Although homecoming is a joyous event for migrant families, it is also fraught with difficulty. Women's routines are disrupted by their formerly absent husbands who now are in the house every day. They must reorient their lives so that their husbands are in charge (or at least give the appearance that they are in charge). Children are reintroduced to their father's parental authority. Families often lament what they have missed in the intervening months or years that they have been separated, but migrant families must get to know one another again.[16] Francisco Castillo, a secondary school teacher, recalled that when his father returned from the United States he and his siblings "always saw him as if he were a stranger. . . . After a while we began to lose our affection for him. . . . We wanted him to assume his natural authority in the family, but it never happened."[17]

More important, these journeys expose what is impermanent as well as what is stable about the pueblo. When an ausente returns home from a prolonged absence, it is not uncommon for others to recognize how he or she has changed. Women in Textitlán often lament the changes they see in their young adult children or grandchildren who have lived in the United States. The act of sending a child back to Mexico, particularly when the family believes that she or he has become too influenced by American culture, is viewed as a means to put the child back on track. In 1999, I was asked by a local social worker to talk the parents of a Mexican Kennett High School student. The family had decided to pull their son out of school and send him to Textitlán to live with his grandmother. The boy's teachers and local social workers were distressed by his parent's decision; they believed that although he was having trouble adjusting, it was better for him to stay in Pennsylvania. When I talked to his mother, however, she explained that she could no longer control her son's behavior. Admittedly, his conduct was unacceptable, but he was rebelling in a manner similar to many American teenagers, experimenting with marijuana and cutting classes at Kennett High School. Although I understood why the teachers were upset, I also recognized that the boy's parents were not accustomed to teenage rebellion, which is uncommon in Textitlán. After watching their son's behavior for a few months, his parents decided to send him back to Mexico.[18] "The United States has changed him," his mother said. "We're sending him back and hope he'll become a nice young man again."[19]

This situation was an extreme case, but it was not unusual for parents in Textitlán to observe the families of their migrating neighbors, pay close attention to the changes that families underwent, and openly wonder whether or not living in the United States was truly the best option for any family. In addition, Textitlanecos who have never migrated resent many of the negative changes in Textitlán that they believe immigrants bring home with them. As Father de los Reyes commented, "Many people who go there [to the United States] come back alcoholics, many that go there come back with drug problems, and they bring the drugs here and use them here."[20]

Textitlán's social problems are often believed to be a result of American influence and migration, and there is no denying that this is in part correct. Mexican immigrant families are under tremendous pressure, and in response to those pressures some immigrants adopt destructive behaviors. At the same time, however, I have never heard anyone consider Textitlán's social problems, particularly among those who have never migrated, as having a local origin. Because of this, when most people speak about the benefits of immigration to the United States, it is also very common for those comments to be followed by statements about the obvious problems associated with working in the north.

Most Textitlanecos who have migrated say that the major disadvantage of working in the United States is leaving home. Homecoming involves returning to the place that was once home and the return to familiarity and comfort. At the same time, homecoming forces the ausentes and non-migrating Textitlanecos to recognize how their pueblo has changed. Although working and living in the United States changes relationships between ausentes and their place in the community, these are not the only changes that take place there. Returning home forces ausentes to take stock of their relationships with their family and friends who have stayed in Textitlán as well as with others who remain in the United States. The result of confronting what was once a familiar place and the memories of its past can contrast sharply with the place as it is in the present. The complexities of individual and community alter the ausentes' feelings of emplacement and, by extension, their legitimate place in the community (Casey 1993).

The annual return trip that migrants and settlers make to Textitlán is an essential aspect of social and cultural life for Mexicans in Kennett Square and Textitlán. Over the course of making this journey with them, I realized two important things about Textitlanecos and their connection to their natal community.[21] The first is that migration raises the status of men and women who live all or part of their lives in the United States, which is due in part to the economic benefits associated with migration. The second is that this change in status gives rise to mixed feelings about the ausentes within the pueblo upon their return, so that migrants are at once envied and revered by their compatriots who choose not to migrate.

These observations are not unique to Textitlán but are common in other migrant communities in Mexico (see Goldring 1997; Hirsch 2003). What is distinct about the return of Textitlanecos is how tenuous their place is in their "home" community. Although Textitlanecos who live in Kennett Square anxiously await their return trips, their homecomings are uncertain times because ausentes are often stigmatized by their life choices, many of which have offered opportunities to their families that exceed those available locally. To the non-migrating residents of Textitlán, particularly the successful merchants and textile factory owners, these men and woman are often viewed as transitory visitors who have forsaken their homeland in search of easy money and excitement. They also pose a threat to the otherwise taken-for-granted position of Textitlán's elites. For instance, it is not uncommon for men who have worked in the United States to marry well above their station; the ease with which returning ausentes ascend the social hierarchy means that these formerly poor, uneducated laborers now vie for position and status that was once a privilege of birth.

Ausentes who return home are in jeopardy of losing their place regardless of whether they are in the United States or Mexico. In order to understand how ausentes and non-migrants come together to form one community, it is important to understand the restoration of their place within the community and how the process of belonging is influenced

THERE AND BACK AGAIN 183

for all members of this community by homecoming. It is through the ritual practices associated with the feria that Textitlán begins to respond to the ruptures brought about by migration and return.

MIGRATION, PROSPERITY, AND FINDING ONE'S PLACE

Although the places of the ausentes are held in their non-migrating family members' hearts and minds, the process of reconnecting with their natal community involves significant effort for all involved. Men and women attempt to reengage the place by spending time with their family and friends as they begin the one- to three-month *descansa* (rest), enjoying the lifestyle and events that they have sorely missed while living and working in the United States. Although this time is a period of great personal comfort and satisfaction, the season of return migration is often fraught with uncertainty beyond the bounds of the family. Just as Mexicans who live and work in Kennett Square are often considered perennial outsiders in their new settlement community, these men and women are also frequently characterized as outsiders at home. The young men who return with new cars and cash in hand succeed in attracting not only the attention of available young women but also the enmity of many others, especially local young men. Clustered together on street corners in the late mornings or early evenings, these *muchachos* are often characterized as show-offs or troublemakers. Admittedly, their presence is a source of frustration for any unescorted woman who wants to walk down the street as they shout commentary on her appearance, but rarely do these young men present more than a petty annoyance.

More significantly, young men eager to flaunt their recently acquired prosperity uncover a long-standing schism in the community between those who migrate and those who stay behind. Envy is not something that is easily overcome. Even well-meaning ausentes can find themselves the recipients of their neighbor's scorn because of their obvious wealth. Merchants who are quick to contest the need to work in the United States openly express the enmity toward returning ausentes. One of the distinguishing aspects of life in Textitlán is the substantial number of prosperous families, the majority of whom have never migrated. Although migration has no doubt provided capital for many locals to start or enlarge their commercial endeavors, businessmen and women often deny that migrant money has ever been used to enhance the local economy. Instead, they insist that the city's thriving garment industry is the result of the hard work and investment of locally earned funds. Elvia Lemos is the owner of a successful jewelry store. She and her husband Emilio have not only supported their own family, but also they have financed the start of two of their daughters' jewelry shops in town. Elvia said, "Listen, there are places in Mexico where there is no work and those men have to migrate to make a living. But here in Textitlán we have jobs. They pay well. I think men migrate from here because they want easy money; they don't want to work hard." Similarly, Portfio Guzmán Zavala, an octogenarian who is now retired from his rebozo business told me, "I honestly think that these young men are looking for *aventuras*. They want to be free of the responsibility that living in this community requires." In this sense, Don Portifio is using the Spanish word *aventura* in a double sense, meaning adventure, exploration, and novelty but also suggesting that migrant men are looking for casual sexual relationships that are not acceptable in this conservative pueblo.

Although I understand and respect the opinions of my non-migrating informants, there are also those who form a modest, but nevertheless significant, middle ground in this debate. These are non-migrants who are not from the merchant class who make every effort to support their families on local employment but nevertheless struggle with the decision of whether or not to migrate. Their stories paint a clearer picture of the economic situation of workers who are not from wealthy families. René Guzmán,[22] thirty-eight years old, is a primary school teacher. His job pays well, and he has migrated to the United States one time, years before he was married. He did this to satisfy a youthful desire to *conocer*, or explore the world outside Mexico. He describes migration between the United States and Textitlán as "a little bit of tradition, a custom, and a little for necessity." Although René has no desire to leave his wife and three small children, he also admits frustration that he cannot seem to keep pace with his local salary. He said, "I'm a photographer, and I'd like to get a good digital camera. I would also like to finish my house, put in a tile floor, finish the second floor. But I don't have the money to do it with what I earn. I earn enough to take care of the family, but if I want anything else, I have to think about going *pa'Norte* to get it."[23]

In this community of migrants, those who stay put rarely mention immigration or remittances of dollars as a contributing factor in their prosperity. When asked, non-migrating locals often deny any significant connections between their communities or businesses and migration. Their world is locally focused; that beyond their national borders, particularly *pa'Norte*, is of little consequence to them, to their businesses, or their local prosperity. During my first trip to Textitlán, I found this outright denial of a visible social reality puzzling until I probed further. The large population of well-to-do non-migrants in Textitlán view working in the United States not as an economic necessity but as a personal choice, and they are rarely sympathetic regarding the hardships confronted by these families. Despite their denials to the contrary, the fact that a significant portion of residents migrates and settles abroad does influence the culture, economics, and daily rhythm of Textitlán for all residents, regardless of whether a particular individual has lived or worked in the United States or not.

The divisions within the community between those who migrate and those who do not are frequently characterized as essential differences between the two groups. When I began this study, I made it clear to everyone in town that I was interested in the influence of migration. When I began seeking more information on Textitlán's history, I encountered a fierce resistance from the merchant class. One gentleman told me, "Débora, you have to understand that migrants, they are not really part of this community and cannot give you a full picture of life here. If you want to understand Textitlán, you must talk to people who live here."

RE-EMPLACEMENT, BELONGING, AND HOMECOMING

In Textitlán the Feria de Esquipulitas emerges as a complex spectacle that at once draws migrants home and functions to reunite the community's post-migration fracture. Participation in the feria is acknowledged as an expression of deep connection to the pueblo of Textitlán and a broader nationalistic identity for all local residents. The celebration that begins on January 8 and ends on January 31 combines secular state-sponsored events and a wide variety of sacred events that are supported by the Catholic Church.

Although nearly every community in Mexico is home to a patron saint that is venerated through a community festival, Esquipulitas's feria has come to dominate the social life of Textitlán; it is the center of cultural activity in the community and almost all major life cycle events are scheduled to coincide with the event. For example, January is the most popular month for couples to marry, as well as for children to be baptized or take their first communions and for young women to celebrate *quinceañeras* (fifteenth birthday parties). Families from all social groups in the pueblo have told me that most families schedule other important events at the same time in order to ensure the largest participation by friends and extended family members who live in the United States. More significantly, the political and spiritual leadership of the pueblo has constructed an event that has become emblematic of local secular and sacred identity. Textitlán demonstrates its resilience in its ability to reunite symbolically through the residents' spiritual connection to Esquipulitas. It is through the communal reenactment of this history that the sense of belonging is re-created. The image, however, is more than a spiritual symbol. Esquipulitas is tied to the founding of the pueblo and the creation of Textitlán as a distinct place.

ESQUIPULITAS, MYTH, AND THE FOUNDATION OF PLACE

It is a fact not overlooked by many in Textitlán that this pueblo that became a sending community of migrants in the twentieth century also hosts a patron who came to Textitlán as the result of a failed, or fated, journey. Esquipulitas has resided in Textitlán since May of 1805. His fortuitous arrival, suffuse with mythical allusion, is attributed to divine intervention that brought Esquipulitas to the village and facilitated its founding as a distinct place. Before Esquipulitas, the Spanish colonial leadership established a small chapel dedicated Saint John the Baptist in the settlement named Congregación, the location that would become Textitlán. There was no priest in residence for the community as the small population was part of a neighboring *municipio*. A priest traveled regularly to the chapel of St. John the Baptist to say mass and attend to the spiritual needs of the residents, but in the early nineteenth century, Textitlán was an outpost. Esquipulitas's arrival facilitated the development of a distinct political and spiritual community, and the mythical tale that surrounds Esquipulitas and Textitlán not only narrates past events, but also it explains how that past influences interpretations of the present and how an amorphous settlement subsequently grew economically to exceed its longer-established neighbors.

El Señor de Esquipulitas is a sculpture of ebony, a replica of the famed Esquipulas of Guatemala. In Textitlán he is always referred to in the diminutive, Esquipulitas. Local scholars in Textitlán indicate that this carving was not created as a true reproduction of the crucifix in Guatemala, but its Spanish sculptor, Alonso de Velasco, was inspired by the black Christ Esquipulas and created a second image that was similar, but not identical.[24] In 1805 Don Alonso de Velasco set off from the village of Esquipulas, Guatemala, en route to the city of Guanajuato in order to present the image as a gift to the Catholic community of Santa Fe. Documents from the period do not explain why de Velasco decided to make this journey or why he selected the capital city of the Mexican state of Guanajuato, but local historian Manuel Ibarra Perez speculates that "[p]erhaps it was because Guanajuato was a famous city, known worldwide for its silver mines."[25]

Alonso de Velasco traveled on foot alone, and during his journey met a traveling merchant, José María Aguilar, known as "Brother Chema" from Quiayo, a small farming community located in what eventually would become the municipio of Textitlán. Brother Chema was well known in Textitlán, as his travels had brought him through from time to time. When the pair reached Valladolid,[26] the capital city of Michoacán, de Velasco fell ill with fever. After a few days rest he recovered sufficiently to continue on to the village of Cuitzeo, Michoacán, where he again became too ill to travel. Cuitzeo is a small island pueblo located in the middle of the *Lago de Cuitzeo* (Cuitzeo Lake), some forty miles from Textitlán. De Velasco was ill for a short time, but recovered after the care of a local *curandero* (folk healer), who treated him with potions and herbs. As his health improved, de Velasco and Brother Chema embarked on their journey again, but they traveled only a short distance when de Velasco fell gravely ill. They were able to reach the community of Congregación (later the pueblo of Textitlán). In 1805 there were no inns in Congregación, but Don Augustín Guzmán, who resided in a house located on the periphery of the central plaza, agreed to accommodate de Velasco for as long as he had need. De Velasco accepted this hospitality, saying that he hoped to improve or completely recover from his illness quickly and to return to his journey (López-López 1945: 49).[27]

Alonso de Velasco's health did not improve, however, despite the efforts of local healers. Brother Chema remained with de Velasco and visited him daily. In early May of 1805, de Velasco's health continued to deteriorate and it became obvious to his host that he would not recover. Brother Chema asked de Velasco if he was ready to call for a priest from a neighboring pueblo so that he could confess and receive his final sacraments. He also asked de Velasco where his family resided, so that they could be contacted regarding his condition. De Velasco told his hosts that he had no family in Guatemala, Mexico, or Spain. In fact, to this day nothing is known about Alonso de Velasco's life, apart from his artistic creation and journey through Textitlán, as historian Miguel Ibarra Perez told me, "de Velasco did not want to reveal anything about himself. His religious devotion and commitment to the black Christ gave Brother Chema and those around him the impression that he must have been a monk, but he never disclosed his personal nor professional identity."[28]

As he lay dying, he offered the "treasure" stored in the cedar box he was carrying to his host, Don Augustín Guzmán, as payment for his care and hospitality. Guzmán refused the gift, telling de Velasco that the care he offered was an expression of his Christian duty, not for personal gain. De Velasco then offered the treasure to the nascent community of Congregación as a gift of thanks, requesting that the image be named the patron of the pueblo and that they build a church in the image's honor. De Velasco also requested that he be buried beneath the altar of the new church after it was built (Ortiz-Ortiz 1993).[29]

Shortly after de Velasco bequeathed his gift to the pueblo, Father Quintana, the priest who had been assigned to Congregación, accepted the gift and requested his bishop's permission to move his ministry to Congregación full time. Soon afterward, construction was underway for the new church, as well as plans to designate Congregación an autonomous municipio and parish in the territory that is now Textitlán, linking the arrival of the image and the historical foundation of the pueblo. For this reason, the story of Esquipulitas's arrival through the efforts of Alonzo de Velasco is viewed with great reverence. The tale is familiar to nearly everyone I have met in Textitlán; only the pueblo's newest arrivals are unaware of this story and its significance for the founding of the community.

In the two hundred years since de Velasco's journey, he too, has become a mythical figure. Historical documents from the era indicate that a man named Alonzo de Velasco did arrive in the community bearing a cedar box with the image of Esquipulitas, and eventually he died there (López-López 1945). Yet these accounts, like the oral histories outlined above, lack specific information about this man and his purpose. Brother Chema's encounter with de Velasco on the road to Congregación allowed him the opportunity to spend many hours with him. Chema reported that de Velasco was unwilling to disclose details about his personal and professional life. He also refused to reveal what was in the cedar box he was transporting, which de Velasco referred to simply as his "treasure" (López-López 1945).[30]

Textitlán historians acknowledge that the lack of detail surrounding this man is curious but the absence of a detailed life story from de Velasco or other sources simultaneously enables him to become more than a mere mortal carrying a piece of art.[31] De Velasco's unwillingness to share his personal narrative increases the mystery of his persona. Absent of any concrete life details, de Velasco's story is open to local interpretation that has shaped his journey into a divine quest. Today de Velasco's status as a mythic hero or quasi-saint remains strong in Textitlán's oral history.[32]

De Velasco's secrecy makes it apparent that he wanted his life's work and story to be closely connected to the image of Esquipulitas. His is not the story of a random sojourner; indeed, his journey is understood by Textitlanecos as fulfilling God's purpose in initiating the founding of the pueblo as a distinct political entity.[33] To Textitlanecos, de Velasco's journey was a miraculous occurrence; Esquipulitas' arrival is seen not only as the origin of the pueblo but also as the event that set in motion the actions that would ultimately shape the community's future.

Esquipulitas, therefore, is not a simple crucifix. The image is the semblance of the Divine with a connection to Textitlán that enables local residents to interpret him as an accessible and vital spiritual guardian. Esquipulitas is personified and recognized, much as Christ is, as a living being. The image is hollow and is said to have small silver lungs and viscera, as well as a pendulum in his chest that, observers note, gives the impression that he has a beating heart (López-López 1945).[34] Little good that happens in the pueblo is not attributed to Esquipulitas. When crisis befalls the community he is called upon to provide aid and comfort. Esquipulitas is not only *in* Textitlán. His coming transformed the amorphous Congregación into a *place* set apart by the arrival of this guardian. Esquipulitas is Textitlán.

FERIA ESQUIPULITAS: CELEBRATING AND ENACTING TRANSNATIONAL IDENTITY

The devotion demonstrated toward Esquipulitas takes place in everyday life through personal devotions, attending mass, church participation, and more formally through the feria of Esquipulitas. The first feria was celebrated in 1806, but the coming war for independence with Spain postponed public celebrations and forestalled the construction of the new church. By 1857, the feria was established as a distinctive combination of secular and sacred events hosted through the cooperative efforts of the municipio government and the Catholic Church. The event remains so today.

According to the few archival documents from the nineteenth century that exist regarding the feria, this event has always included a grand celebration that observes both secular and sacred events. The feria has two major events around which the entire month is structured: a bacchanal street fair on January 16 and a solemn pilgrimage on January 31, where the image of Esquipulitas is paraded through the main streets of the pueblo. During the feria the pueblo is alive with activity every day. It would be impossible, as well as prohibitively expensive and exhausting, for any one person to attend most of these events. But the range of entertainments offered is intended to provide diversion for every age and socioeconomic group in the pueblo.

What distinguishes Mexican community celebrations of local patron saints from place to place are the ways in which patrons are venerated and how the community interprets these events. These events enact distinct local histories so that local history has a deeper meaning in the lives of participants. The feria of Esquipulitas is the pueblo's defining event. Much as Esquipulitas represents Textitlán, the feria's elaborate spiritual events, cultural celebrations, and popular entertainments enact a unique ritual that expresses local identity for residents and a distinct sense of place for the pueblo. For Textitlán's citizens, participation in the event is emblematic of their belonging and their place in the pueblo.

The feria is a distinguishing feature of Mexican social life. When asked about what they miss about their old lives, Textitlanecos in Pennsylvania mention the feria most often after family and friends. "I can't tell you how sad I am," recalled Gloria Serato, "when I'm in el Norte during the feria. I think about my family and all of the things I am missing [in Mexico]."[35]

FIESTA SAGRADA/FERIA PAGANA: FESTIVAL—SACRED AND PROFANE

The Feria de Esquipulitas has always been a combination of secular (*pagana*) events hosted by the local municipio government and religious (*sacrada*) events that are sponsored by the church. To the casual observer, it can be difficult to determine which organization hosts the events. For example, the large pyrotechnic *castillos* (fireworks)[36] are church sponsored, but *teatro del pueblo* (theater commemorating local historical events) is hosted by the municipio. The secular events include *bailes* (dances), *jaripeos* (bull riding), *Charreada* (a stylized Mexican rodeo), *corrida de toros* (bullfights), concerts, mariachis, *torneos de gallos* (cock fights), a carnival, and an all-night street fair on January 16.[37]

Feria participation takes many forms. Clearly the most popular events are the bailes and jaripeo-bailes, which occur once or more per week. These events draw young and old participants, from those looking for marriage partners to longtime married couples on a night out. The dances are surprising in that they feature well-known Mexican performers, which are likely to be bands that perform norteño or banda music, the musical styles most popular in western Mexico.[38] These groups often sing of the issues that are closest to the hearts of immigrant families: loyalty to one's homeland, love, and betrayal. Of the latter there are literally hundreds of songs dedicated to women who leave a solid relationship in search of a man who can offer more affluence or a higher social position. These songs point to the anxiety on the part of some regarding migrant influence and suggest that the economic distinctions that divide migrants and non-migrants are pervasive beyond the pueblo of Textitlán.

The two main events of January 16 and 31 are by far the most widely attended, and the contrasting experiences that they offer provide the foundation of unity within the pueblo. What is most important about street fair on January 16 is the way in which it minimizes the social structure of the community, particularly for ausentes. The main events of the evening take place in the village's central plaza, with bands, parades, folk dancers, and food and souvenir vendors. In addition, nearly every block in the pueblo has its own party; a returning migrant's family often hosts these parties. The block parties are not small events; they typically include large volumes of food, tequila, and a live band that begins playing when the street fair in the center of town dies down, around 1 a.m., and continues until dawn. January 16 is much like a Mardi Gras celebration in that it provides a release from the bounds of normal obligations, but the general behavior overall is no more boisterous than a street fair after a major athletic victory in the United States. At the same time, the feria offers a culturally sanctioned way for migrants to demonstrate, and share, their economic success. When an ausente hosts an event for his neighbors and friends, it fosters a sense of community and camaraderie for everyone who lives within the vicinity of the party.

Although many of the feria events are free or inexpensive (such as the street fair and carnival), most of the entertainments are extremely expensive for the average Textitlaneco. The income for a *cosera* (seamstress) or *obrero textil* (garment factory worker) is approximately 1,000 pesos per week (approximately $100 U.S.), but many make much less. Tickets for a jaripeo can range from 120 to 200 pesos (approximately $12–$20 U.S.); torneo de gallos range from 200 to 300 pesos ($20–$30 U.S.), depending on the musical artist performing after the gallos; and bailes cost between 180 and 200 pesos ($18–$20 U.S.). The events are typically populated by the pueblo's more prosperous residents and always many who have returned from a stint working in the United States. For some, the feria is a time when spending to excess is common. Emilio Guzmán noted, "I remember many years that men would lament how much money they spent at the feria. Many overspend and are left to suffer for the next month. Still, they had a good time while it lasted."[39]

Since my first feria in 2000, I have returned to Textitlán every year but one to celebrate with the returning ausentes. I have attended nearly every event offered over the years, and although each festivity gives insight to local culture and history: the feria of January 16 and the *peregrinación* (pilgrimage) of January 31 are the most significant events of the feria. I discuss each of these events in turn.

FERIA PAGANA: TRANSGRESSION AND IDENTIFICATION

The feria is a much-anticipated event. On January 15, the day of Esquipulas in Guatemala and anywhere the image resides, Textitlán hosts a mass with the bishop presiding. The holy day is followed the next evening with the feria, an all-night street fair that begins at ten o'clock in the evening and continues until dawn. The feria combines expressions of religious devotion and carnal excess; the evening's events are sponsored by the church and municipio.

The feria begins in the jardín near the Presidencia, the seat of the municipio government. Here there are folk dancers, clowns, and *mojigangas* (large dancing puppets) parading in the street. Every time I have attended a feria, my research assistant Felipe Ortega accompanied me on the street. A parade begins with *carros alegóricos* (allegorical floats) around ten o'clock; these carros emphasize the role of the church in the community. Many of these carros carry young women dressed as heavenly creatures: angels who serenade the revelers with songs about Esquipulitas and the blessed church or young women dressed as Mary, the virgin mother. There is also a carro carrying the holy family. Dispersed throughout the carros are folk dancers and mojigangas, as well as *charros* (horsemen) in full mariachi-style regalia upon their prized steeds. The *reina* (queen) and *princesas* (princesses) of the feria are typically daughters of wealthy merchants and garment factory owners; they follow in the final carros. In 2004, the reina was seated in front of an image of the basilica of Equipulas, Guatemala, emphasizing the connection between her pueblo and the historic origins of Textitlán's Equipulitas.

As the parade ends, people move into the streets and take up positions in the plaza and the street with their families and friends, and Felipe and I follow the crowd, watching the events from different places on the plaza. The use of space or preferred spaces is not restricted by economic or political status; groups form wherever they find room in the crowded streets and sidewalks. Similarly, there is no correct way to enjoy the evening. The only necessary ingredient is the gathering of friends and family, although nearly all of the groups drink tequila or beer, and most people purchase food to share among their group.

All of the restaurants located on the plaza are open, and the street hosts dozens of vendors selling food and souvenirs; the feria attracts performers and vendors from great distances. The mood of reserve and restraint of the previous day is replaced with unbridled merriment. As midnight approaches, parents and their small children begin to depart. Many families return to find their streets blocked off and bands playing on makeshift bandstands. Others remain on the street dancing, drinking to excess, and enjoying the chaos that is common on this day.

The street noise is impenetrable with the resonance of dozens of bands playing in close proximity. The feria always draws uncommitted banda and mariachi bands wandering about, hoping a reveler will decide to hire them for the evening or even an hour. I spoke with several *jefes* (managers) of mariachis who came to Textitlán looking for employment. They charge between 1,000 and 1,500 pesos ($100–$150 U.S.) per hour. Once they are employed, the bands follow their employer as he (or rarely she), his family, and friends walk through the street. It is a mark of distinction to have a band on the night of the feria, an obvious demonstration of one's wealth and status in the community. One need not be wealthy, however, to enjoy a particular band. Bands are also often followed by groups of revelers who are known as *colas* (tails). They have not paid for the performances but are often friends of the individual who has hired the band and trail behind the band singing and dancing to the music.

Given that the feria is a street fair, it is not surprising that the limits of acceptable behavior are much more broad than usual, and in some cases the mores of the community are temporarily suspended. Nevertheless there are limits regarding what is tolerated. For example, public drunkenness by men and women is tolerated, but physical violence of any type is not. And whereas men are free to demonstrate their amorous feelings openly for women on the street, women are frequently cautioned to be on guard of any man who might go too far. The release from the normal standard of strict social regulation is surprising but nonetheless well managed within the crowd. If a situation gets out of hand, and it sometimes does, the municipio police are on hand to remove intoxicated revelers from the streets.

The mood on the street is jubilant and free but as the evening draws on, the crowds diminish and it becomes apparent that the good-natured festivities of the early evening can develop dark consequences. Men and women who are still on the street by three in the morning are typically profoundly intoxicated. As Felipe and I move through the streets, we pass more than one young man passed out drunk on the street. Making our way back to the home of Elena and Pedro Fernández (with whom I was living), we avoid the men staggering around, in some cases urinating on the walls along side streets. The following morning the streets will be deserted until late afternoon, and the remnants of the previous night, a sea of discarded plastic and glass bottles, paper, and other garbage, will fill the street until the municipal workers sober up and come out to clear the debris. It is clearly not the pueblo's best moment. But the night is still not quite over for us; it is only 3 a.m.

As we round the corner to arrive at Don Pedro's house, we hear the half-hearted efforts of a band that is just about played out. Don Pedro's son Omar, who works half the year in Pennsylvania and returns to see his wife and four children every winter, has hired a small banda group. The entire family is still on the street. The women are clustered tightly around Omar's wife Teresa on the stoop of their home and the men are gathered a few feet away sitting around Omar and Don Pedro.

When the band begins their next tune, Omar takes Teresa's hand and they begin to dance, and he leads her masterfully on the dimly lit street. Several of the men tentatively move forward and ask other women to dance. One older man wearing a white cowboy hat approaches me, but I hesitate. I always feel ambivalent about how to respond when I am asked to dance in Mexico. I love to dance, but an affirmative response might be interpreted as romantic interest, a complication I have worked hard to avoid. At the last moment, I move into the doorway under the pretense of looking for tequila. I pour myself a drink and watch the dancers. When the next song begins, Teresa encourages me to dance with Omar. Instead, I dash to the bathroom, but when I return I realize that I cannot avoid this any longer, and I dance with Omar, but only after Teresa's neighbor Lola explains that because this is a house party, dancing with someone other than one's spouse is acceptable behavior, so long as all parties involved agree. After my dance with Omar, several of the other men come forward as the band plays on. Then a sufficiently tipsy Don Pedro makes his way toward me. Doña Elena and her daughter Rosa had retired to bed half an hour earlier. Don Pedro takes my hand to lead me to the street, then we dance while the other men hoot and tease him from the sidelines. Doña Elena is a sweet gentlewoman, but the neighbors know she would not approve of Don Pedro's boldness. The night wears on and by 6 a.m. the party begins to break up, the exhausted band members pack up and slowly move toward their car, massaging their tired lips. I retire to my room in Doña Elena's home by 6:30. Exhausted, I fall into a restless sleep, my mind processing all that I've seen and heard. This is the third feria I've observed. Once the parties have ended, I will wait for the most holy of days.

THE PILGRIMAGE OF THE AUSENTES

The celebrations that culminate with the feria continue through the end of the month, although in a more subdued manner. It is strange, in a way, that the penultimate celebration, the one that is the most raucous and free takes place in the middle of the month. But the placement is crucial: after the solemn mass but two weeks before the pilgrimage. The feria is a means of cleansing one's soul, of flushing out sin and sensuousness common to the human condition. For the next two weeks, there is contemplation and prayer. There are also people arriving from and then departing to the United States as vacations end and parents usher their school-age children back to their schools. As the end of the month approaches, the mood in Textitlán becomes more reserved, perhaps pensive. Although thousands of people descend on the pueblo for the feria, equally large numbers return for the pilgrimage. During the month people are constantly coming and going in Textitlán, some of their own volition, some at the request of a harried employer who cannot survive an entire month without his most reliable employee.

I witnessed the pilgrimage for the first time on January 31, 2000. I had been living in Textitlán for nearly two months, and as the end of January approached, nearly everyone I met insisted that I should observe the pilgrimage. I remember talking to José Ortega one afternoon while my children were playing in his video arcade and indoor recreation station, La Bandera.[40]

He described the pilgrimage as a remarkable and very solemn spectacle. Later he invited me to come to his house to watch from his second-floor balcony. José and I became acquainted through the many visits I made to his business with my children. In the months leading up to the pilgrimage, he had brought photographs and books detailing the events. His images were of dimly lit streets crowded with pilgrims carrying what seemed like thousands of flickering candles. In one image, the litter carrying Esquipulitas glowed ethereally from the center of the photograph, the ebony crucifix surrounded by flowers, his gold crown sparkling in the muted light.

Although I was keen to know as much about Textitlán as possible, I must admit that at first I found it difficult to understand what could be so important about a procession with a crucifix. I had seen similar events during Good Friday services in the United States, but as José and others described the event and its importance to the local community, I realized the pilgrimage had a special meaning for everyone in the pueblo. From what I had been told, the entire town, along with thousands of returning ausentes, would take to the streets for the second time in a month. While the event I had participated in on January 16 was a raucous street festival, this was described as a spiritual event. I knew that Payal Gupta, a colleague with the Mexican Migration Project, would join me in the field early on January 31, so I made arrangements to have my babysitter, Erica, sleep over so Payal and I could attend the procession.

Payal and I set out walking through the streets shortly after nine o'clock en route to José's home. We soon found ourselves lost. José lived in a part of town I had not visited often, and although I was certain I would find the house, our quest was hindered because most of the houses had no street numbers to identify them. As we moved through the streets we were surprised by the elaborate decorations that had been put out that afternoon. Textitlanecos had used leftover Christmas lights to adorn their houses and the streets with enormous twinkling archways, erected twelve-foot panels with painted images of Esquipulitas adorned with flowers, and displayed signs that read "Viva el Señor de Esquipulitas" (Hail the Lord Esquipulitas). We also saw a street altar that covered the front of two houses. When we finally arrived at José's home, he and his wife escorted us to the balcony of their nineteenth-century home where we waited for the procession to begin. The street was full of people walking north, away from the center of town, but the streets seemed uncharacteristically quiet. There were no cars or motorcycles and the mood was solemn, as if someone had just died.

Within an hour small groups of men, women, and children began to walk southward down the street toward the central jardín. Each person carried a large lit candle. Some groups recited the rosary, others sang, still others passed silently in the streets as if engaged in prayer. Soon a steady throng of pilgrims replaced the intermittent groups. The street was lit with the soft glow of hundreds of candles as the crowd swelled, eventually filling the street and sidewalk. Shortly before midnight the *cargadores* (those men and women entrusted with carrying the crucifix) came into view bearing a large flower-laden litter with Esquipulitas at its center. The people softly sang the "Hymn to the Lord Esquipulitas":

> We come, Oh Lord Esquipulitas! with our humble gift.
> You are our King. With infinite yearning we yield our pueblo to you,
>   Textitlán.

> Hail Jesus Christ! All of the children of this happy pueblo sing your
>   praise.
> We rejoice in the blessings of Your love, a love without end.

When the hymn ended the voice of a priest, amplified from a loudspeaker, began to recite prayers, giving thanks for the many blessings of Esquipulitas. When the image and the crowd had passed, José encouraged us to go to the jardín to see the procession a second time. I was moved by what I witnessed, but nevertheless, I was confused. What is it about this crucifix that inspires such devotion?

As we walked to the center of town, we came face to face with the crowd, arriving just in time to see the procession pass in the center of the pueblo. The crowd was much more intense at the street level, and we were forced to take refuge in a doorway to avoid being pushed along with the crowd instead of simply observing on the sidelines. I had taken my video camera and had been filming from the balcony all night, and I continued to film the procession from just a few feet away. I realized as the participants came into focus through the camera lens that there were many men here, and there were scores of migrants. Later I learned that this group that lead the procession was the *peregrinación de los ausentes* (the pilgrimage of the pueblo's absent). Ausentes are given a special place in the procession that sets them apart from other pilgrims. They lead the way for Esquipulitas, but theirs is not the most prestigious place in the procession. That place is taken by the men and women who carry Esquipulitas and stand closest to him, and they are the Textitlanecos who live in the village year-round. On the street I saw that the large candles that the pilgrims carried melted freely; the hands that bore them were covered in molten wax. The procession passed us, and we followed behind them as they moved slowly toward the central plaza where merchants were set up to vend food to the returning pilgrims. Esquipulitas and his followers disappeared ahead of us into the dark night.

Payal and I decided to go to the jardín to buy tamales. We sat in reverent silence as we ate. I remember looking up at the inky black sky to admire the moon, contemplating what I had witnessed. I recall being certain that the pilgrimage was not entertainment. I was equally certain, having just experienced my first feria for Esquipulitas, that there was more to this monthlong event than diversion, but it was not yet clear to me. I spent the next five years returning to Textitlán again and again, puzzling it out.

PILGRIMAGE AND RE-EMPLACEMENT

During the pilgrimage, the streets are Equipulitas's and his symbolic dominion is established as faithful followers move him through the heart of the pueblo. Church officials and citizens alike acknowledge that the procession is a useful tool to inspire devotion from Esquipulitas's flock, a devotion that is demonstrated through church attendance and adherence to church doctrine. The pilgrimage is also a reason to return to Textitlán. For migrants who regularly make the journey north, homecoming is often characterized as a return from exile and a time to celebrate family homecoming and local traditions. Much as the Esquipulitas is emblematic of local identity, participation in the feria in his honor is an indicator of belonging to Textitlán. The feria is a time set apart to enact ritual practices that recall and commemorate Esquipulitas's arrival and Textitlán's creation as a distinct place.

The rituals surrounding the feria have evolved as a means to reunite Textitlán's ausentes with the pueblo's year-round residents. In Textitlán, much as in the United States, immigration is a divisive topic; it is unlikely that Textitlanecos will ever reach consensus on their opinions about migration and its effects on life in the pueblo. What binds this community together, however, is not consensus but compliance and participation in a series of ritual activities during the feria. Participation in the events of the feria has the effect of drawing attention away from the divisive social issues that are attributed to migration and redirects attention toward Esquipulitas, a powerfully evoked representation of local identity and spiritual devotion.

Transnational migration presents a stark reality that compels Textitlanecos to reaffirm the rightful place of their exiled and resident sons and daughters, but they are not alone in their need to reaffirm belonging. "There can be no society," writes Émile Durkheim, "which does not feel the need of upholding and reaffirming at regular intervals the collective sentiments and the collective ideas which make its unity and personality" (quoted in Bell 1997: 83). The social practices enacted through the feria, particularly the pilgrimage, reconstitute the boundaries between ausentes and non-migrants, but they also give license to the transgressions brought about by migration. The feria restores the rupture in the community, but it also legitimizes the hierarchy that places ausentes in a subordinate position vis-à-vis the wealthy elites who have never been forced to migrate.

Esquipulitas is an emblem of an immediate and local god whom one can petition, and he is the source of miracles. Pilgrimage sites are often believed to be places where miracles have happened and are likely to occur again. Miracles, coupled with the reaffirmation of faith, are the reward for making the sacrifices one endures in undertaking the pilgrim's journey. It is an individual decision, an "inward movement of the heart" that requires the separation of the pilgrim from everyday life (Turner 1978: 8) and moves him or her into fellowship with like-minded people. In making this choice, Textitlanecos' return is a form of penance that reconciles ausentes to the community of believers (Turner 1978; Harpur 2002). Textitlán's miracle, in this sense, is that the migrants/pilgrims can renew their belonging through their devotion, and that they can be away but still be part of the natal community.

A perceived dedication to the image of Esquipulitas, in fact, can emplace newcomers as well as ausentes. The small replica that that René Guzmán sent to my father was indicative of this. Esquipulitas accompanied my father through a long illness that required two surgeries and transfers to three hospitals. His experiences cannot be counted among Esquipulitas's miracles; he passed away three agonizing months after my return from Mexico in January 2003. I returned to Textitlán the following January to complete the work that was left unfinished the year before. In the midst of an interview, I asked Emilio Guzmán if he knew of any Textitlanecos who lived abroad and returned annually to participate in the feria. He paused for a minute to consider my question, and then he replied, "No, no one. Except, of course, you."

SEVEN

The Ambivalent Welcome

CINCO DE MAYO AND THE PERFORMANCE OF
LOCAL IDENTITY AND ETHNIC RELATIONS

On May 5, 2002, I drove to Kennett Square with a queasy sense of apprehension. It had been nearly a year since I had completed my full-time fieldwork in this rural farming village. I had taken a job and moved to suburban Washington, DC, and had been back to Kennett only occasionally for fieldwork and to visit, but these trips were infrequent. I was returning to document and observe the second annual Cinco de Mayo. The year before I was in the midst of a move and the start of a new job, and therefore I was unable to attend the first annual festival. I had observed the groundwork that led up to the festival during the term of my fieldwork, and I was eager to observe the event. At the same time I was uncertain about what this festival, created by Kennett Square's English-speaking majority on behalf of Mexican settlers, would reveal about the places of Mexican families in Kennett Square, and more important, how

Mexicans and their American-born hosts would each respond to the event.

Being keenly aware of the history of ethnic relations in Kennett Square, my apprehension about the festival, and particularly the festival's organizers (drawing almost exclusively from the English-speaking majority), was not unwarranted. I had witnessed the angst and frustration that Mexican settlers and their English-speaking neighbors had experienced for nearly a decade as they endeavored to coexist peaceably in this small community. I was also fully cognizant of the magnitude of the event when I arrived at Kennett Square that spring morning. I recalled wandering into Kennett Square in October 1995, when I could not find a single Mexican on the street; now the town was celebrating local Mexican heritage for the second year in a row. I was at once apprehensive and hopeful about what the day would represent as I pondered the transformations that led to the Cinco de Mayo celebration in Kennett Square.

The questions that inform this chapter have developed from my exploration of festivals in Kennett Square and examine the concepts of community and belonging. In order to examine Kennett Square's transition from a community that historically housed seasonal migrant workers to one that became a settlement for Mexican families, I analyze several of Kennett Square's public display events, including the Cinco de Mayo festival. Although Kennett Square hosts up to a dozen street fairs and family events throughout the year, the Cinco de Mayo festival in 2001 was the first time the town officially recognized its growing Mexican population through a large-scale public celebration. The festival commemorates the victory of Mexican forces over the French in the Battle of Puebla on May 5, 1862. The initial response by the local elected officials and the English-speaking majority to the early years of Mexican settlement in the late 1980s and early 1990s was an attempt to forestall Mexican settlement and to segregate the Mexican population. The Mexicans that I interviewed in the mid-1990s shared stories about living in a community where they were not wanted, and most often, these narratives provided insight into the boundaries that had emerged between Mexicans and others in the town.[1] Immigrant workers and their families were considered transients and were routinely excluded from community events, such as the annual Mushroom Festival. Thus the Cinco de Mayo festival was hailed as a turning point for Kennett Square's majority English-speaking population, who for years had openly expressed ambivalence, and at times hostility, toward the Mexican families who settled in the area.

This appraisal of the Cinco de Mayo festival is not overstated, but the event was not only a turning point for Kennett Square's English-speaking population. The Cinco de Mayo also marked a major shift in the position of Mexicans in the Kennett Square community. When the English-speaking citizens decided to celebrate Mexican participation, the Cinco de Mayo simultaneously opened the door to encourage Mexican emplacement and belonging. During the first decade of settlement, acknowledging that Mexicans belonged in Kennett Square was unthinkable for English-speaking residents, but the Cinco de Mayo festival marked a shift in social relations. Not only was the majority population willing to openly recognize Mexican cultural heritage as part of *their* community, but also the festival provided an occasion for Mexicans to begin the process of incorporation and shape the sense of place in Kennett Square.

RITUAL BELONGING: THE COMMUNITY FESTIVAL

During the course of my fieldwork in Kennett Square, longer-term residents often lamented that small-town festivals were less common that they once were in Chester County. This idea was based in part by the fact that Kennett Square was the only town in this corner of Chester County, with the exception of Chadds Ford,[2] that regularly held community festivals and parades. When the Mushroom Festival was scaled back significantly in 1999, with no parade and only a modest street fair, it was rumored that within a few years Kennett Square's biggest festival would soon be cancelled. The Mushroom Festival organizers did this to cut costs, as festival expenses had become prohibitive. The following year, however, the festival parade and large street fair was reinstated, due largely to the desires of the local community.

Scholars frequently overlook festivals because they can appear apolitical and innocuous to the casual observer, but the process of determining which communal features are to be celebrated and under what circumstances reveals much about community attitudes and priorities. In the places where they are celebrated, festivals offer insights to the community's values and priorities. Festival celebrations are expensive and time consuming; they require the coordination of the municipal government and sometimes state government, citizen volunteers, and local entrepreneurs (who often underwrite the event) and participation by local residents. The fact that Kennett Square continues to host many public festivals, particularly when many of its neighboring municipalities do not, is a feature that draws some middle- and upper-class English-speaking families to settle in the town. During a Mushroom Festival parade in 1998, a married couple told me that they moved to Kennett Square because "we wanted our children to grow up in a community where there they still have parades and people know each other."[3]

Although there are other ways that communities can display collective identity, festivals carry particular weight as public display events. Festivals require communal participation and therefore cannot take place in locales that lack people with a strong commitment to the event and sense of corporate identity. They also hark back to notions of a past that sharply contrasts with contemporary life. Such associations are suffused with romantic ideas of rural America, where face-to-face interaction and strong communal ties were the norm. Yet given the organizers' efforts to initiate and sustain festivals, these events represent more than a day of family fun and entertainment. Festivals are cultural performances that reference intensified expressions of how their organizers—be it a family, community, or social group—sees themselves. Cultural performances call attention to local values and "highlight the multiple roles an individual [or group] plays in shifting configurations of community" (St. George 1998: 7). These celebrations "attempt to manifest, in symbolic form, what [the community] conceives to be its essential life, at once the distillation and typification of its corporate experience" (Turner 1982: 16).[4]

Despite their folksy associations, festivals are expressions of power and resistance. In the United States, festivals typically represent a group's ideas of itself and the community's values; an example of such values may be the ideal of the harmonious multicultural community. Festivals are also used to demonstrate the organizers' image of their community or social group. More significantly, festivals reflect how organizers would like others to see them and their community.[5] Thus, as a cultural performance the festival provides a means to allow a group to extract select attributes of the community, such as a particular tradition or cultural practice, and display it as if it were a true representation of the entire group. Festivals showcase cultural differences while simultaneously allowing disparate groups to access one another's normally isolated worlds. Robert Cantwell (1993) argues that in a festival's most positive expression, it offers the possibility of mutual understanding, but is just as likely to sanitize and reshape the group it endeavors to represent, stripping away less-desirable features such as poverty and discrimination.

At their core, festivals are multisense events that can express divergent, contradictory, or ambivalent meanings. Festivals such as Kennett Square's Cinco de Mayo are not merely sources of entertainment; they are also complex events that expose social and political relations in the communities where they are celebrated.[6] They also offer an opportunity to examine local change in the making. People are attracted to festivals because of what they represent: liberation from social constraints, the ability to contest the social order, and conviviality among friends and strangers. These events break with the mundane aspects of daily life and foster a sense of *communitas*, the sense of local identity and the relationships formed through sharing a common space (Turner 1969: 96). This identity is frequently expressed in terms of power relations within the community. Festivals are spectacles replete with music, food, dance, and drama, but they do more than entertain: they also validate and contest the established social order. In short, they are occasions that are "intimately and dynamically related to the political order and to the struggle for power within it" (Cohen 1993: 4).

The Cinco de Mayo festival in Kennett Square is an opportunity to shape local ethnic relations and articulate the English-speaking community's ideas and attitudes about their Mexican neighbors and their place in the local community. The event is best understood as a cultural performance, an "occasion in which as a culture . . . we reflect upon and define ourselves, dramatize our collective myths and history, present ourselves with alternatives, eventually change in some ways while remaining the same in others"(MacAloon 1984: 1). The festival as cultural performance is not only a demonstration of how a group imagines itself, but also it is a means to reconfigure intergroup relations and to integrate those who are outside the boundaries of the group (St. George 1998). During the Cinco de Mayo festival, Kennett Square's State Street became a stage where local actors performed their identities in relation to their perceived place in the community and to one another (Schechner 1993), and the festival unexpectedly became a tool to facilitate Mexican incorporation by reshaping locality for Mexicans and their English-speaking neighbors.

The Cinco de Mayo celebration was intended to be an unequivocal welcome to Mexican families and to celebrate Mexican contributions to the local community; to work toward constructing a totality from disparate groups who need to find a way to share a social space and coexist harmoniously.[7] It was also viewed as a means to set right past transgressions against Mexican families, who had been overlooked or excluded in the planning and execution of other community events. As is the case with other large-scale public display events, the Cinco de Mayo festival expressed more than these positive virtues and, in fact, gave voice to a deep ambivalence in community sentiment: the English-speaking population's conflicting emotions regarding Mexican settlement, particularly the changing sense of place in Kennett Square.

INTERCULTURAL AMBIVALENCE

Everyone has felt ambivalent at one time or another, whether toward a job, family member, or neighborhood. Emotions are often mistakenly considered to be the opposite of reason, but in fact emotions are complex bodily feelings that result in part from judgments that are directed toward someone or something. We feel our emotions, but they are informed by mental acts of understanding or judgment. Thus an individual's rea-

soning is not overcome by his or her emotions; emotions are bodily perceived feelings that are informed in part by intellectual processes. For
instance, the emotion of falling in love is rooted in part in judgments
made on the basis of interactions with another person and an appraisal
of his or her behavior (Koch 1987).

Ambivalence can arise on the communal as well as personal level,
when broader community or cultural values conflict with individual wants
or desires or when the interests of one faction of a community or group
conflict with communal principles of inclusion, justice, or equity. For
example, a political candidate may support a woman's legal access to
abortion but also maintain that her values would prohibit her from personally exercising that choice. Or a small business owner may agree with
current U.S. immigration laws that prohibit low-skilled workers from
entering the United States legally but also hire undocumented workers in
order to maintain his profit margin or to keep his small business afloat.
Similarly, a family may purchase a new home in a subdivision that was
once a family farm and at the same time oppose any further development
of existing open land in their community. In these instances, the beliefs,
and the exceptions to these beliefs, are not merely instances of ethical
duplicity but also constitute a "dilemma of competing virtues or evils"
(Shore 1999: 171). The ideals that are the basis on which principled choices
are made often have competing standards that, at first glance, seem to
undermine them. It is possible for the broader values of a community,
such as acceptance, equality, and inclusion, to run counter to the individual preferences for a community that is familiar and unified in class,
language, or ethnicity. These instances of conflict between the communal
value of acceptance and the desire for constancy are what I call "intercultural ambivalence."

CHANGE AND THE CRAFTING OF LOCAL IDENTITY

The central conflict in Kennett Square has long been between the appropriateness of welcoming Mexican settlers as part of the community and
the certainty that their permanent settlement inevitably means change.

Kennett Square's communal identity is strongly associated with agriculture and the local mushroom industry; it is regionally known as the Mushroom Capital of the World. Although the industry relies on Mexican labor, the permanent settlement of Mexican families has produced a mixed reaction from the English-speaking population. Furthermore, this once out-of-the-way farming community has been experiencing growth and change from two directions: an influx of wealthy, highly educated Anglo-American professionals who work in Philadelphia and Wilmington and an influx of a population that is predominantly Mexican and low income and has had limited access to education.

Not surprisingly, Kennett Square's older, longer-term English-speaking citizen community has been more receptive to the growing suburban population than to the Mexicans, a fact outlined on the Kennett Square Borough Web site.[8] Like leaders in many other growing municipalities, Kennett Square's elected officials are interested in attracting people to the area who can provide a stable tax base and whom they believe will be productive members of the community. As a means of setting the tone of the community, the official Web site stresses Kennett Square's Anglo-European heritage and its connections to significant historical events, such as the Battle of the Brandywine and the town's role in the Underground Railroad. In addition, the Historic Kennett Square Web site emphasizes that "[m]any talented individuals have been attracted to the town and found Kennett Square a good place to make their home. For a borough that has always been less than five thousand in population, a surprising number of private educational and cultural activities have flourished."[9] More recently, the site has been updated to include important statistical information, including Kennett's median household income, $51,149, and compares this with the average household income for the Commonwealth of Pennsylvania for the same time period, which is $29,069. The site also notes that 31 percent of the population over the age of eighteen are college graduates and "two-thirds . . . have taken additional graduate or professional training."[10] For anyone researching the area as a possible future home or business location, these statistics craft an image of Kennett Square's population as wealthy, well educated, and culturally sophisticated.

The Kennett Square Borough Web site anticipates that the town will be a growing community well into the next decade and notes an expected population increase to 6,713 by 2010, but there is no mention of the fact that Mexican migrants are chiefly responsible for the past and predicted population increases. The calendar of events does list the Cinco de Mayo as a "family celebration of Mexican food and culture," but the celebration is in no way explicitly linked to the actual Mexican residents in town. In fact, there is no mention of the Mexican settlers or their influence on the local culture anywhere on the site.[11]

For over a century, Kennett Square has been home to a thriving agribusiness. Although the mushroom industry has always attracted newly arrived U.S. immigrants and other low-wage workers, Kennett Square has rarely become a permanent home to mushroom laborers.[12] Mushroom pickers from a variety of ethnic and minority groups, especially Puerto Ricans, eventually moved away from picking mushrooms and also moved out of Kennett Square to find better employment. Today the sizable population of Puerto Ricans in Wilmington, Delaware, is one result of this. The historical flow of low-wage mushroom laborers out of the area has allowed Kennett to maintain its Anglo-European character. The Mexican farmworkers were the first to settle permanently in and around Kennett Square, even as many of these men have moved into more lucrative work, such as landscaping and construction. The fundamental reason for this shift is the availability of work. The rapid suburbanization of Kennett Square's surrounding county has produced a demand for cheap local labor, particularly in construction and landscaping, thus eliminating the need for laborers to move away to acquire better, reliable employment.[13]

Why would local governing officials minimize or hide Kennett Square's growing Mexican community, particularly in light of an influential social movement dedicated to incorporating them into the community? The information provided on the official Kennett Square Web site exposes an underlying class tension that has been evident since the early days of Mexican settlement and that I also observed during my fieldwork in the community. Mexican families on the whole are low-income households and the average Mexican settler has only 5.4 years of education.[14] The class distinctions between Mexican settlers and their citizen neighbors are great and are reinforced by the fact that both populations are largely monolingual. These incongruities are only compounded in the differences in the two groups' cultural tastes.[15] In spite of these marked differences, neither group has shown signs of wanting to leave Kennett Square to escape the other. Thus the initiation of the Cinco de Mayo festival was indeed significant in that it created an opportunity for these two groups to come together and symbolically share the community through a public festival.

CONCEPTUALIZING PUBLIC AND PRIVATE SPACE

In the early years of my fieldwork, Mexicans who spoke to me often lamented the life they had left behind. Many of these women and men, even after years of living in the United States, still reported that they had never felt "at home." Most told me they still owned homes in Mexico and hoped one day to return. Although I understood the concept of homesickness and feeling out of place, it was not until I lived in Textitlán that I fully realized what these families had lost in their pursuit of economic opportunities north of the border.

When I reflect on my own experiences in Textitlán, the images I have are of the street life at dusk. It is several hours before *cena* (dinner), and the families have reconvened and moved into the streets in front of their homes. Neighbors stroll down the streets to visit friends. Chairs are pulled onto the sidewalks and women gather to discuss the events of the day, family life, and local gossip. Men are also on the streets, but they stand together in small groups apart from the women and children. Earlier in the day, young men—*muchachos*—gather at certain street corners throughout the town's *colonias* (neighborhoods). I have unpoetically named these places "muchacho stands," simply because that is what the muchachos do there: stand, hang out, chat, and whistle at the young women who walk by. In these ways the street becomes an extension of the home, and because the space is used in common, the sense of individual ownership is lessened. While I lived in Textitlán it was not uncommon for my neighbors to congregate on my stoop and talk for most of the night, leaving a pile of garbanzo bean hulls and beer cans on the sidewalk in front of my home. The refuse would mysteriously be swept away in the morning by one of the *señoras* on my street. As I worked late into the night on my field notes and transcriptions, I often heard the muffled whispers of my neighbor's daughter Lilia as she and her sweetheart sat talking by my front door.

In contrast, day-to-day life in Kennett Square is dramatically different because family life is much more isolated and work centered. After I moved to Virginia, I returned to Kennett for a field visit in 2002 as the guest of the Espinosa family. I had rented their house when my family lived in Mexico, and our families had become close in the course of my fieldwork. Their oldest daughter, Celia, who was getting ready to return for the spring semester at Penn State, kindly offered me her room, as she was departing in a few days. The Espinosa house was a small, two-story single-family home with three bedrooms and one bath. The first floor consisted of two large rooms: a living room and an eat-in kitchen. Upstairs Mario and Ofelia shared the master bedroom with their youngest son, Miguel. Celia, the oldest, occupied the smallest bedroom alone, and her younger sisters, Rosa and Lisa, shared another room. During the summer months, Ofelia's brother rented a room in their basement. From time to time other extended family members, primarily one of Mario's siblings and their families, shared the house as well. It was rare for so many people to be living in the house for more than a few weeks. Like many Mexican families, particularly those who were established in their own homes, the Espinosa family felt obligated to help their relatives when they arrived in the United States.

During my first night with the Espinosa family, I woke up unexpectedly. Although it was early January, the room I was in was so hot I could not sleep. The Espinosa home was heated by an ancient furnace, Ofelia explained to me earlier, and the rooms in the house alternated between too hot or too drafty. I looked up and saw a dim glow of stars on an unfamiliar ceiling. The stars were press-on glow-in-the-dark disks that I imagined Celia must have put on her ceiling years ago. Celia's room was small and full of furniture, old stuffed animals, dried flowers and remnants of old bouquets, and a variety of used textbooks. I sat up in bed and reached for the window, feeling guilty for opening the window in the dead of winter, but the room was insufferable. I compromised with myself and cracked the window slightly and left the bedroom door ajar, hoping to coax in enough air to make the room temperature bearable.

After a few minutes I began to doze off, but then I heard someone moving in the hallway. Checking my watch, it was 3 a.m. After a few minutes I realized that Mario had gotten up to get ready for work. He had told me that he went into his job at a restaurant early to prepare food for the day. He drives a food truck for a Mexican restaurant that vends Mexican food to several mushroom farms. A few minutes later, he left the house, and I realized this early work call was why he was always so tired in the afternoons.

Ofelia was up by 7 a.m. to get the younger children fed and ready for school. After the children were off, she would spend the morning cleaning the house and cooking. Ofelia, an outstanding cook, worked at the same nearby Mexican restaurant as Mario, and she would sometimes bring food home with her at the end of the day. Other times, she would prepare a dish that Mario could easily heat up for dinner when he returned in the afternoon.

Mario and Ofelia made arrangements so that one of them would be home with the children after school. Mario's day ended around two o'clock in the afternoon, and he would drive back to the house and take Ofelia to work, as she had never learned to drive. He would then return to the house and wait for the children to return from school at 3:30. It was not unusual to find Mario napping on the sofa in the afternoons. Mario and Ofelia made a commitment to be the primary caregivers of their small children, but it was obvious that he was too exhausted after a normal workday to be actively involved in his children's lives. Most often, Miguel and Lisa would play in the house or watch television. Each evening Ofelia would return from the restaurant near eleven o'clock, usually driven by a co-worker. Her children might be waiting up for her; Mario would retire to bed by eight o'clock most evenings. Because the parents worked opposite schedules, it was rare for the family to eat dinner together, except on Tuesdays, the weekly day of rest that Mario and Ofelia allowed themselves.

While visiting with the Espinosa family, I often stayed up late chatting with Ofelia when she returned from work. Like her husband, she often complained of being exhausted, and I asked her if she ever considered working less. She explained, "We earn well, Mario and I, but we have to work so many hours. I always worry that there are so many expenses living in the United States. We have to pay for our house, our car, and for Celia's college. The children need things, too, always toys, clothes, something. We have to work, because we never know if we'll need money for something."

I understood Ofelia's concern for keeping ahead: she and Mario were minimum-wage employees, and they needed the income they earned working six days a week. Like many of their peers in Kennett Square, they had to work long hours if they wanted to maintain their modest, but comfortable, lifestyle. Their work lives also essentially eliminated any possibility of a social life, however. Ofelia said that they were willing to take a day off for a special occasion, such as when Celia graduated from high school, but these occasions were atypical.

In contrast to the everyday life in Textitlán where the street life was an important part of social life, the absence of this and other communal aspects of their lifestyle was a source of distress for Mexicans in Kennett Square. There have been complaints from the English-speaking community of Mexicans "loitering." Such gatherings are seen as threatening or undesirable. Although these families have homes and apartments, their access to common or public spaces has been limited by long work hours, zoning laws, community disapproval, and a decade of hard feelings. Opposition to Mexicans moving into what was previously an exclusively English-speaking space no doubt discouraged other activity at communal events or in public places. The activities of Mexicans who lived in Kennett Square's apartments were an example of this. Although some young men congregated in the parking lots and the patchy unkempt yard in front of the apartments, families typically remained inside and avoided public interaction.

Separated from their extended families and friends, unable to re-create a semblance of the life they had in Mexico, Mexican families have been understandably frustrated by the lack of community life and have felt out of place in Kennett Square. Thus, the initiation of the Cinco de Mayo festival was an important event for Mexicans as well as the majority population, as nearly everyone in Kennett recognized the Mexican community's need for this type of social recreation.

SOJOURNERS AND NEIGHBORS

Festivals are common occurrences in Kennett Square. This is due in part to the community's commitment to its rural heritage. Neighboring towns have similar agricultural histories, but Kennett has a particularly strong attachment to folk customs typically associated with rural America, parades and festivals being the most frequently observed. Thus it is not surprising that the community decided to celebrate a festival to acknowledge their Mexican neighbors. The town hosts nearly a dozen annual public events, including the Mushroom Festival, which usually draw large crowds from Kennett and the surrounding county.

What is surprising, however, is that the English-speaking community decided to celebrate the Mexican population at all. Unprepared for the rapid expansion of Mexican settlement in the early 1990s, these long-term residents of Kennett Square resisted changes in their community related to Mexican settlement, including neighborhood and school integration and bilingual services. Before 1986, the Mexican men who lived and worked in Kennett Square were carefully hidden out of sight on mushroom farms where they lived in barracks or trailers; these men were seen as transients and not included in local events. Although these men were vital to the mushroom industry, they were essentially invisible to the English-speaking community. Peggy Harris, a nurse practitioner who has worked at the local migrant clinic since 1976, described the situation in 1995, saying, "Well, the [Mexican] community is basically a hidden community. I'm not sure how . . . what happens in the school system. The kids seem to be pretty much okay there. But I know that in all other aspects it doesn't seem . . . there's no mixing. I'm not seeing much of the Mexicans being involved in the community life overall here. They're still a hidden community."[16]

Although a sizable Mexican population was well established by 1995, the English-speaking majority was simply unwilling to share their neighborhoods and public spaces with Mexican families. As Mexican families moved in, long-term residents joined together in an attempt to forestall settlement.[17] Although they began as scattered events, the effort to keep Mexicans out of Kennett Square did not go unnoticed by Mexicans who were settling in town.

These actions eventually brought accusations of racism from within the English-speaking community and exposed fractures within the majority population. Those who had participated in the protests bristled at the idea that their actions were racist and insisted that their actions were misinterpreted. Although it is difficult to determine exactly how many of the English-speaking majority participated in activities to create obstacles to Mexican settlement, these events were frequent enough to provide ample evidence of a racist sentiment on the part of those who had organized the protests. Nevertheless, for those who did not take part in the actions, including local advocates of the Mexican population, social service providers, and citizens who simply refused to get involved in such activities, the notion of being labeled a racist community did not fit the image that most Kennett Square residents had of themselves or their town, and many insisted that Kennett was still a progressive and inclusive small town (Lattanzi Shutika 2005).

In 1997, the Bridging the Community movement, led by the community activists from the English-speaking majority, was initiated to deal with community conflict and successfully quieted most of the overt opposition to Mexican settlement. At the same time, Bridging the Community leaders attempted to reframe the discussions surrounding Mexican settlement, emphasizing the positive features of having a diverse, multiethnic community. Members of the movement also launched a variety of volunteer programs to help the youths of the community and encouraged locals to incorporate Mexican families into the life of the community. Bridging the Community helped Kennett Square rehabilitate its image and encouraged a sense of openness (Lattanzi Shutika 2005).[18] It was in this context that the idea for a Cinco de Mayo festival took shape.

LA FIESTA AGRINGADA: CINCO DE MAYO IN KENNETT SQUARE

Why did the predominantly English-speaking population opt to put on a festival in order to embrace and promote Mexican culture in their community? To fully appreciate the Cinco de Mayo celebration that was initiated in May 2001, we must first look back a few years to 1998, the year of the formation of the *Alianza Cultural Latina*, the Latino Cultural Alliance.

Alianza was formed through local efforts of primarily Mexican families and the Catholic priest serving the Mexican population, but the group expanded to include a Latino college professor, a social services director, and two graduate students conducting research in the area, of which I was one. I joined Alianza in the summer of 1999 to assist with the second annual celebration of Mexican Independence Day, the *16 de Septiembre* (September 16). Much like the Fourth of July, this is a large-scale national celebration, but it is celebrated not only in Mexico but also in areas in the United States where large populations of Mexicans have settled. Although the Mexican consulate in Philadelphia hosts an impressive event on Penn's Landing every year, most Kennett Square Mexicans lacked transportation to the city so they rarely took part. The Alianza board decided to celebrate the 16 de Septiembre locally because it provided an opportunity for Mexican settlers to freely express and celebrate their identity as Mexicans in a community that seldom offered such opportunities.

The first two years of the event, 1998 and 1999, were well supported by Alianza and local Mexican families. The first year about three hundred attended; the next year about fifteen hundred. After the first year the event was moved to Anson B. Nixon Park, located centrally in Kennett Square and within walking distance from many Mexican families' homes. The Alianza board invited food vendors, organized a program of volunteer performers from the area, and paid a Mexican band to play at the event. By 2000, the successes of the previous two celebrations were well known in the community, and the number of participants increased to four thousand. The event had grown to an extent that Alianza's president decided it was time to request underwriting from the English-speaking business community, especially those that interacted the most with Mexican families, such as grocery stores, drug stores, and mushroom farms.

The board's attempts to raise money were unsuccessful. Local entrepreneurs expressed discomfort about celebrating a Mexican national holiday in the United States. One farm owner told me, "It just doesn't make sense. They're in America now," implying that celebrating the 16 de Septiembre indicated that the settler community lacked proper allegiance to the United States. Although Alianza raised enough money to pay for the event by vending sodas and selling souvenirs, the 2000 event was the last time the organization sponsored the celebration. The group folded later that year as the board members, overwhelmed by the work of staffing the event, concluded that Alianza lacked widespread community support. They also recognized that sustained support for the organization was unlikely.[19]

Although not willing to offer financial support, several members of the English-speaking community nevertheless considered Alianza's work to make Mexican settlers feel welcome a worthy endeavor. The English-speaking business community was hesitant to underwrite an event by the Mexican-led Alianza, but they were enthusiastic about sponsoring the Cinco de Mayo. Cinco de Mayo is a well-known holiday among Americans in the United States, but is not widely celebrated in the Mexican Republic outside of central Mexico in the states of Puebla and Mexico. For the Mexicans living in Kennett Square who are from western Mexico, this date had little significance before the initiation of the Kennett Square celebration.[20]

This is not to say the holiday cannot represent Mexican identity in the United States. In fact, Mexicans and Chicanos in other parts of the United States often employ Cinco de Mayo for this purpose. Festival organizers frequently employ Cinco de Mayo parades and other organized public display events as a means of exhibiting community identity. Often the festivals function to expand ideas of inclusion and belonging, a fact documented in the evolution of the Cinco de Mayo festival in Corona, California (Alamillo 2003). In the early 1930s, Mexican Americans used the festival to redefine the interests of their ethnic community and to demonstrate that they had become a political force. The festival was transformed

in the post–World War II era and became a bicultural event with participation by Mexicans and English speakers to promote "good neighborly"
relations (72).

A similar evolution took place in the transformation of the Cinco de
Mayo celebrations in San Francisco in the 1980s. This festival was an exclusively Mexican and Chicano celebration that grew to include many
Central and South American cultural forms. These changes were self-
consciously initiated to express a broader Latino solidarity when the Central and South American populations in the city increased. In these cases,
the Cinco de Mayo festival was initiated and directed by a core Mexican
American group that self-consciously elected to transform the festival to
meet political objectives and to promote pan-ethnic relations (Sommers
1991). In fact, academic studies of Cinco de Mayo festivals in the United
States document this pattern: a Mexican or Chicano leadership initiating
a festival and adapting its direction to fit a particular cultural or political
milieu (Sommers 1985, 1991).

Although Cinco de Mayo is a Mexican holiday, it is much more widely
celebrated as a popular ethnic crossover event in the United States than
in most regions of Mexico. During the last two decades it has grown
from an obscure regional Mexican holiday most frequently celebrated in
California and the southwestern United States to a national event that
is commemorated by Latinos, African Americans, and Anglo-Americans
in a variety of contexts. Actively promoted by restaurants, bars, and beverage companies, Cinco de Mayo has become particularly popular among
English-speaking Americans as a means of "understanding" or acknowledging Mexican culture (Saxton 1992; Turcsik 1996).[21] It is not uncommon
for schoolchildren throughout the United States to celebrate Cinco de
Mayo as part of a multiethnic curriculum or for young adults to mark
the holiday at a local bar that hosts a "fiesta." However, its popularity
among the general population, along with the commercialization of
the day, is a cause for concern for some Mexicans and Chicanos. For example, the California-based campaign *Cinco de Mayo con Orgullo* (Cinco
de Mayo with Pride) is actively trying to reclaim the holiday as a celebration of ethnic pride and distance it from its current associations with the
alcohol industry (Staples 2001). Despite this and similar efforts, many

Anglo-Americans continue to believe mistakenly that Cinco de Mayo is Mexico's Independence Day and to associate the day with excessive alcohol consumption.

The conceptualization of Cinco de Mayo by the population celebrating the event is the most likely factor in shaping the meaning of the event for participants. Cinco de Mayo can be used effectively to accurately represent Mexican identity, but this is most likely to happen when the festival is initiated, or at least governed, by a Mexican leadership. Yet the meanings of Cinco de Mayo festivals are multiple, ranging from a true cultural representation to a commercial endeavor to promote the sale of Mexican-brand beers. In Kennett Square, the Cinco de Mayo festival is associated with a particular *idea* of Mexican culture and identity as understood by the English-speaking majority and is not necessarily associated with other conceptions of the event in other parts of the United States. It is a cultural symbol that is easily misread as a neutral and an objective representation and "celebration of Mexican culture," as Historic Kennett Square states it on its Web site,[22] rather than as an interpretation of Mexican culture by English-speaking citizens, or a "fiesta agringada," which is how one Mexican woman described the festival to me. [23]

The reasons that the English-speaking community in Kennett Square selected Cinco de Mayo as their means of celebrating Mexican settlement are multiple. The timing of the event, in spring, is convenient, as there are no other festivals scheduled at that time. The community's largest festival celebrating the mushroom industry takes place during the second weekend in September, which effectively rules out the possibility of a 16 de Septiembre celebration. Perhaps more significant, as a Mexican celebration in the United States, Cinco de Mayo has fewer associations with Mexican nationalism than the more popular 16 de Septiembre.[24]

Cinco de Mayo has long been a pliable symbol of Mexican identity in the American imagination. Vince Ghione, the chairman of the Kennett Square Cinco de Mayo festival put it succinctly when he said, "Cinco de Mayo is a function of the Anglo community. . . . It's a commercial venture."[25] What Americans "know" about Cinco de Mayo often reflects common stereotypes about Mexican culture. But Kennett Square's Cinco de Mayo celebration does not adhere to the stereotypes of drinking and partying, the idea most commonly promoted by the alcohol industry and Mexican-themed restaurants. Instead, it has been conceived as a family event with the hope of drawing members from all facets of the community.

Planning for the first Cinco de Mayo festival began shortly after what turned out to be the last 16 de Septiembre festival in Kennett Square, in 2000, and was sponsored by a broad community coalition, including the Kennett Square Borough Council, the mushroom industry, and local residents. The first Cinco de Mayo festival, in 2001, was well attended and so was then added to the list of annual events that would be sponsored in the community. Although Kennett Square hosts many family-oriented fairs throughout the year, most have been poorly attended by Mexican families. In fact, the Cinco de Mayo was the first Kennett Square festival widely attended by Mexican families. The first Cinco de Mayo was held from one to six in the afternoon on May 5, 2001, and was located on State Street, the main thoroughfare in town. It was attended by approximately one thousand people. The second year the event organizers invited three Mexican-owned restaurants to sell food, and the borough also sponsored free activities for children, including pony rides and face painting. The local Giant grocery store donated two hundred ears of sweet corn, which were steamed and served on sticks covered with cheese and chili powder, Mexican style. There were also a number of invited vendors, some of whom sold Mexican-themed crafts and souvenirs, including straw sombreros and wooden maracas. Many of the vendors, however, were social service agencies and companies who serve, or would like to serve, Kennett Square's Mexican population. For example, Project Salud and La Comunidad Hispana, the local migrant clinic and social service center, had booths promoting state-funded health insurance for children and information on the prevention of AIDS and Lyme disease. State Farm Insurance was on hand to provide information on auto and home insurance, complete with bilingual materials demonstrating the company's effort to attract Mexican clientele. On the south end of State Street there was a stage for a rotation of Mexican popular and folk performances by a folk dance troupe, a mariachi band, and a Mexican deejay.

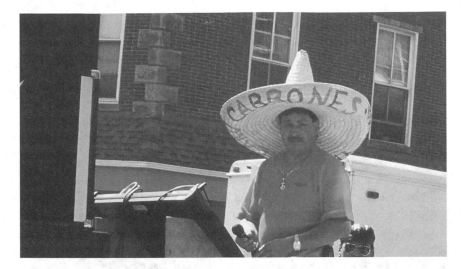

Figure 7. "Viva Cabrones" (Photograph by Debra Lattanzi Shutika)

Some of the performers were from the local Mexican community. On the surface, these were standard entertainments. The folk dancers were a group of local Mexican middle and high school students who wore bright indigenous costumes emblazoned with the image of the Virgin of Guadalupe across the back, signifying the combination of Mexico's Spanish and indigenous roots. The costumes, purchased in Mexico, were an apt symbol of contemporary Mexican nationalism. The Mexican deejay donned an unusually large straw sombrero with *Viva los Cabrones Mexicanos* (Long live the Mexican bastards) embroidered in red across the brim—in essence a caricature of Mexican culture. Many English-speaking festival participants also wore such sombreros, without the embroidered message. The embroidered message on the deejay's sombrero was emblematic of the type of dissent made possible by the festival. To the festival organizers and English-speaking participants, the deejay appeared to be engaging in the same kind of "fun" as many of the non-Mexican participants who wore sombreros. But the rude message inscribed across the brim simultaneously subverted the playfulness of his action, indicating a subtle rebellion obvious only to those who understood Spanish.

Figure 8.   Lyme Disease Float, Cinco de Mayo 2002 (Photograph by Debra Lattanzi Shutika)

In the afternoon there was also a short parade featuring the same Mexican folk dancers, a float highlighting the insidious dangers of Lyme disease, and a parade of flags. There were national flags representing the countries of origin of the English-speaking Kennett Square population.[26] The events culminated with a dance at the north end of State Street with live music from a popular local Mexican band. By the end of the day, the street was packed with Mexican families and couples wearing T-shirts imprinted with the Mexican flag, the Virgin of Guadalupe, and other Mexican national symbols.

Two other aspects of the event are noteworthy. First is the bilingual information that the Chester County Republican Party provided. Chester County is overwhelmingly Republican, and this booth provided information on the party and voter registration forms in Spanish. Second is that the ever-present bicycle police were outfitted with uniforms clearly marked "POLICIA." The presence of the Republican recruiter indicates that, to the GOP at least, the Cinco de Mayo represented more than a friendly gesture to the Mexican community.[27] In their attempt to include Mexicans in the then-majority political party, the GOP not only acknowledged their presence in the community but also assumed that they would eventually become a political force in the county and were working to attract them to their party. Similarly, by inscribing "POLICIA" on the police officers' uniforms, while other official signage is not bilingual, the local government indicated that it felt the need to make Mexicans aware of the local police and perhaps encourage them to manage their behavior carefully during the festival.

The booths dedicated to social services and the Lyme disease parade float are also telling. To festival organizers, the Cinco de Mayo festival was an occasion to educate the Mexican population about available social services and how to avoid unsafe health behaviors, elements that were not part of the other festivals during the year. These exhibits not only demonstrated the English-speaking community's paternalistic attitude toward Mexican settlers, they presumed that Mexicans were less informed about health issues than other members of the community and that the English-speaking community was responsible for protecting and educating them. Thus the festival was utilized as an opportunity to influence what festival organizers considered deficiencies in Mexican health behavior.[28]

According to the *Kennett Paper*, festival organizers and local business owners along State Street were pleased with the 2002 event. The estimated attendance was some six thousand people, an increase from one thousand in 2001. The majority of the participants were Mexican or Latino (Barber 2002). The day ended with one small hitch. When Vince Ghione, the festival chairperson, at 5:55 p.m. instructed the band to play their last song so the event could end at six o'clock as scheduled, the "final" song they played went on for about twenty-five minutes, causing a slight rift between the Kennett Square chief of police and Ghione.

Participation by the English-speaking population was essential for the festival to succeed as an example of the community's acceptance of Mexicans, an image that Kennett Square was anxious to present. The festival was advertised as an "authentic" Mexican fiesta in hopes of attracting participants from all groups, but particularly the English-speaking community. Vince Ghione explained that Cinco de Mayo "is something different. We will never do anything that is artificial . . . [but will have] the authentic Mexican food . . . the folk dancers . . . because the people who are going to come are the Anglos. There are only so many Latinos in the area, and they're all welcome, but the people who will drive the attendance will be the Anglos."[29] Ghione went on to explain that his primary goal is to create a large festival that is also a commercial success, and strong participation is central to achieving this. His strategy for accomplishing this is to draw attention to the distinct cultural aspects of the festival, such as Mexican folk dancers, food, and mariachis, and to emphasize that these entertainments are not available at other venues. The participation by the English-speaking population is particularly important in order to maintain widespread support of the event. Given the community's history with the 16 de Septiembre celebration, it seems unlikely that the community would be willing to underwrite any event that primarily serves the Mexican population.

Despite the efforts to attract a multiethnic crowd, the majority of participants at the 2002 festival were Mexican and Latino. There were a few English-speaking families present, but they were more numerous early in the day and participated in the children's activities, such as face painting, pony rides, and watching the parade. As the afternoon progressed, the street was packed with Mexicans who had come to hear the band and dance. The event transformed Kennett Square's typically peaceful, quiet streets into a loud, exuberant celebration. It was remarkable in that for the first time since they began to settle in Kennett Square, Mexicans were given free rein in the streets, and they took full advantage of the opportunity to express their national heritage and pride, and simply to be comfortable being Mexican in Kennett Square.

Although the event began and ended much earlier than a true Mexican fiesta, which would typically begin after dark and end in the early morning, even my informants who have typically been unhappy with life in Kennett Square were pleased that the event took place and that the English-speaking community made the attempt to make them feel welcome, although few were willing to comment extensively on the festival. "This was a really nice fiesta," said Marta Zavala.[30] Her comment was representative of the majority of the Mexicans I spoke to on the street. The Cinco de Mayo provided an opportunity for Mexican settlers to lay claim to their place in the community; their numbers alone indicating that they were a force that must be recognized and that they were ready to take part in the community.

FESTIVAL, BELONGING, AND THE SENSE OF PLACE

The influence of a public festival extends well beyond the day of the celebration. Festivals and the memories they produce communicate the participants' ideas regarding local identity and the sense of place throughout the year, yet they rarely express a seamless local identity. In fact, they often do the contrary and illuminate social distinction and discord. The Cinco de Mayo festival emerged at the start of the new millennium and was envisioned by its organizers as a means to call attention to Kennett Square's evolving community, promote social cohesion, and reinforce the idea that the town's majority population community values inclusion and accepts its newest neighbors. At the same time, the festival brought to light several complex, and often contradictory, expressions of local identity. Most important, the Cinco de Mayo clearly articulated the English-speaking majority's ambivalence about Mexican settlement.

These contradictions were obvious in the 2002 festival, which demonstrated that the English-speaking majority's agenda for the festival, while partially an entertainment event, was strongly suffused with unsubtle lessons for Mexicans regarding how to become responsible and productive members of the community. This paternalistic tone also highlighted a palpable sense of superiority on the part of the English-speaking population toward the new settlers. Using the festival to "educate" the Mexican settlers also suggested tension on the part of the festival organizers toward the changes that Mexican settlement was bringing to the community. As a cultural performance, the festival communicated acceptance conditioned on the Mexican settlers acculturation to customs and values of the established community.

I would not, however, characterize this festival as a mere hegemonic expression. True, the organizers were rigid in their interpretation of a "celebration of Mexican culture," but there are always implicit risks when access to public space is opened, particularly to those who have lived on the margins of the community and whose access to public space has been limited. Even festivals where the events are strictly prescribed can have unintended consequences and at a minimum provide a venue for a temporary social inversion. Historically, authorities have used festivals consciously to channel the ambitions of the disenfranchised and have used festivals to prevent social unrest by ceding power, for a brief time, to the disenfranchised (Brandes 1988; Cantwell 1993).

Kennett Square's Cinco de Mayo served a similar political purpose in that it provided a token welcome. Although Mexicans were not given access to the public life of the community on their own terms, the festival provided a means of civic engagement that approached cultural familiarity. State Street was previously the exclusive domain of the American-born citizen population; for three consecutive years it was also the site used to celebrate Mexican cultural and national heritage.

The Cinco de Mayo festival allowed Mexicans symbolically to be in possession of the heart of the town, albeit temporarily. Once this access was granted, no matter how brief or partial, the majority population's ability to control the public space was changed. The festival organizers could set a time for the festival to end, but they could not enforce it; they could host an Americanized festival, but Mexican participants were nevertheless free to use the event to display their commitment to their Mexican identity and to poke fun at the cultural stereotypes paraded by the English-speaking majority. The festival became an example of "the traditional and temporary conquest of official society by the . . . [sub]culture that lives within it" (Cantwell 1993: 97).

Yet is it accurate to characterize the Cinco de Mayo, or any regulated public festival, as an opportunity to shift the balance of power in a multiethnic community? And if so, is such a "conquest" necessarily temporary? Public display events bring diverse groups together to share public space, and they have a variety of intended and unintended consequences. Festivals can create lasting changes, regardless of whether they were intended to do so.

In the United States, public spaces are presumed to be open to all, yet access to the public sphere is often regulated. The means to limit access are not always visible: some are formal, such as legislation that limits the times, places, and number of people who can congregate; some are informal behavioral mores, the unwritten rules that govern the use of space. Whenever a large crowd is allowed to congregate in a public arena, the participants' very presence legitimizes their right to that place. It is no coincidence that groups "take to the streets" to protest racial or economic injustices. The significance is even greater when sacrifices are made to enact the transformation, such as interruptions in commerce, or decreased convenience for those who typically control public space, or when a major thoroughfare is blocked off (Schechner 1993).

The infusion of Mexican settlers into Kennett Square's town center not only legitimized their presence in the community but also introduced the possibility that Mexicans could begin to shape the community and therefore transform Kennett Square's place identity. Place identity is the perceptible distinctions that are used to describe the difference between one place and another and that are used to situate or symbolize interpretations of individual or group identity (Cuba and Hummon 1993). It is based on a variety of factors including the natural landscape (e.g., seaside or mountain), the built environment (e.g., historic structures or modern development), and, most important, the people who dwell in the locale. Edward Casey (1993, 1996) argues that local sense of place and place identity correspond directly to the people who dwell there, and he argues that the very idea of place is only understood in the context of some*body* having resided there. He writes, "Bodies and places are connatural terms. They *interanimate* one another" (Casey 1996: 24). The identity of a particular place is directly related to the people who inhabit it, and as people bring particular places into existence, so, too, do places shape the people who inhabit them. The qualitative differences that one experiences in different places, the actual attributes that distinguish one place from another, however, vary according to who is given access to the place and under what conditions.

Until the first Cinco de Mayo festival, the English-speaking population had assumed de facto ownership of Kennett Square's centrally located public spaces. Kennett Square's downtown property is held in common, of course, but in cases where the ownership is collective or ambiguous it is typical for the social group that has the longest history in the area to assume proprietary ownership of the public space (Fried 2000). For many years Kennett Square's majority population was the only population, therefore it is not surprising that they would claim the town center as their own. As the long-standing (predominantly Anglo-European) identity of Kennett Square was slowly challenged by Mexican settlement, the English-speaking residents could no longer assume they would continue to have preeminence over the public space. This was demonstrated in the ways they routinely excluded Mexicans from festivals and public events until 2001. Thus, placing a festival celebrating Mexican cultural heritage into the heart of Kennett Square's downtown was a dramatic shift in the public face of the community. Consequently this seemingly small step in local ethnic relations made way for a shift in the place identity of Kennett Square.

Festivals such as the Cinco de Mayo as well as the 16 de Septiembre before it offer opportunities for settlers to develop a sense of themselves as a distinct group. Although the majority of Mexican settlers in Kennett Square are from the same home community, Textitlán, this hometown is large enough that many settlers do not know one another or have friendships and social networks that draw upon from their experiences in Mexico. Even when settlers do know one another, they may not live in proximity to their former friends and neighbors, and their new day-to-day and work routines in Pennsylvania can limit social contact with old friends. Even in 2002, the settler population was very much a nascent community trying to find its place in a new home. Collective experiences such as the Cinco de Mayo lead to shared memories of place and as a result work to construct a new local group identity.

The development of shared experience and memory in place is significant. Festivals and other common experiences provide a break from day-to-day routines and enable participants to engage one another. Such experiences connect people to the place in significant ways. Just as humans live their lives someplace, memories are always rooted to particular places so that the places in return hold memories and facilitate what Anthony D. Smith has termed the "territorialization of memory" (1996: 25). After the festival, the location of the event will be associated with memories of what was experienced that day. As a result, the connections made during the festival are likely to be recalled whenever the participant passes through the festival site at other times. A similar process occurs in the creation of historic sites as the location of particular significant collective memories. Vacationers visit historic places in order to connect with the events associated with the site; the sites in turn cultivate the recollection of significant past events.

Some of the changes brought about by the Cinco de Mayo festival were quite obvious. It made the Mexican community's visibility more acceptable. Since the first festival in 2001, Mexican businesses and agencies have moved into space on State Street, something that was unthinkable just a decade earlier. The first was La Comunidad Hispana, the social service agency for migrants, which moved its offices from an obscure space behind a heating oil company on the far edge of town to offices in the center of town on State Street. Two additional Mexican-owned businesses opened in the center of town. For a few years it appeared that things were changing in Kennett Square and that the Mexican population was on its way to being incorporated as full members of the community. In addition, the festival continued to grow and was successfully celebrated on State Street through 2003. The following year, however, local support for the event apparently began to moderate.

I arrived in Kennett Square in the early afternoon of May 2, 2004, with my sister Susan to conduct research on the 2004 Cinco de Mayo festival.[31] I was surprised to find State Street open to traffic and no indication of a festival in progress. It had rained that morning; at first I thought the event had been cancelled. We decided to head to Mi Casa Su Casa, a gift shop that specialized in Latin American arts and crafts.[32] When I asked the shop cashier about the festival, she told me it had been moved into the parking lots and alleys behind State Street and explained that the merchants didn't want the street closed because they thought it would be bad for business. As we talked, I found that this decision not to close State Street was not part of an overall policy change and that the street would be closed for the Mushroom Festival in the fall. When I inquired why the merchants would allow the street closed for one festival and not the other, the shop cashier said that the crowds would be bigger for the Mushroom Festival and thus would not negatively affect business.

This change had a significant effect on the 2004 Cinco de Mayo. Tucked away in the parking lots and alleys, it was much less impressive than the 2002 event had been. Gone also were the booths promoting public health issues; in their place were vendors, many Mexican, selling arts and crafts. There were also more refreshment options. The same Mexican-owned restaurants that were present in 2002 were back, and joining them were a vendor from an Anglo-owned Mexican-style restaurant and an ice-cream vendor, *Paleteria La Michoacana*, a locally owned franchise that is based in Mexico.

Because the alleys were too narrow for a parade, instead there was a walking procession. The Mexican folk dance troupe returned to perform, and once again there was a parade of flags; but these flags did not represent English-speaking Kennett Square's heritage and were instead from each of the Mexican states. They were carried by Anglo-American and Mexican teenage girls wearing regional Mexican costumes. There was also a procession of Anglo-American school-age children carrying masks that they had made in preparation for the festival. Festival organizers had asked two local elementary schools to have the children create masks that represent what they thought about Mexican culture. The masks were bright and colorful, in some cases bearing skeletal images that resembled those of Jose Guadalupe Posada, which are associated with the Days of the Dead. However, most of the masks bore no resemblance to any Mexican cultural icon.

The masks were followed by the "March of the Sombreros." Papier-mâché hats had been crafted and were worn by English speakers and were disproportionately large—their brims up to three feet in diameter—and decorated in a variety of ways, almost all brightly colored in a style that was clearly a stereotype of a common Mexican symbol. There was no explanation of the purpose of the sombreros, nor was it obvious what constructive messages those wearing the hats might be trying to communicate to or about their Mexican neighbors. I call masks and sombreros used in these ways "pseudosymbols," that is, material objects that are used to represent a poorly understood aspect of Mexican culture. Later Mr. Ghione explained that the sombreros and masks were included to represent Mexican cultural heritage and because "that is what they do in Mexico."[33] Here Ghione was referring to the Mexican custom of parading giant puppets during fiestas. The masks created by the Kennett Square children were flat and were carried on poles during the procession. Although they bore little resemblance to the Mexican puppets, I found the connection that Ghione made to Mexican festival masks intriguing. Festival masks, such as the ones carried by the Kennett Square children and the sombreros worn by Anglo revelers, are often used in festivals and signify transformation (Napier 1987).[34] Masks hide the identity of the wearer, but in the process they also reveal other cultural personae. In masking their Anglo-European identity, these Anglo festival participants symbolically adopted a Mexican persona in the form of a common Mexican stereotype.

The transformation in the Cinco de Mayo in this two-year period articulates the ambivalence that the English-speaking community has had toward the Mexicans who are settling in Kennett Square. Having shed its paternalistic impulse, the Cinco de Mayo was more festive than educational and, therefore, more analogous to other Kennett Square festivals. The change in the parade of flags indicates that there is recognition of Mexico as a diverse nation, just as the parade of Kennett Square flags at the 2002 festival represented the town's English-speaking "diversity."

Nevertheless, the mixing of the Mexican folk traditions with the pseudosymbols is indicative of how little the English-speaking community understands about their Mexican neighbors' culture. In this sense, the Cinco de Mayo is a true instance of what Cantwell (1993) termed "ethnomimesis": a point of convergence where the majority English-speaking population engages the Mexican minority and for a moment imagines itself as part of the minority culture. This is temporary for the majority culture, however, which can just as easily set the Mexican aspect of their

Figure 9. Street Crowd, Cinco de Mayo 2002 (Photograph by Debra Lattanzi Shutika)

Figure 10. View from State Street, Cinco de Mayo 2004 (Photograph by Debra Lattanzi Shutika)

Figure 11. Student Masks Representing Mexicán Culture, Cinco de Mayo 2004 (Photograph by Debra Lattanzi Shutika)

Figure 12. The March of the Sombreros, Cinco de Mayo 2004 (Photograph by Debra Lattanzi Shutika)

community aside. As there is not consistent basis of association between the two groups, the festival provides a false sense of understanding, one that comes from the dominant culture projecting, or perhaps looking for, itself in the other. The most revealing attribute of the 2004 festival was the choice of location. By moving the event to less-visible alleys and parking lots, locations considered unthinkable for any other community event, the festival represented how Mexicans are "placed" in the broader community. The Su Casa Mi Casa shop cashier's statement suggested that there was a bias on the part of the merchants when it came to closing the street. Later, Vince Ghione acknowledged that some State Street merchants do not see Mexicans as potential customers. He explained that moving the festival was "my idea from the start. The conflict, and it's really not a conflict, but the merchants just howl when you close the street. And you know if you close the street and you bring enough people in, they still complain. Even with the Mushroom Festival, it's like, you put the wrong thing in front of me and no one can get to my store. So I decided to try this, this other idea."[35]

Though he took responsibility for this decision, Ghione indicated that his prior experience with the State Street merchants had influenced his decision to avoid the potential conflict of closing the street in 2004. He continued, "You being familiar with Mexico should understand this. Someone, I can't remember right now who, came up to me and said, 'This is just like Mexico, all the little plazas'. Now with everything, we have different plazas [parking lots]."[36] The distinction here is that in Mexico festivals typically take place in central plazas and not side streets or alleys.

When the mayor of Kennett Square made his customary remarks to the crowd, he emphasized "all are welcome here."[37] Standing beside me, my sister whispered, "That's right, you Mexicans can come use this parking lot any time you want."[38] Her appraisal echoes Cantwell (1993) in that this festival is a type of "street theater that makes a major statement of cultural identity" (99). Mexicans are "welcome," but they should remain barely visible on the fringe of the community.

These changes, I believe, resulted from the English-speaking community's discomfort with the experience of opening up the center of town to the Mexicans and realizing that they had set a precedent for the Mexicans to associate their own memories with the locus of the English speakers' own traditional memories. This can be considered the territorialization of memory. Shared memory is linked to a particular place for all participants, not only Mexicans. The festival brought these two groups together, but the organizers did not anticipate that the English-speaking community would not experience "Mexican culture" in the abstract, distilled version advertised for the festival. Instead they experienced Mexicans, the live flesh and blood people who are now part of Kennett Square and whom the festival publicly acknowledged as such.

Moving Mexicans from the fringe of the community for the first three festivals emplaced them and facilitated the process of belonging for Mexicans and their English-speaking neighbors. Once this process began to take hold, it became evident that Mexicans were as likely to shape the future direction of Kennett Square as the community was to shape or assimilate them. Moving the festival to the alley was an attempt to reposition Mexicans vis-à-vis others in the community.

CONCLUSIONS

The process of integration requires more than one day set aside to acknowledge newcomers. It must also incorporate the development of meaningful relationships and social networks from all parts of the community. Mexicans have assumed ownership of the community symbolically and materially, through communal participation in the festival and ownership of homes and businesses. As newcomers, Mexicans in Kennett Square are no longer seen as transients, but by 2004 they were not yet "people who belong."

I see the shift in the content and location of the festival as an indication that the first years of the Cinco de Mayo were successful in creating a point of convergence between Kennett Square's English speakers and Mexicans. Perhaps the festival was too successful in the sense that it may have required English speakers to engage the Mexican population to the point of discomfort. This would explain the decision to withdraw the event from its central location and include stereotypical representations of Mexican culture. Both actions restructure relations between English speakers and Mexicans. They increase English-speaking control over public space and interpret Mexican culture in ways that conform to American sensibilities. Other changes are also revealing. The move away from a social services and heath education event to an entertainment event and the parade of Mexican state flags are both significant transformations. These changes suggest that local Mexicans are beginning to shape the festival, albeit slowly. They are changing the margins of the event even while the main authority rests with the English-speaking majority. These changes suggest that the Cinco de Mayo festival is a cultural performance of the Kennett Square that the English-speaking community would like it to be: a rural American town with a Mexican flavor, but one that is not too noticeable.

Epilogue

I'm sitting with Doña Elena, as I often do, on her patio this afternoon. It is early May, and the day has been pleasantly warm. I'm in Mexico for a brief visit this time, and although I just arrived Doña Elena is already asking me when I will return. It's a question she asks every time, but today I stall, hoping to avoid giving her a straightforward answer. Unlike in past years, I'm no longer certain when I'll be back. My research here is essentially complete, and this visit is simply one to see a dear friend.

We've known each other for six years now, and although I no longer live with her when I do fieldwork in Mexico, when I am here I still stop by nearly every day to talk. Doña Elena is a skilled *cuentista* (raconteur) and a bit of a *chismosa* (gossip). Her stories are so richly detailed that I feel like I can catch up on a year's worth of news in an afternoon. Today she is recounting the successes of her granddaughter Celia, who recently graduated from Penn State University. As she explains the work that Celia does, her voice cracks with emotion. This too, is not unexpected. Different members of Doña Elena's family have been migrating to the United States for over sixty years. They live in Textitlán and in Kennett Square, journeying back and forth sometimes for visits, sometimes to stay. The most remarkable aspect of the Fernández family's experience is that, like many of the families I have met here, they have set down roots in both places (many family members even own homes in Textitlán and Kennett) and yet never fully belong to one place or the other.

When she finishes her stories there is a silence, then I ask her a question that I realize I have never asked before, although I'm not sure why. "Doña Elena, what do you think of migration between the United States and Mexico?"

"What do I think?" she responds in surprise. "Débora, what I think isn't important. I've never been to school. Besides," she says with a smile, "you're the one writing the book [about migration]." I assure her that her opinion does matter, that her experiences are far more valuable than my own. She sighs and begins, "What do I think of migration to the United States? Well, I would love to have every one of my children here with me, but they cannot; they have to go out to find a living for their families. That's what I think."

"My children want to be with me," she continues, "but it's impossible. My son, the *güero* (fair skinned), he says, 'Mamá, I am so sad to be so far away from you and Papá.' His sister-in-law asked him once 'Why are you unhappy? You are with your family [in the United States], your wife and children. You have a good job. What more could you want?' He explained that he feels alone in *el Norte*; his parents and two of his sisters don't live with him, so he feels alone. You see, he has his children with him, but not his parents, and someday when he comes back to Mexico, he'll have his mother and father, but be away from his children."

.   .   .   .   .

My conversation with Doña Elena took place during my final field trip to Textitlán. I have often reflected on this moment and related it to friends because Doña Elena's account seemed to perfectly encapsulate the sentiments of Mexicans I had been working with over the last decade: a combination of thankfulness for the economic opportunities that living in the United States provided and a deep regret that their families were separated and that they were forced to leave their home. The distress Doña Elena was experiencing, that she attributed to separation from family and homeland, was compounded by the fact that her children and grandchildren were settling in a new destination community. Although Mexicans have been settling in Kennett Square for two decades, there are still challenges to adjusting to life in the United States.

During that trip to Textitlán, I also met the latest generation of immigrants who were either considering a trip or on their way to Kennett Square. While visiting another friend a few blocks from Doña Elena's house, I was introduced to another young man. He was twenty-two years old and said he had worked as a mushroom picker until December 2004. He came home for the feria, and when he tried to return to the United States in early February, he found that he could not make it back across the border. "I couldn't believe it," he recalled. "I was on that border for two weeks. I went to Tijuana, Mexicali, Nogales, Matamoros. I paid one coyote $2,000, but even he couldn't get me into the United States." When I asked about his plans for the future he said, "I don't know. I'd like to work in the United States to earn some extra money, but it was tough on the border. I don't want to die."

As we were chatting, another young man who introduced himself as Ramón joined our group. Ramón's father had worked in Pennsylvania and Delaware, but when Ramón turned sixteen he decided to go to Utah with a friend. When I met him, Ramón had recently been deported from Salt Lake City and was still reeling from the disruption of being forcibly removed from his new home and friends. "I did everything they told me to, you know?" he recalled. "In Utah, you can get a driver's license, so I did. I owned my car and it was insured. One afternoon I was driving home from work, not doing anything wrong, you know, but the police, they stopped me. They asked me for my license and passport. I didn't lie, 'cause, you know, I liked living in Salt Lake and I didn't want to break the rules. But, they, they arrested me! Man, I didn't do anything wrong.

They picked me up because I looked Mexican, and they thought, well, you know, we'll check him out. I don't know what I'm going to do. I left my car there, my clothes, everything. I really liked it there, but man, I don't know. I don't want to go through that again."

As our conversation continued, other young men joined us. They asked if I thought there might be another amnesty. For these men, an amnesty is their best hope of establishing a legal foothold in the United States. They hope for an amnesty so they can avoid the precariousness of entering the country and working illegally; not one of the men takes pleasure in living a clandestine life in the United States. There was a strong sense of anticipation in the group as they discussed their prospects about going north, whether or not it was worth the risk, and if so, if they would try to take their families with them. They also considered what their lives would be like if they decided to remain in Textitlán. This last idea became a kind of running joke as the conversation wore on, the comic relief in an otherwise extremely serious discussion. Eventually, they all acknowledged that when the inevitable need arises, to buy a house, to make a business investment, or to pay for family expenses, they will try again.

·   ·   ·   ·   ·

In Kennett Square, the rapidly growing Mexican population continues to pose challenges for settlers and their citizen neighbors alike. The English-speaking residents of Stenning Hills have been complaining about overcrowding in the neighborhood again, but this time there have been no yellow ribbons or organized protests. Instead, two of the more vocal residents have run for the Borough Council, vowing to "clean up" Kennett Square. Although many of the issues are the same ones raised ten years ago, including better enforcement of the housing code, no one has mentioned Mexicans specifically as a problem. It seems obvious from reports in the *Kennett Paper*, however, that immigrants are at the heart of the controversy. Nick Perigo, a strong advocate for Mexican residents, lost his reelection bid for his Borough Council seat, and residents who sent the letters to the editor of the local newspaper expressed regret that his loss may indicate increased ethnic tensions in town.

Similarly, the Cinco de Mayo celebration on May 1, 2005, was a disappointment to most everyone who attended. A Latino gang had been spotted in the area in the months before the festival, and the organizers decided to dramatically scale back the event to discourage gangs from attending. Unfortunately, there was so little to do that most of the Mexican families were unenthusiastic about the event. I bumped into Erica, a young woman I have known since 1999, and a few of her friends that day. I was surprised to see her and learned that she and her parents recently moved to Pennsylvania. "Why is there nothing to do here?" she asked. "I thought there would be a band and dancing today." She and her friends walked around the parking lots and left early, along with many of the others who attended that day.

Although in some ways, Kennett Square seems to have changed little, in other respects, the town is certainly not the same place I wandered into in 1995. Fewer Mexican families I've met show signs of being displaced in their new home, more continue to purchase homes in Kennett Square's neighborhoods, and some have started to move into other nearby communities. Las Rosas, a newly constructed townhome community that had been planned for years, was finally finished in June 2006. Eighteen low-income families, the majority Mexican, purchased the new homes. When Samuel Fernández moved into his recently purchased house in the neighboring community of Oxford, Pennsylvania, his was the first Mexican family on the street. His neighbors have been friendly and welcoming, even though they do not speak the same language and can barely communicate. Mexican families are also acknowledged positively in the local press more often. For instance, the *Kennett Paper* reported on a group of Migrant Education students who were commended for painting murals on commercial buildings and for the volunteer work they do in the community.

Moreover, several young women have completed college and started professional careers in the area. These women are held up as models for the Mexican community. Several years ago I asked Celia Espinosa if she intends to return to Kennett Square to live after she graduates from Penn State University, she hesitated and changed the subject. She no longer imagines herself returning to her life in Mexico, but she is not certain what will come next. Celia is happy at the university where she has friends and is a successful student, and most important, she is not treated differently simply because she is Mexican. Celia believes that women in the United States have more freedom and opportunities, and while she expresses a desire to one day marry and have children, she also wants a life beyond those roles. Now that she has lived outside of Kennett Square, she has come to realize that living in the United States is not what bothers her, it is the feeling of being unwelcome and out of place in Kennett Square.

As one of several Mexican children from Kennett Square who have pursued a university education, Celia and her cohort would seem to be in an ideal position to one day return to Kennett Square and become active members of the community. They are bilingual, college-educated, and in most respects that they have successfully assimilated and would be exactly the type of people that the English-speaking neighbors would like to see living in their community. They also have exceptional insight into the problems and perspectives of their *paisanos* (countrymen) who have recently arrived as well as those who have lived in Kennett Square in the long term.[1] Yet the opportunities afforded them by the sacrifices of their parents and years of hard work have also provided the option of living away from Kennett Square. In the process of successfully adapting to American life and adjusting to the mainstream customs and values, Celia has incorporated one crucial aspect of American culture: she knows that she has rights and she is willing to express them. The process of becoming more "American" allows her to recognize that she no longer has to settle for the marginal place that Mexicans were relegated to in Kennett Square, a place that she and her family had reluctantly accepted. Ironically, what may be the determining factor that allows her to be accepted by the citizen community in Kennett Square may well be the path to her departure altogether. Although Celia's story is not representative of all Mexicans in Kennett Square, her perspective is nonetheless telling. Inasmuch as I have characterized the stories of Mexican settlers as an account of belonging and emplacement, these perceptions have inevitably pointed to experiences of exclusion and alienation.

Kennett Square's past, however, does not appear to be its future. It seems that there is a mutual recognition that much as Mexicans have had to work to find their place there, the English-speaking community also must adapt and assimilate to the emerging community that Kennett Square will become. In May 2006, when Latino activists across the United States marched in mass numbers to protest proposed changes in American immigration laws, an estimated five hundred Mexican and Latino immigrants marched peacefully through downtown Kennett Square. Their message to Kennett Square was unequivocal: undocumented immigrants are productive members of American society and should have a path to legalization. For all the difficulties they have experienced in Pennsylvania, Kennett Square's Mexican community never suffered the denigrating actions and opinions that are common in other new destination communities. They were never regarded as criminals, whether or not they were undocumented. The English-speaking community acknowledged the appropriateness of the march, and Kennett Square Police Chief Albert McCarthy said it was example of "real American democracy at work" (quoted in Barber 2006).

The Cinco de Mayo celebration continues to be an annual event in Kennett Square. The event is now planned by a Mexican-led organization, Casa Guanajuato. It has reemerged from the back alleys and is now celebrated on State Street. The organizers predict crowds of some ten thousand people, and the event showcases local musicians, dances, food and crafts (Weigel 2009). Like so many things I documented in Kennett Square, this small step forward was met with a setback. A few days before the scheduled celebration in 2009, the mayor cancelled the event at the last minute, citing health department concerns about a possible swine flu outbreak. This fear was heightened, the *Kennett Paper* reported, because one of the bands scheduled to perform was coming from Mexico and thus was believed to increase the chance of a swine flu transmission (Maye 2009).

Here in Virginia, the controversy surrounding immigration continues as local governments attempt to address the "crisis" that became apparent when Congress failed to pass an immigration reform package in 2007. Herndon closed its once successful day-labor center in September 2007, after a federal judge ruled that the town could not exclude undocumented workers from using the site, regardless of the community's desire to prevent using tax dollars to help "illegal aliens." In July of the same year, neighboring Prince William County's Board of Supervisors passed a series of anti-immigrant resolutions, effectively alienating the county's large Latino population by making it easier to arrest people who are suspected of being undocumented. Loudon County, known for its wealthy suburbs and pristine farmland, passed similar measures. The anti-immigrant movement here has found a voice in the "Help Save Virginia" movement, which consists of a number of local organizations across the state dedicated to pushing immigrants out of their communities. One of the primary goals of the Help Save movement is to "take back" communities from the "invasion" of "illegal aliens."[2]

At the time of this writing, Senators Lindsey Graham and Charles Schumer are attempting to draft a framework for comprehensive immigration reform, but their efforts have not yet found momentum. The move to "take back our country" is the stated goal of several movements bearing the same name, as well as the Tea Party movement. Although the "take back" movements are not singularly anti-immigrant efforts (they oppose many issues), they are at their core fighting many changes associated with immigration. Their ideal nation is one that looks back to a time when immigrants were less numerous and certainly less visible.

It is no less difficult for me today to observe the reactions to other new destinations. It seems that the controversies taking place in my backyard are destined to be expressed with increasing anger, intensity, and hostility at home and across the nation. As I reflect on my work in Kennett Square, I know that the reactions to the growing number of Mexican families in town were not necessarily typical of American communities in general. At times reactions to Mexican families were openly racist; at other times, they were simply disappointing. Yet Kennett Square offers an example of how a community can adapt to the transformations brought about by the settlement of a significant number of immigrants. It demonstrates that these transitions are not easy for citizens or their newly arrived neighbors. Kennett Square's example is typified by mutual change, often undertaken begrudgingly, but nevertheless residents accepted the certainty that their town had forever changed. While every community will have a distinct experience, the demographic changes that occurred in Kennett Square are not unique. The residents of new destinations across the nation must decide whether they want to facilitate the process of belonging for immigrants and participate in a new assimilation: mutual change. They can, of course, choose other paths and risk antagonizing their new neighbors. But they will not ultimately alter the demographic certainty of a changing community and a changed nation.

When asked to comment on the changes in Kennett Square and the image of the community, Guillermo Rivera, a Puerto Rican housing activist with the Alliance for Better Housing, put it best: "It's time to add a Latin face to the [American image of the Norman] Rockwell portrait" (quoted in Corchado 1999). In this case, what is true of Kennett Square is true for the nation.

April 2010

Notes

CHAPTER ONE

1. The majority of Mexicans living in Kennett Square at the time of this study were from one community.

2. Textitlán is a pseudonym derived from the Nahuatl meaning "place of textiles."

3. The term "new destination" was coined by Zúñiga and Hernández-León (2005).

4. Examples of sense of place studies in folklore include *The Written Suburb* (Dorst 1987); *Homeplace* (Williams 1991 [2004]); *A Place to Belong* (Pocius 1991); *Chaseworld* (Hufford 1992); and *Mapping the Invisible Landscape* (Ryden 1993). Each of these texts examines small rural or suburban towns where face-to-face interaction is the norm.

5. Recently, the term assimilation reemerged as a vital concept in the scholarly considerations of immigration, with attempts to reconsider its meanings and

interpretations. Works such as those by Kivisto (2005) and Alba and Nee (2003) have provided new means of theorizing assimilation in order to acknowledge immigrant enculturation and incorporation in the host society while recognizing that the mainstream population is also evolving as a result of immigration. For further analysis of the concept of assimilation and its varying interpretations, see also Park (1930); Social Science Research Council Summer Seminar on Acculturation (1953); Park and Burgess (1969); Teske and Nelson (1974); Gans (1979, 1992, 1999); Portes and Zhou (1993); and Portes (1995).

6.   Singer (2004) identifies six categories of immigrant gateways since the 1990s: Former Gateways, which attracted immigrants in the early twentieth century; Continuous Gateways, which have been and continue to be popular destinations for newly arrived immigrants; Post-World War II Gateways, which have attracted immigrants in the last fifty years; Emerging Gateways, which have experienced growth in the last twenty years; Re-emerging Gateways, which are locations that were popular in the early twentieth century but had a waning immigrant population mid-century and are now experiencing increased settlement; and finally Pre-emerging Gateways, which I refer to here as new destinations. These locations have experienced a significant increase in their populations since the 1990s.

7.   Proposition 187 was a California ballot initiative passed in 1994. The law included a number of provisions, most notably those designed to prohibit undocumented residents from receiving public assistance and health care (with the exception of emergency care), and mandated that law enforcement agents report suspected undocumented persons to the state attorney general and the Immigration and Naturalization Service (Martin 1995).

8.   Interestingly, women from Textitlán had a distinct aversion to taking work in the house cleaning industry, although the demand for these services were clearly on the rise during the time I was working on this project. When asked about why they were resistant to this type of work, most women said it was "trabajo indecente," or inappropriate/indecent work for a woman. There was marked cultural bias against working in a stranger's home, which was consistent with attitudes about the type of work that women could do in Textitlán.

9.   Among these texts, Fink (2003); Millard et. al. (2004); and Jones (2008) focus on issues most similar to those I examine here, specifically the increasing number of immigrants settling in small towns across the U.S., adaptation, discrimination, migrant ties to local communities, and other issues common to new destinations. Fink focuses on the events surrounding the organization efforts of workers at a chicken processing plant, while Millard et al. offer a collection of multidisciplinary essays on issues of settlement in the rural Midwest. Jones' text is a collection of eleven case studies. The others listed also address new destination settlements: Lamphere (1994) documents the influence of immigration on

the transformation of the American workforce in three U.S. regions; Hirsch (2003) examines the redefinition of marriage and courtship among a community of transnational Mexicans settling in Atlanta; Smith (2006) explores the dynamics of a Mexican transnational community in New York City and migrants' influence in their home community.

10. Peggy Harris, interview December 1, 1995.

11. I discuss the mushroom industry and the fallout of the worker strike in Chapter 5.

12. The fact that returning Textitlanecos were seen a disloyal to their home community is not unique to this population (see also Smith 2006). What was unique about this particular situation was that the economic situation in Textitlán was stable and thriving, thus migrating for work was viewed as unnecessary. I discuss this in further detail in Chapter 2.

13. Scholarship on sense of place draws from a variety of disciplinary perspectives, including folklore, geography, philosophy, and anthropology.

14. This idea is commonly referred to as a translocal, a local-to-local spatial dynamic, which is discussed below (see also Mandaville 1999; Ma 2002; McKay 2006b).

15. "Localized displacement" is a term used to reference the nearby relocation of residents after a natural disaster has permanently altered the landscape (Levine, Esnard, and Sapat 2007). I use the term here to signify the perceptions of displacement and loss expressed by longer-term residents in Kennett Square.

16. Examples of community-based sense of place studies include *The Written Suburb* (Dorst 1987); *Mapping the Invisible Landscape* (Ryden 1993); and *The Lure of the Local* (Lippard 1997), as well as many of the works of Wendell Berry (1990, 1991, 2001).

17. Allan Pred takes a similar position here, arguing that humanistic geographers, including Edward Relph, Yi-Fu Tuan, and Anne Buttimer, also portray place as little more than "frozen scenes of human activity" (1984: 279) and calls for an examination of place as a historically contingent process.

18. Commonly referred to as "salvage folklore" (Jackson 1987) or "eleventh hour ethnography" (Kirshenblatt-Gimblett 1998), academic studies of this nature are rare today, although it is still common for local governments or public agencies to hire folklorists to document traditional cultures in areas that are threatened by outside influences, such as when local industries are moved off shore or when farmland or forests are sold and developed into residential or commercial properties.

19. Roger Abrahams (1993: 9–10) describes this inclination: "Because American folklorists have long used folk to refer to a group that has developed traditions because of its perceived isolation or special interests and practices, we [folklorists] have tended to forget the ways [folklore] . . . arose within a political

environment in which specific bourgeois peoples sought to assert political power in the face of international, cosmopolitan domination."

20.   I describe American notions of local identity in Chapter 5.

21.   Media and scholarly accounts of new destinations indicate that many communities characterize immigrants and the changes they bring as a problem for the community, regardless of whether there is actual proof that immigrants have effected negative changes in the community. This was true of Manassas, Virginia (Walker 2008), Hazelton, Pennsylvania (Legomsky 2007; Ludden 2007), and Freehold, New Jersey (Cleaveland and Kelly 2008), among others.

22.   I argue in subsequent chapters that Kennett Square's longer-term population exhibited all three reactions at different times between 1995 and 2005.

23.   Richard Florida (2002, 2005) expands this idea in his work on the "creative class." He argues that specific open social and economic conditions are more likely to attract a dynamic, creative workforce and points to "global talent magnets," such as large cities and college towns, that are in competition to attract members of the creative class with other places in the U.S. and abroad.

24.   Many of Kennett Square's longer-term residents viewed assimilation as the means through which Mexicans would be incorporated into the community. This has been consistent with my more recent work in Manassas, Virginia (see also Constable 2007; Walker 2008).

25.   I am intentionally avoiding the term assimilation in the discussion of emplacement and belonging as it relates to new destinations of Mexican settlement. Belonging is a process that is common to the human experience of place, and not limited to immigrants and new arrivals. I have elected instead to employ the term incorporation when I speak of integrating and including immigrants in new destinations because the term accurately emphasizes the process I describe, and unlike assimilation, is not linked solely to immigrants and their experience of place (Kivisto 2005).

26.   Rouse (1992) was one of the first ethnographers to define Mexican transnational communities as one population in two places. Similarly, Hirsch (2003) notes that Mexican families in Atlanta described their homes in the United States and Mexico as one community.

27.   This was determined through the survey work I completed in Textitlán and is discussed in Chapter 2.

28.   San Miguel Arcángel is also a pseudonym.

29.   Mexican settlers from these other communities are often related in some way to people from Textitlán. For instance, many are the spouses of Textitlanecos; others have cousins or in-laws from Textitlán and have immigrated to Kennett Square as a result of these relationships.

30. Although my original intent was to study migration and its effects on the family and health, my focus changed within the first six months in the field to an examination to the effects of migration on the sense of place.

31. The first Mexicans to make their way to Kennett Square in significant numbers were replacing Puerto Rican workers who were beginning to move out of mushrooming and into industrial employment in nearby Wilmington, Delaware, and Philadelphia (Bustos 1994a; John Swayne, interview August 3, 2002).

32. The census data indicate the population recorded as I was ending fieldwork in Pennsylvania. I reference public school enrollment data later in this chapter to indicate the rapidity with which the Mexican population was growing.

33. There were two mayors in office from 1995 to 2005. Both were African American. The 2000 census indicates that only 10.3 percent of the town's population was African American.

34. The Kennett Consolidated School District includes all of the borough of Kennett Square, Kennett Township, New Garden Township, and a small portion of East Marlborough Township.

35. This response was consistent with all of the men I interviewed between 1995 and 2000.

36. While conducting fieldwork in Mexico, I met one man who told me he believed he was the first Mexican to travel to Kennett Square to pick mushrooms, and he arrived with a few friends in early 1958.

37. The oral histories mentioned here were collected primarily in Textitlán in 1999–2000.

38. Although October–March is the peak season, Dr. David Beyer of the Pennsylvania State University School of Agriculture indicated that growers have used air conditioning in mushroom houses since the late 1960s and early 1970s to extend the growing season year-round. Nevertheless, in the warmer months (particularly April through September), crop yields are much lower, as is the labor demand (Beyer, personal communication, April 30, 2002).

39. Municipio literally means "township," but the local government in Textitlán better resembles a United States county rather than a township.

40. This point is explored in Chapter 2 along with the history and development of the pueblo.

41. Herndon's mayor, Steve J. DeBenedittis was elected in 2006 and promised to return Herndon to its historic "roots." Aside from promising to end the controversy surrounding the day labor center by closing it (which was accomplished in September 2007), he has offered no details regarding how he plans to accomplish this plan (Rein 2006: B05; Turque 2007).

42. Since I began this study in 1995, a number of new volumes have been published that examine new destination communities. They include: Hirsch

(2003); Millard, Chapa, and Burillo (2004); Zúñiga and Hérnandez-Léon (2005); Smith (2006); Massey (2008).

43. In determining who should be selected for an oral history, I elected to focus on older, more experienced informants for the oral histories for several reasons. Most significantly, their life experiences offered a long-term perspective on migration between Kennett Square and Textitlán, and they were able to contextualize many of the recent changes that they had witnessed in both locations.

44. The Mexican Migration Project has since relocated to Princeton University. All data are available online at http://mmp.opr.princeton.edu/.

45. A copy of the survey instrument I used for this study is available at http://mmp.orp.princeton.edu/databases/ethnosurvey-en.aspx.

46. For further information about the use of the ethnosurvey in migration research, see Massey 1987 and 2000.

CHAPTER TWO

1. San Miguel Arcángel is a pseudonym.

2. For other accounts of "typical" Mexican village life, see Gonzalez (1994); Hellman (1994); Reyes (1997); and Grimes (1998).

3. After successfully establishing themselves in the United States and improving their economic situation, many immigrants return and invest money into community projects in Mexico, which increases their importance in the home community (Goldring 1997).

4. Smith's (2006) work with Mexicans in New York City reveals a complex interdependence between the Mexican immigrant population in the United States and their support of public works projects in their home community in Mexico.

5. The Lafayette and Center Street apartments were long neglected complexes where many Mexican families lived in their first years in Kennett Square.

6. Much later I learned that Deborah would be correctly pronounced with a strong accent on the first syllable, "Débora."

7. Colonia in this case indicates a neighborhood. Neighborhood boundaries are formed informally, but then later incorporated by the municipio. Neighborhood sizes vary, and El Bordo was one that was located on the edge of the village and growing rapidly.

8. Mexican secundaria is literally translated "secondary school," but it is the equivalent of United States middle school and ends after ninth grade. After completing secundaria, students who are interested in pursuing further education enroll in prepatoria, the equivalent to grades ten through twelve.

9. *Cosera* is the local slang for seamstress. The more common word in Spanish is *costurera*.

10. Overlock is a type of sewing machine that sews a seam and finishes the edge. Overlock machines require specialized training, and seamstresses who work with them make the highest salaries, generally 800–1,000 pesos (approximately $80–$100 U.S.) per week. Straight (rectas) sewing machines are standard sewing machines that sew a straight stitch. These seamstresses make 500–700 pesos (approximately $50–$70 U.S.) per week. Most experienced seamstresses own both of these machines. Terminadas (finishing work) seamstresses are women who could not afford or did not have access to a sewing machine. Often these women are older (over age forty) than Overlock or recta seamstresses.

11. The terminology "jefe de casa" was set in the research methodology of the Mexican Migration Project. As a fieldworker for that project, I was obligated to follow their research protocols, which focused on male heads of household.

12. I do not know the exact number of families who have been purposefully abandoned, but this is a fear that is constantly discussed among migrant wives and the chief reason many women want to accompany their husbands to the United States.

13. *Calidad Superior*, meaning "first quality," is a pseudonym of one of the dozens of mushroom farms that are located in and around Kennett Square.

14. El Bordo literally means "reservoir." One of my informants said that there was a reservoir located in what is now the center of the colonia, but it has since dried up.

15. To complete a random sample of these households, I followed the research protocols established by the Mexican Migration Project (MMP) at Princeton University (formerly located at the University of Pennsylvania). I did a complete count of the total number of homes in the colonia, assigning each a number. Then, using a random number table, I selected a random sample of households for the survey. Full information on the research protocols of the MMP, along with the complete data sets from the 118 communities that have been surveyed can be found at the following URL: http://mmp.opr.princeton.edu/.

16. I collected the statistical data on Textitlán with the help of my colleague Payal Gupta from December 1999 through March 2000. Another researcher collected the data on San Miguel Arcángel in 2001.

17. The major distinction I draw between a migrant and a settler (or immigrant) is based upon whether or not these workers have moved their families to the United States. Migrants in this sense are typically single or married men who come to the United States every year alone for part of the year. Settlers are those who live full time with their wives and children in the United States.

18.   Although at first glance this seems unusual, there are many similar municipalities in the United States where new neighborhoods from bordering townships grow into one another and the residents can elect to say they are from either place.

19.   This custom is discussed in detail in Chapter 3.

20.   Vicente Zavala, interview October 28, 1999.

21.   This is compared to San Miguel, where 46 percent of the respondents reported having at least one family member who had migrated to the United States.

22.   Migration to the United States continued after the Bracero Accord ended for several reasons. Piore (1979) and Mines and Massey (1985) note that working abroad for a time allows migrants to develop a clear picture of the relative risks and rewards of temporary work abroad. With each subsequent trip, the risks and costs of migration decrease because the workers learn how to become more efficient migrant workers; they develop a network of contacts for work and accommodations and learn how to manage their lives abroad. As men and women continue to migrate, they return to their home communities with invaluable information that they share with others of their acquaintance. Sharing this information has a twofold effect on the sending community: the information gives aspiring migrants a better idea of the relative risks and rewards of migrating, increasing the possibility that others will migrate. As some migrants settle abroad, they expand the support networks for later migrants, which further encourages the migration process (Massey et al. 1987; see also Piore 1979; Mines and Massey 1985).

23.   Pedro Fernández, interview January 31, 2000.

24.   Ibid.

25.   Ibid.

26.   Alfonzo Ramírez, interview January 27, 2000.

27.   Pedro Fernández, interview January 31, 2000.

28.   I am not the first to recognize that migrants and non-migrants occupy distinct social worlds (see Massey et al. 1987; Goldring 1997). However, what is distinct about Textitlán is that the pueblo's elite citizens, particularly wealthy *comerciantes* (business owners), also do not mix with well-to-do Textitlanecos who migrate. I return to this community distinction in the discussion of the *Feria de Esquipulitas* (Festival of Esquipulitas) in Chapter 6.

29.   Although there is no concern about American-style foodways and their influence on local culture, the effects of immigration on family life is a great concern for Textitlanecos. This is discussed in detail in Chapter 6.

30.   The lack of consistent development is common throughout urban and rural Mexico.

31.   The limited use of these appliances is in part due to the fact that they are expensive to use. Refrigerators and clothes dryers, for example, use inordinate

amounts of electricity and thus their expense includes not only the purchase price but also their operational costs for day-to-day use.

32. Televisions are the only nonessential appliances that are common to nearly all households.

33.

Household Amenities Reported	Textitlán Yes (%)	San Miguel Yes (%)	Significance Level (chi-square)
Electricity in household?	100	99	N.S.
Running water in household?	99	98	N.S.
Sewage in household?	99	98	N.S.
Television in household?	99	95	N.S.
Stove in household?	97	97	N.S.
Radio in household?	94	91	N.S.
Refrigerator in household?	86	79	N.S.
Washing machine in household?	70	68	N.S.
Stereo in household?	59	44	.006
Telephone in household?	45	18	.0001
Sewing machine in household?	44	32	.024

SOURCE: Mexican Migration Project (MMP) 118 (housefile), http://mmp.opr.princeton.edu/.

34. All electronic equipment, such as stereos, hair dryers, and computers, are typically twice as expensive as they are in the United States, and thus they much less common in the typical Mexican home.

35. The different levels of migration experience are the only significant statistical difference between these two communities.

36. T-test comparisons for all three U.S. migration variables (above) by community are statistically significant at $p < .0001$. A significant difference between the two communities is said to occur when the test yields a P value of .05 or less. The "p" or P value represents the probability that the difference between the groups is due to chance alone. For example, $p < .001$ means that the odds that a difference between the communities is due to chance are less than 1 in 1,000. Thus the differences in mean scores can be attributed to real differences between the communities rather than due to chance. In the behavioral sciences, $p < .05$ (probability of chance less than 5 in 100) is usually considered significant. All statistical testing (regardless of the test) uses the "$p < .05$" probability level when assigning statistical significance.

37. MMP 118 (housefile). mmp.opr.princeton.edu.

CHAPTER THREE

1.   Many homes in Textitlán do not have refrigerators and it is unusual to find a kitchen with a sink and running water. Most homes have a sink outside the kitchen with running water where all household cleaning tasks are completed, including washing dishes and cleaning clothes by hand. See Chapter 2 for a list of common household amenities.

2.   Municipio literally means "township," but the Mexican municipios in Guanajuato more closely approximate the county government common in the United States.

3.   This question elicited two responses, depending on the length of time the settler and I had known one another. In general, most Mexican settlers correctly presume that Americans have little or no knowledge of their home community. Thus, if the settlers and I were first-time acquaintances, their response to the question, "Where do you feel most at home?" would be "Mexico." However, once they were aware of my familiarity with Guanajuato and the municipio of Textitlán, they were more likely to respond "Textitlán."

4.   In both of these cases, I am referring to the first generation of Mexican settlers. Recall from Chapter 2 that this settlement began in the early 1990s and new arrivals continue to settle in Kennett Square every day.

5.   This courtship practice is not common among Mexican families who now reside in Pennsylvania. Typically both mother and father work outside the home in the United States, and extended family members are not living in the same household. This leaves many young women unattended at home and is a cause of considerable worry for Mexican parents who live in Pennsylvania.

6.   The notable exception here would be the person who is abused within their home. In this case, the home becomes a metaphorical prison. See Lawless (2001).

7.   Vince Ghione, interview August 2, 2002.

8.   Jesús Juárez, interview August 3, 2002.

9.   See also Levitt (2001); Espiritu (2003); and Hirsch (2003).

10.   Lilia Ramírez, interview January 16, 2005.

11.   Maintaining a house in Mexico is economically possible because home mortgages are still relatively uncommon in Mexico, although in the last few years they have become more available than in the past. Thus most homeowners have purchased their homes outright. Not having a mortgage makes keeping the house less of a financial burden for families who are in the process of purchasing homes in the United States.

12.   Celia López, interview May 12, 2005.

13.   Cory Thorne, personal communication July 16, 2005.

14.   Julio Pérez, interview May 12, 2005.

22. The yellow ribbon campaign is discussed in Chapter 5.

23. Leo Chavez (1991) describes a similar situation in San Diego, California, where the undocumented Mexican residents were simply excluded and viewed as outsiders. Through interviews with undocumented residents, he confirms that the host community's attitudes do prevent them from being incorporated into the community.

24. Peggy Harris, interview December 1, 1995.

25. Every child treated in the clinic who was under the age of nineteen was referred to La Comunidad Hispana (a social service provider) to enroll them in PA CHIP (Pennsylvania Children's Health Insurance Program). At the time of this study, all low-income children (including the undocumented) were eligible for comprehensive health insurance through this program. Most of the children initially treated at the clinic were eligible for health insurance through this insurance program regardless of their documentation status. For more information on PA CHIP, see www.chipcoverspakids.com.

26. LCH was founded by Sheila Druily in 1973 with the support of farmworker advocates and local clergy.

27. Alfonzo Ramírez, interview January 27, 2000.

28. Ibid.

29. The average single-family home in Kennett Square is approximately 1,200 to 1,400 square feet.

30. A typical rent in 1995 for a well-appointed apartment in Kennett was $700–$800.

31. In 2000, the Center Street complex was sold to a new owner, who renovated the building over several years and then renamed it Santa Maria Court. The renovated apartments provided decent affordable housing for low-income families.

32. This changed in 2005 when Chester County introduced the SCOOT bus lines between Kennett Square, West Chester and other locations in Southern Chester County.

33. This changed in 1998 with the initiation of the 16 de Septiembre celebrations. A full account of this and other Mexican-themed festivals is discussed in Chapter 7.

34. In 1994, the Mushroom Festival included a large number of recreational events that spanned two weeks and featured the selection of a Mushroom Queen, performances by two rock bands, a flea market and dozens of food stalls, all with many types of mushrooms prominently on display (Clark 1994).

35. Fictive kinship refers to social relationships that are approximate family relationships but are based on religious rituals or close friendship ties rather than through blood or marriage (Foster 1953). Ebaugh and Curry (2000) argue

that these relationships constitute an important part of immigrant social networks and support.

36. Local health and social service workers often remarked that loneliness and depression were commonly associated with the settlement process in southeastern Pennsylvania and confirmed my observations. This was a major issue when I began my fieldwork in 1995, and it continued to be an issue in 1999 (Peggy Harris, personal communication April 17, 1999).

37. Urry (1987) emphasizes that the sense of belonging to a place is influenced by three factors: the relationship between social relations and access to space, the nature of communal social relations, and residents' different "senses" of place.

38. It should be noted that bringing one's family to the United States is typically viewed as husband's decision. I have met many women in Mexico who were anxious to join their husbands and sons in the United States but were unable to do so because their husbands refused to apply for their legal residency status.

39. Alma Bedolla, interview January 27, 2000.

40. Vélez-Ibáñez (1983) describes the Mexican cultural construct of confianza as a relational aspect that "designates generosity and intimacy as well as a personal investment in others" (11).

41. Alma Bedolla, interview January 27, 2000.

42. Ibid.

43. This is not a pseudonym.

44. Loretta Perna, interview January 7, 2002.

45. Maria Elena Gutiérrez, interview June 1, 1999.

46. Although women in particular expressed concerns about their personal safety when Mexican men were seen hanging out on street corners in Kennett Square, during the time of this study there were no incidents of violence or even threatening verbal exchanges (such as cat-calling) between Kennett Square women and Mexican men.

47. Hagan's (1994) study of a Guatemalan Maya community in Houston accounts a rapid development of a settler community and Hondagneu-Sotelo's (1994) ethnography of Mexican women in Los Angeles similarly chronicles the transition to settlement for recently arrived Mexican women and their reliance on established social networks.

48. I discuss Mexican attempts to establish recreational spaces, and the long-term community's responses, in Chapter 5.

49. Mulgan (2009) identifies ten feedback circuits that he describes as areas where people receive messages regarding whether or not they belong. They include: 1) strong ties of family and friendship; 2) participation in organizations

such as religious institutions, clubs, and organizations; 3) economic opportunities, particularly adequate employment; 4) an accessible political system that represents the group; 5) cultural sensitivity to differences and the ability to express oneself culturally; 6) feeling safe in one's community; 7) accessible public spaces; 8) access to and responsiveness of public services; 9) affordable and adequate housing; 10) fair and responsive law enforcement.

50.   Though Buena Vista was eventually seen as a welcome addition to Kennett Square, the process of obtaining approval of the township required the consensus of the longer-term residents. The Kennett Square borough's zoning board required that the Alliance for Better Housing locate their offices on the property, as Howard Porter noted, "to keep an eye on things" in the community (Howard Porter, personal communication July 4, 1999).

51.   Buena Vista was the first new construction project undertaken by the Alliance for Better Housing. The houses were subsidized through a program with the U.S. Department of Agriculture. To qualify to purchase a home in Buena Vista, a potential homeowner had to meet qualifications of low income, steady employment, and a favorable credit history. Of the original twenty-four homeowners, twenty-two were Mexican, one was Puerto Rican, and one was African American. Howard Porter explained that residents' loans were subsided so that they could afford their monthly payments, but they were required to return part of their home's equity should they sell the homes within ten years of purchasing them.

52.   See also Chapter 5. ABH was a spin-off organization founded by Sheila Druily as part of La Comunidad Hispana (LCH) in 1993. Druily was also the founder and director of LCH until her death in 1996. Before ABH developed Buena Vista, the organization had worked to assist Mexican and other low-income families purchase homes through a loan subsidy program of the U.S. Department of Agriculture.

53.   This is not a pseudonym.

54.   In Chapter 5, I describe the controversy surrounding ABH's purchase of a dilapidated duplex in Kennett Square and the protests that erupted as a result.

55.   Mexicans who did not live in Buena Vista were also invited to events there. More significantly, the success of the project seemed to encourage other Mexicans who were looking to purchase homes in the area to go to ABH. Enrique and Julia Pérez, for instance, mentioned earlier in this chapter, both told me that they might not have considered buying a home before Buena Vista was built.

56.   Manuel López-Peña, personal communication Febrary 17, 2001.

57.   Although overt and organized protest against Mexicans had ceased by 2001, there were clearly residents who held onto prejudices against Mexicans. Still others expressed an ambivalent acceptance, as I discuss in Chapter 7.

58.   A quinceñera is a celebration of a young woman's fifteenth birthday. It is commonly viewed as a right of passage to womanhood (Cantú and Nájera-Ramírez 2002).

59.   The Red Clay Room, the reception facility owned by the Kennett Fire Company, offered an Italian menu and standard American reception foods (i.e., carved roast beef and baked chicken) but could not provide pork carnitas (a braised or roasted pork dish), which was the preferred dish served at family celebrations.

60.   As our Mexican friends in Kennett Square started to buy homes, our family was frequently invited to attend parties at their homes. We reciprocated, inviting our Mexican friends to our home for parties and dinner, but these invitations were almost always declined. The reason why they could not attend our parties was not surprising: most Mexicans worked on weekends and could not take a day off for a social gathering. Luís and I worked together at Project Salud, and thus he worked Monday through Friday.

61.   The major difference between this party and those we had attended in Mexico was the use of plates and utensils. Typically, in Textitlán, paper plates and plastic utensils were seen as an unnecessary expense, and therefore were not common at the parties I attended. Instead, guests would share a large plate of carnitas, which they would wrap with a corn tortilla.

62.   After the party, Luís and I discussed this decision again. He told me that he felt confident that the residents had not felt compelled to exclude piñatas from their celebrations but saw this as one of the inevitable compromises that they would make living in the United States.

63.   In Chapter 5, I note that Kennett Square residents would commonly emphasize how their community and residents were exceptional, such as being well educated or maintaining a friendly community. In this regard, it is not surprising that the local community would identify Mexicans who were also seen as exceptional and emulating the core values of the community.

64.   Pennsylvania State University operates a large main campus in State College and many local branch campuses. The majority of students complete two years at a branch campus before completing their education at the main campus. At the time that Celia was admitted to Penn State, a small percentage of the total number of students admitted were invited to attend at the main campus as freshmen.

65.   Although Mario and Ofelia were relatively well off, both were afraid that their expenses would one day exceed their incomes, which I discuss in detail in Chapter 7.

66.   An open container law prohibits both possession of any open alcoholic beverage container and consumption of any alcoholic beverage in a moving vehicle.

67.   After graduating from college, Celia elected to stay in the United States, but she did not return to Kennett Square. She took a job in a nearby state that was within driving distance to Kennett Square.

68.   Loretta Perna, interview January 7, 2002.

69.   The ambivalence of their welcome is discussed in Chapter 7.

CHAPTER FIVE

1.   Although leaders of The Minuteman Civil Defense Corps deny that their organization operates outside the law, the Minutemen volunteers do claim to "use every legal means at our disposal to assist law enforcement authorities in identifying and apprehending those who violate our borders." Their organization is the most common example of vigilantism. MinutemanHQ.com, "The Minuteman Pledge," www.minutemanhq.com/hq/mmpledge.php, accessed October, 28, 2006.

2.   There has been a substantial increase in the number of nativist groups since 2004, well after research for this project was completed. The most recent nativist movements are small-scale grassroots organizations (sometimes consisting of as few as one or two members) that use Web sites and blogs to recruit members and establish initiatives to stop illegal immigration in their local communities. These organizations have grown substantially since 2004, according to the Center for New Community, a Chicago organization that tracks immigration issues, and they are on the rise because there is widespread frustration with the federal government's failure to develop a comprehensive immigration policy. Although several nativist groups have been identified in southeastern Pennsylvania, Bridging the Community has not been named among them. Center for New Community, "Mapping the New Nativism," www.newcomm.org/, accessed September 27, 2006.

3.   Organizations that promoted Americanization of immigrants were sometimes state sponsored, but many were nongovernmental organizations, and some were lead by immigrant leaders (Graham and Koed 1993).

4.   New nativist movements typically refer to immigration as a "crisis" and employ the language of war, referring to immigrants as "invaders" or "foreign enemies" who must be "battled" and "defeated" (Chavez 1997; Santa Ana 2002; Massey 2007). This type of anti-immigrant rhetoric was amplified under President Ronald Reagan, who framed undocumented immigration as a threat to national security (Nevins 2002: 62–68).

5.   I use the terms "Hispanic" and "Latino" together to reflect the changes in the U.S. Census Bureau's terminology for this group of people. In 1990, the term "Hispanic" was employed, but "Latino" was adopted for the 2000 Census.

6.   Rents in Kennett Square have long been higher than in the surrounding countryside. In the neighboring communities of Avondale and West Grove, rents are approximately half of those in Kennett Square.

7.   Guillermo Rivera, interview June 4, 1999.

8.   In her ethnographic analysis of the 1992–1993 riots in Bombay, Radhika Subramaniam (1999) argues that the construction of differential identity between "Muslim" and "Hindu" "acquires habitual forms and circulate as every day beliefs," which promote fear, and as a consequence, collective action (97). These beliefs regarding the other coalesce in what she terms a "culture of suspicion," • typified by "dread and unease that does not throb with overt hostility but is fleeting" (101). Although fleeting, these cumulative emotional responses form the basis of what would otherwise be implausible beliefs about the other, and ultimately they encourage collective action, in this case, collective violence. Subramaniam argues that the culture of suspicion is grounded in experiences and encounters that are "located at the crossroads where memory and habit collide daily and where banal routine can momentarily render an experience unfamiliar" (101). Such unfamiliarity creates an emotional state that makes the implausible plausible, so that even unsubstantiated, fantastic rumors of social instability or violence provoke fear and then, ultimately, group action.

9.   Howard Porter, interview July 22, 1999.

10.   LCH and ABH were granted approval for the renovation project, and the duplex was rented to two Mexican families. However, Porter encountered similar resistance in his attempts to develop Buena Vista, a low-income townhouse community in Toughkenamon, a borough adjacent to Kennett Square. That community was completed in 1999. The first residents in Buena Vista included twenty-four families, of which twenty-one are Mexican, one African American, and two Puerto Rican. Porter also attempted to develop similar properties in neighboring West Grove but was unable to obtain zoning approval. ABH initiated another low-income housing project, Las Rosas, within Kennett Square Borough in 2002. Although the agency has received permission to build on property in town, approval for the project was delayed for three years. The project was completed and residents moved into the new homes on June 8, 2006 (Barber 2006).

11.   United States Census Bureau data (2000) indicates that the average household income in Kennett Square was $85,975 per year and 10 percent of the adult population had a graduate or professional degree. Mexican workers who earn well took home less than $40,000 per year and the average level of education for adults was 5.5 years (MMP 118 [persfile], mmp.opr.princeton.edu).

12.   There has been a general shift within the social sciences to consider the role of emotion in social contexts. In addition to those mentioned here, the work

on emotion includes Shott (1979); Thoits (1989); Barbalet (1992); Lawler and Thye (1999); Corenblum and Stephan (2001); and Massey (2001).

13.   Corchado's 1999 article in the "Reshaping of America" series in the *Dallas Morning News* places the timing of the yellow ribbon campaign four years prior to the publication of his series, in 1995. However, the events in Stenning Hills are chronicled in the *Kennett Paper* in October, 1997.

14.   Parsons notes that in 1979, Penelope Laingen tied yellow ribbons around her tree in Bethesda, Maryland, as a way of remembering her husband, an embassy staff member who was held hostage in Tehran. Laingen indicated that her inspiration for her use of the yellow ribbon was the song "Tie a Yellow Ribbon 'round the Ole Oak Tree," which was recorded by the pop vocal group Tony Orlando and Dawn in 1973 and was a number one hit. The song is based in part on a legend that songwriter L. Russell Brown heard in Vietnam about a returning prisoner who asked loved ones to tie a white kerchief in the front yard if he was welcome to return home. Brown co-wrote the song with Irwin Levin in 1972 and changed the color of the kerchief from white to yellow to better fit their music (Parsons 1981).

15.   Although I made several attempts, I was not able to secure an interview with any of the yellow ribbon organizers.

16.   A brief Internet search on "yellow ribbons" produced a plethora of Web sites dedicated to the use of yellow ribbons as symbols of hope, particularly for military families.

17.   The issue of cultural superiority versus cultural difference is discussed in detail in Chapter 7.

18.   Please be aware that the purpose of this discussion is not to evaluate whether or to what degree individuals have had a sincere change of opinion regarding Mexican settlement. What is at issue here is the particular process that was engaged in this transformation and how these processes roused social action.

19.   Lois Maharg, a reporter for the *Kennett Paper* from 1998 to 2001, confirmed these observations. In an interview and electronic correspondence, she stated that when she was able to report on the positive aspects of community the response of "people in the white community—at least the ones who spoke to me about my articles—liked seeing them in the paper because they showed evidence that Kennett was a diverse and inclusive community." Lois Maharg, interview January 20, 2002; electronic mail correspondence January 24, 2002.

20.   Gossip often fulfills a similar purpose in small communities where face-to-face interaction is the norm. Simply the fear that one's actions will become the subject of communal disapproval through gossip can be an effective means of maintaining certain social mores. To avoid the shaming associated with gossip,

community members are cautious in their behavior, and behavioral norms are held in check (Abrahams 1983).

21.   This is the exact terminology employed by Bridging the Community leaders to explain their particular emphasis on community development. However, the movement is not solely focused on Mexican settlers. Teenage motherhood, for example, is no longer referred to as a community problem; rather teenage mothers are viewed as community members who still have the potential to make positive contributions to local life. Joan Holliday, personal communication February 17, 2001.

22.   I have no doubt that in my presence many in the community were cautious about what they said about Mexicans and Mexican settlement.

23.   Joan Holliday is not a pseudonym.

24.   The initial name of the organization is telling, as Bridging was not conceptualized as a multiethnic community integration movement. This fact may be indicative of the trajectory of the movement since.

25.   Of course, there are people in Kennett who are still unhappy about Mexican settlement. However, most of the residents involved in the protest, particularly the yellow ribbon campaign, now say they regret their participation.

26.   Although Joan Holliday's role in Bridging the Community is central, she often distances herself from her central role in the organization. For example, after reading a draft of my description of the organization, Holliday telephoned me to encourage me to rewrite this section to emphasize Bridging as a community effort and not dependent on any one person. At the same time, she shifted the format of the bimonthly meetings so that other community members now lead the forum. Despite these changes, during the eighteen months that I observed the group and its activities, Holliday remained the driving force behind the movement. It is understandable, given the principles of the movement, that her role as the group's leader would be problematic because it is thought of as a community initiative, rather than one driven by individual interests.

27.   It should be noted that the composition of this group has changed over time. Although members came and went, the demographics of the group remained consistent during the time of this study.

28.   I address scholarly approaches to this way of thinking about place in Chapter 1.

CHAPTER SIX

1.   The word "feria" is derived from the Latin root meaning "abstinence from work in honor of the gods" (Falassi 1987: 2). In common usage it refers to a

fair or carnival to describe an event that has religious and secular activities. In contrast, "fiesta" in this context means religious feast day. January 15 is the fiesta (feast day) of Esquipulitas.

2. Francisco Castillo, interview January 12, 2004.

3. However, it is not uncommon for Textitlanecos in this group to have visited the United States on vacation.

4. The most obvious changes include the influence of U.S. clothing and fashion trends, as well as the Spanglish slang that returning families use in normal conversation.

5. This is the case even when long intervals have separated journeys between the United States and Mexico. Ausentes, even after they return to Textitlán to live permanently, are nevertheless identified (by themselves and others) as a distinct group because they have lived in the United States.

6. The journey ausentes experience is something akin to that of mobile American professionals who move from one coast to another, following career opportunities and gathering skills with each move. They differ in that Textitlanecos move between two places instead of many and, in the process, they accumulate the experiences and memories of these two locales over a lifetime.

7. I draw on Babcock's (1978) notion of symbolic inversion, where expressive behavior presents an inversion or contradiction of what is expected. In this case, some ausentes become symbolic insiders, but only for the course of the feria. For those who express a more sustained or deeper commitment to the pueblo through their devotion to Esquipulitas, as I argue later in the chapter, incorporation is not symbolic, but it is a qualified incorporation.

8. For instance, Nájera-Ramírez's (1997) study of the Fiesta de los Tastaones considers how internal conflicts between indigenous and Mestizo populations are performed during community fiestas. See also Harris (2000).

9. Olvin's (2000) analysis of the Gaúcho movement in Brazil is an example of this.

10. This is not a pseudonym.

11. Jesús Elena de los Reyes, interview May 13, 2005.

12. *Miracles on the Border* (Durand and Massey 1995) examines the tradition of creating votive paintings to commemorate a favor granted by Christ, the Virgin Mary, or a saint. Durand and Massey's research indicates that most migrants face similar dilemmas and are very likely to request divine assistance in time of need.

13. Patricia Zavala, interview January 12, 2000.

14. *Pa'Norte* is a Mexican vernacular expression meaning "to go to the north" (referring to the United States).

15. Rámon Ramírez, interview January 28, 2000.

16. See Hirsch 2003 for a detailed account of marriage in transnational Mexican families.

17. Francisco.Castillo, interview January 12, 2004.

18. This family's decision to send their son back was a means of protecting him from his objectionable friends in the United States, but it was also a means to keep him out of serious trouble with immigration authorities. His mother understood that if her son were arrested in possession of marijuana, he could permanently lose his legal residency status. Based on this understanding, she and her husband believed it was best to send the boy back to Mexico.

19. Marta Sánchez, personal communication.

20. Jesús Elena de los Reyes, interview May 13, 2005.

21. The changes I note are not unique to Textitlán but are common among returning migrants in most communities in Mexico. The significant difference here is not the change in the economic situation of the migrants but the position of migrating families relative to the numerous wealthy non-migrating families.

22. This is not a pseudonym.

23. René Guzmán, interview January 17, 2004.

24. Manuel Ibarra Pérez, interview January 12, 2004. The names of the local scholars mentioned here, along with the historical personas Alonso de Velasco and José Maria Aguilar are not pseudonyms.

25. Ibid.

26. Valladolid was later renamed Morelia in honor of José Maria Morelos, a hero of the Mexican Revolution.

27. Manuel Ibarra Pérez, interview January 12, 2004; and Nicolas Ruíz Rodriguez, interview January 9, 2004.

28. Manuel Ibarra Pérez, interview January 12, 2004.

29. Today no one can confirm exactly where Alonso de Velasco is buried, although the oral tradition maintains that he was buried beneath the altar of the small chapel located in Textitlán in 1805, and that his body was moved and is buried beneath the altar of the current church, which was built in 1846. Ibid.

30. Manuel Ibarra Pérez, interview January 12, 2004.

31. Ibid.; and Nicolas Ruíz Rodríguez, interview January 9, 2004.

32. Those who came to pay respects upon de Velasco's death noted that far from looking like a dead man, de Velasco's face gave onlookers the impression that he was a saint lying at rest (López-López 1945: 20).

33. During the colonial period in Mexico the Roman Catholic Church established local parishes and assigned each a saint. During the nineteenth and early twentieth centuries, it was not uncommon for communities to install patrons who were more compatible with local sensibilities. It is not surprising that Tex-

titlán, at its foundation, was inclined to adopt a more personal, relevant image to represent the pueblo and its people.

34. Juan Rico García, interview January 10, 2003; and Manuel Ibarra Pérez, interview January 12, 2004.

35. Gloria Serato, interview January 16, 2003.

36. The Spanish word *castillo* literally means castle, but in this case they are two to three story wooden structures with moving fireworks displays. They include images of Christ on the cross, the Eucharist, and other Christian imagery, such as doves.

37. Very few events take place without music. Jaripeos, for example, are followed by dances and the torneos de gallos are followed by live concerts. Each event hosts well-known Mexican bands.

38. Banda is a musical style usually consisting of ten to twelve musicians playing woodwinds and brass instruments, including clarinets, trumpets, trombones, tubas, percussion, and often a vocalist. Mariachi bands traditionally are string bands featuring violins and guitars, but sometimes also incorporate brass instruments and vocalists (Simonett 2001).

39. Emilio Guzmán, personal communication, January 19, 2003.

40. José Ortega is not a pseudonym.

CHAPTER SEVEN

1. For details of these narratives, see Chapter 4.

2. Chadds Ford is a small suburban community some five miles north of Kennett Borough. The community celebrates "Chadds Ford Days," an annual festival commemorating local history and identity. For a detailed account of this festival, see Dorst's *The Written Suburb* (1989).

3. Mary Stevens, personal communication September 12, 1998.

4. For further explorations of the concept of cultural performance, see Hymes (1975); Bauman (1984); Bauman et al. (1991); and St. George (1998).

5. The process that was undertaken in Kennett was a self-conscious effort to demonstrate, through the Cinco de Mayo festival, Kennett's "core principles" (as discussed in Chapter 5) of progress and inclusion, and as such the festival organizers carefully selected aspects of Mexican vernacular culture that they wanted to emphasize in the community. Using the festival in this way is not an isolated incident. In their discussion of American folk festivals, Bauman et al. (1991) argue that festivals reproduce "symbolically constructed image[s] of the popular foundations of American culture by traditionalizing, valorizing, and legitimating *selected aspects* of vernacular culture drawn from diverse . . . groups that are seen to make up American society" (289, emphasis mine).

6.   The idea that festivals expose deep and sometimes obscured social relationship is commonly acknowledged in festival scholarship. For instance, Abrahams (1983) notes that festive celebrations offer opportunities for a deliberate display of various economic, social, and political aspects of a community, and Handelman describes the social and power relations that are expressed through festival as "events that present the lived world" (1982: 41). More recently, Picard and Robinson argue that contemporary festivals become an "important social vector for the reformulation of ethnic, regional, diasporic, or national narratives and identities" (2006: 6).

7.   Dorothy Noyes's (2003) examination of the Patum of Berga, a festival to celebrate Corpus Cristi in Catalonia, is an example of how cultural performance is used to construct identity.

8.   Kennett Square Borough, www.kennett-square.pa.us/, accessed November 12, 2005.

9.   Historic Kennett Square Web site, www.historickennettsquare.com/, accessed November 15, 2005.

10.   Kennett Square Borough, www.kennett-square.pa.us/business.htm, accessed August 15, 2007.

11.   Kennett Square Borough, www.kennett-square.pa.us/, accessed November 15, 2005.

12.   Italian laborers are a notable exception to this. They not only remained in Kennett Square, but also they became the majority of current mushroom farm owners.

13.   The first permanent Mexican settlers were those who were legalized under the Immigration Reform and Control Act of 1986. Subsequent settlement has been fueled through job growth that resulted from Chester County's rapid suburban development in the early years of the 2000s.

14.   MMP 118 (housefile), mmp.opr.princeton.edu.

15.   For example, there has been considerable dispute in the community regarding proper property management, the number and types of persons who should be allowed to live in a single-family home, and aesthetic preferences for exterior home decoration. For an account of these issues, please see Chapter 5.

16.   Peggy Harris, interview December 1, 1995.

17.   These events are discussed in detail in Chapter 5. The most significant events occurred between 1995 and 1997. Kennett's citizen population organized and protested the redevelopment of dilapidated properties in town that would eventually house Mexican families in 1995. A year later a local dance hall that had become a favorite gathering place for Mexican couples was closed and later torn down, and a vacant field where Mexican men gathered in the evenings after work to play soccer was plowed under. Then, in early 1997, a neighborhood

association organized English-speaking residents, asking them to place yellow ribbons in front of their homes to protest Mexicans who were purchasing houses and moving into their neighborhood.

18.   The conflict that erupted between members of the English-speaking community, along with the Bridging the Community movement, is detailed in Chapter 5.

19.   It should be noted that the Latino Cultural Alliance was a well-organized group and was registered as a 501(c)(3) nonprofit organization.

20.   During the time of this study, Alianza was the only Mexican-led organization in Kennett Square.

21.   Alvar Carlson (1998) notes that the growing number of Cinco de Mayo festivals in the United States is closely related to the expansion of Mexican American populations throughout the United States.

22.   Historic Kennett Square Web site, www.historickennettsquare.com/, accessed April 12, 2002.

23.   Fiesta Agringada is slang meaning a gringo-style festival.

24.   Sommers (1985) notes that the emergence of Cinco de Mayo as a major Latino cultural performance is directly related to the fact that it is not a clear symbol of Mexican nationalism. Instead, the holiday can be interpreted as a significant day to persons of Mexican ancestry, but it also works effectively to represent multicultural experiences in the United States.

25.   Vince Ghione, interview September 6, 2004.

26.   The parade of flags did not begin with the Cinco de Mayo but as a regular event in Kennett Unity Day, a festival created a decade ago to highlight community diversity and to promote unity among the town's population.

27.   The Democratic Party also had a booth at the event, but their materials were available only in English.

28.   This is not to say that information presented at the festival is not necessary or useful. Public health education is an essential part of all communities. I do take issue with the choice of venue in which it was presented, however, and the fact that these types of displays are not common at other Kennett Square festivals. Furthermore, these organizations have other opportunities to reach this population. Every April local social service organizations host an Expo Latino, where they present similar information about local services.

29.   Vince Ghione, interview September 6, 2004. Ghione's concern here is that the attendance has to reach certain levels to maintain sponsorship support, and thus Anglos must to attend in order to reach that goal.

30.   Marta Zavala, personal communication May 5, 2002.

31.   The Cinco de Mayo festival is held on the Saturday that falls closest to May 5.

32.   Mi Casa Su Casa was owned and operated by La Comunidad Hispana. The shop sold handcrafted Latin American goods to generate income for the agency. The shop has since closed.

33.   Vince Ghione, interview September 6, 2004.

34.   A mask need not completely cover one's face to create its desired effect. Partial masks, such as those worn at masquerade balls, achieve similar effects.

35.   Vince Ghione, interview September 6, 2004.

36.   Ibid.

37.   Leon Spenser, public address during Kennett Square Cinco de Mayo, May 2, 2004.

38.   Susan Lattanzi, personal communication May 2, 2004.

EPILOGUE

1.   I define a long-term settler as one who has lived in Kennett Square or the surrounding area five years or more.

2.   This information was found at the Help Save Manassas Web site, Help Save Manassas, http://helpsavemanassas.org, accessed January 10, 2010.

References

Abrahams, Roger D. 1983. *The Man-of-Words in the West Indies: Performance and the Emergence of Creole Culture.* Baltimore, MD: Johns Hopkins University Press.
———. 1993. Phantoms of Romantic Nationalism in Folkloristics. *The Journal of American Folklore* 106 (Winter): 3–37.
Agnew, John A. 1987. *Place and Politics: The Geographical Mediation of State and Society.* Boston: Allen & Unwin.
Alamillo, Jose M. 2003. More Than a Fiesta: Ethnic Identity, Cultural Politics, and Cinco de Mayo Festivals in Corona, California, 1930–1950. *Aztlan* 28: 57–86.
Alba, Richard, and Victor Nee. 1997. Rethinking Assimilation Theory for a New Era of Immigration. *International Migration Review* 31 (4): 826–874.
———. 2003. *Remaking the American Mainstream: Assimilation and Contemporary Immigration.* Cambridge, MA: Harvard University Press.
Alleyne, Brian. 2002. An Idea of Community and Its Discontents: Towards a More Reflexive Sense of Belonging in Multicultural Britain. *Ethnic and Racial Studies* 25 (4): 607–627.

Álvarez, Julia. 2007. *Once Upon a Quinceañera: Coming of Age in the USA*. New York: Viking.

Anderson, Benedict. 1994. *Imagined Communities*. London: Verso.

Andreas, Peter. 1998. The Escalation of U.S. Immigration Control in the Post-NAFTA Era. *Political Science Quarterly* 113 (4): 591–615.

———. 2000. *Border Games: Policing the US-Mexico Divide*. Ithaca, NY: Cornell University Press.

Andreas, Peter, and Timothy Snyder. 2000. *The Wall around the West: State Borders and Immigration Controls in North America and Europe*. Lanham, MD: Rowman & Littlefield.

Babcock, Barbara. 1978. Introduction. In *The Reversible World: Symbolic Inversion in Art and Society*, 16–36. Ithaca, NY: Cornell University Press.

Bachelard, Gaston. 1969. *The Poetics of Space*. Boston: Beacon Press.

Barbalet, J. M. 1992. A Macrosociology of Emotion: Class Resentment. *Sociological Theory* 10, (2): 150–163.

Barber, Chris. 2002. Cinco de Mayo Delights Crowd. *Kennett Paper*, May 9.

———. 2006. Las Rosas Opens Housing with a Ceremonial Rose Presentation. *Kennett Paper*, June 15.

Basch, Linda G., Nina Glick Schiller, and Christina Szanton Blanc. 1994. *Nations Unbound: Transnational Projects, Postcolonial Predicaments, and Deterritorialized Nation-States*. Langhorne, PA: Gordon and Breach.

Basso, Keith H. 1996. Wisdom Sits in Places: Notes on a Western Apache Landscape. In *Senses of Place*, ed. Stephen Feld and Keith Basso, 53–90. Santa Fe, NM: School of American Research.

Bauman, Richard, ed. 1984. *Verbal Art as Performance*. Prospect Heights, IL: Waveland Press.

Bauman, Richard, and Patricia Sawin. 1991. The Politics of Participation in Folklife Festivals. In *Exhibiting Cultures: The Politics and Poetics of Museum Display*, ed. Ivan Karp and Steven Lavine, 288–314. Washington, DC: Smithsonian Institution Press.

Bauman, Richard, Patricia Sawin, and Inta Gale Carpenter. 1992. *Reflections on the Folklife Festival: An Ethnography of Participant Experience*. Special publications of the Folklore Institute, no. 2. Bloomington: Indiana University.

Bauman, Richard, Patricia Swain, Ivan Karp, and Steven D. Lavine. 1991. The Politics of Participation in Folklife Festivals. In *Exhibiting Cultures: The Politics and Poetics of Museum Display*, 288–314. Washington, DC: Smithsonian Institution Press.

Baumeister, Roy F., and Mark R. Leary. 1995. The Need to Belong: Desire for Interpersonal Attachments as a Fundamental Human Motivation. *Psychological Bulletin* 117 (May): 497–529.

Beck, Ulrich. 2000. *What Is Globalization?* Malden, MA: Polity Press.

Beezley, William H., Cheryl English Martin, and William E. French. 1994. *Rituals of Rule, Rituals of Resistance: Public Celebrations and Popular Culture in Mexico.* Latin American Silhouettes. Wilmington, DE: SR Books.

Bell, Catherine. 1997. *Ritual: Perspectives and Dimensions.* New York: Oxford University Press.

Bell, Vikki. 1999. Performativity and Belonging: An Introduction. *Theory Culture Society* 16 (April 1): 1–10.

Ben-Amos, Dan, and Kenneth S Goldstein, eds. 1975. Breakthrough into Performance. In *Folklore: Performance and Communication.* The Hague: Mouton.

Benson, J. 1995. For Two-Steppers, the Party's Over: A Popular Dance Spot Ceased Latin American Music Nights after Township Pressure. *Philadelphia Inquirer,* November 28, 1995, W-1.

Berry, Wendell. 1990. *What Are People For? Essays.* San Francisco: North Point Press.

———. 1991. *Standing on Earth: Selected Essays.* Ipswich, UK: Golgonooza Press.

———. 2001. *A Place on Earth.* Washington, DC: Counterpoint.

Bono, Marisa. 2007. Don't You Be My Neighbor: Restrictive Housing Ordinances as the New Jim Crow. *Modern American* 3: 29.

Bourdieu, Pierre. 1992. Rites as Acts of Institution. In *Honor and Grace in Anthropology,* 79–90. Cambridge: Cambridge University Press.

Brandes, Stanley H. 1988. *Power and Persuasion: Fiestas and Social Control in Rural Mexico.* Philadelphia: University of Pennsylvania Press.

Brimelow, Peter. 1995. *Alien Nation: Common Sense about America's Immigration Disaster.* New York: Random House.

Broom, Leonard, Bernard J. Siegel, Evon Z. Vogt, and James B. Watson. 1954. Acculturation: An Exploratory Formulation: The Social Science Research Council Summer Seminar on Acculturation, 1953. *American Anthropologist* 56 (6): 973–1000.

Buonfino, Alessandra. 2007. Integration and the Question of Social Identity. In *Rethinking Immigration and Integration: A New Centre-Left Agenda,* 111–130. London: The Policy Network.

Buonfino, Alessandra, and Louisa Thompson. 2007. *Belonging in Contemporary Britain.* Wetherby, West Yorkshire, UK: Communities and Local Governments Publications. Communities and Local Government, www.communities.gov.uk, accessed March 9, 2010.

Bustos, Sergio. 1994a. For Farmworkers, a Year in Limbo: The Mushroom Workers' Union Battle is off the Streets and in the Legal Arena. Today, Federal Hearings Begin. *Philadelphia Inquirer,* May 18, B01.

———. 1994b. Mushroom Workers Struggle. *The Progressive* 58 (10): 14.

Cantú, Norma Elia, and Olga Nájera-Ramírez. 2002. *Chicana Traditions: Continuity and Change*. Urbana: University of Illinois Press.

Cantwell, Robert. 1993. *Ethnomimesis: Folklife and the Representation of Culture*. Chapel Hill: University of North Carolina Press.

Carlson, Alvar W. 1998. America's Growing Observance of Cinco de Mayo. *Journal of American Culture* 21 (2): 7–16.

Casey, Edward. 1993. *Getting Back into Place: Toward a Renewed Understanding of the Place-World*. Bloomington: Indiana University Press.

———. 1996. How to Get from Space to Place in a Fairly Short Stretch of Time. In *Senses of Place*, ed. Steven Feld and Keith Basso, 13–52. Santa Fe, NM: School of American Research.

———. 1998. *The Fate of Place: A Philosophical History*. Berkeley: University of California Press.

Castles, Stephen, and Alastair Davidson. 2000. *Citizenship and Migration: Globalization and the Politics of Belonging*. New York: Routledge.

Certeau, Michel de. 1984. *The Practice of Everyday Life*. Berkeley: University of California Press.

Chavez, Leo. 1991. Outside the Imagined Community: Undocumented Settlers and Experiences of Incorporation. *American Ethnologist* 18: 257–278.

Cho, David. 2005. $400,000 to Aid Day Laborers. *Washington Post*, May 12, sec. Fairfax Extra, T03.

———. 2005. Herndon Confronts Immigrant Tensions. *Washington Post*, July 18, A1.

Chow, Henry P. H. 2007. Sense of Belonging and Life Satisfaction among Hong Kong Adolescent Immigrants in Canada. *Journal of Ethnic and Migration Studies* 33 (3): 511–520.

Clark, Keith. 1994. Growing Fancy in Fungi but Domesticating Truffle Is No Trifle. *Chicago Tribune*, October 3, Final edition, sec. Business.

Cleaveland, Carol, and L. Kelly. 2008. Shared Social Space and Strategies to Find Work: An Exploratory Study of Mexican Day Laborers in Freehold, N.J. *Social Justice* 35 (4): 51–66.

Cleaveland, Carol, and Leo Pierson. 2009. Parking Lots and Police: Undocumented Latinos' Tactics for Finding Day Labor Jobs. *Ethnography* 10 (December 1): 515–533.

Cohen, Abner. 1993. *Masquerade Politics: Explorations in the Structure of Urban Cultural Movements*. Berkeley: University of California Press.

Conradson, David, and Deirdre Mckay. 2007. Translocal Subjectivities: Mobility, Connection, Emotion. *Mobilities* 2 (July): 167–174.

Constable, Pamela. 2007. For Many Immigrants, No Answers: Manassas Legal Clinic Aims to Assist Hispanic Community. *Washington Post*, March 20, B01.

Corchado, Alfredo. 1999. Growing Together: Struggle for Pennsylvania Town, Mexican Immigrants to Accept Each Other May Signal Path for Other Agricultural Areas (The Reshaping of America Series). *Dallas Morning News*, September 24, 1.

Corenblum, B., and Walter G. Stephan. 2001. White Fears and Native Apprehensions: An Integrated Threat Theory Approach to Intergroup Attitudes. *Canadian Journal of Behavioural Science* 33, no. 4 (October): 251–268.

Cresswell, Tim. 1996. *In Place/Out of Place: Geography, Ideology, and Transgression*. Minneapolis: University of Minneapolis Press.

———. 2004. *Place*. Oxford: Wiley-Blackwell.

Cuba, Lee, and David Hummon. 1993. Constructing a Sense of Home: Place Affiliation and Migration across the Life Cycle. *Sociological Forum* 8 (4): 547–572.

Della Porta, Donatella, and Mario Diani. 1999. *Social Movements: An Introduction*. Oxford and Malden, MA: Blackwell.

Dench, Geoff, Kate Gavron, and Michael Young. 2006. *The New East End: Kinship, Race and Conflict*. London: Profile Books.

Dorst, John. 1989. *The Written Suburb: An American Site, an Ethnographic Dilemma*. Philadelphia: University of Pennsylvania Press.

Duncan, James, and Nancy Duncan. 2003. Can't Live with Them; Can't Landscape without Them: Racism and the Pastoral Aesthetic in Suburban New York. *Landscape Journal* 22 (January 1): 88–98.

Durand, Jorge, and Douglas S. Massey. 1995. *Miracles on the Border: Retablos of Mexican Migrants to the United States*. Tucson: University of Arizona Press.

Durand, Jorge, Douglas S. Massey, and Chiara Capoferro. 2005. The New Geography of Mexican Immigration. In *New Destinations: Mexican Immigration in the United States*, ed. Victor Zúñiga and Ruben Hernández-León, 1–20. New York: Russell Sage Foundation.

Durand, Jorge, Douglas S. Massey, and Fernando Charvet. 2000. The Changing Geography of Mexican Immigration to the United States: 1910–1996. *Social Science Quarterly* 81 (1): 1–15.

Ebaugh, Helen Rose, and Mary Curry. 2000. Fictive Kin as Social Capital in New Immigrant Communities. *Sociological Perspectives* 43 (Summer): 189–209.

Elias, Norbert. 1982. *The History of Manners*. 1st ed. New York: Pantheon Books.

Ernst, Carol T. 1995. Kennett Square's Soul Is Dying. *Kennet Paper*, February 16, A6.

Espiritu, Yen Le. 2003. *Home Bound: Filipino American Lives Across Cultures, Communities, and Countries*. Berkeley: University of California Press.

Faist, Thomas, and Eyup Ozveren. 2004. *Transnational Social Spaces: Agents, Networks and Institutions*. Burlington, VT: Ashgate.

Falassi, Alessandro. 1987. Festival: Definition and Morphology. In *Time out of Time: Essays on Festival*, ed. Alessandro Falassi, 1–12. Albuquerque: University of New Mexico Press.

Feld, Steven, and Keith H. Basso, eds. 1996. *Senses of Place*. School of American Research Advanced Seminar Series. Santa Fe, NM: School of American Research Press.

Fernández-Kelly, Patricia, and Douglas S. Massey. 2007. Borders for Whom? The Role of NAFTA in Mexico-U.S. Migration. *The ANNALS of the American Academy of Political and Social Science* 610 (March 1): 98–118.

Fink, Leon. 2003. *The Maya of Morganton: Work and Community in the Nuevo New South*. Chapel Hill: University of North Carolina Press.

Florida, Richard L. 2002. *The Rise of the Creative Class: And How It's Transforming Work, Leisure, Community and Everyday Life*. New York: Basic Books.

———. 2005. *The Flight of the Creative Class: The New Global Competition for Talent*. New York: Harper Business.

Fortier, Anne-Marie. 1999. Re-Membering Places and the Performance of Belonging(s). *Theory Culture Society* 16 (April 1): 41–64.

Foster, George M. 1953. Cofradía and Compadrazgo in Spain and Spanish America. *Southwestern Journal of Anthropology* 9 (Spring): 1–28.

Fried, Mark. 2000. Continuities and Discontinuities of Place. *Journal of Environmental Psychology* 20: 193–205.

Furedi, Frank. 1997. *Culture of Fear: Risk-Taking and the Morality of Low Expectation*. London: Cassell.

———. 2005. *Politics of Fear*. London: Continuum.

Gans, Herbert J. 1979. Symbolic Ethnicity. In *On the Making of Americans: Essays in Honor of David Riesman*, ed. Herbert J. Gans, 193–214. Philadelphia: University of Pennsylvania Press.

———. 1992. Comment: Ethnic Invention and Acculturation: A Bumpy-Line Approach. *Journal of American Ethnic History* 12 (Fall): 42–52.

———. 1999. *Making Sense of America: Sociological Analyses and Essays*. Legacies of Social Thought. Lanham, MD: Rowman & Littlefield.

García, Victor Q. 1997. Mexican Enclaves in the U.S. Northeast: Immigrant and Migrant Mushroom Workers in Southern Chester County, Pennsylvania. Julian Samora Research Institute, Michigan State University.

———. 2008. Silvia Tlaseca and the Kaolin Mushroom Workers Union: Women's Leadership in the Mexican Diaspora. *Signs: Journal of Women in Culture and Society* 34 (1): 42–47.

García Canclini, Néstor. 1995. *Hybrid Cultures: Strategies for Entering and Leaving Modernity*. Minneapolis: University of Minnesota Press.

Glassner, Barry. 1999. *The Culture of Fear: Why Americans Are Afraid of the Wrong Things*. New York: Basic Books.

Glick Schiller, Nina, Linda Basch, and Christina Szanton Blanc. 1992. *Towards a Transnational Perspective on Migration: Race, Class, Ethnicity, and Nationalism Reconsidered*. New York: New York Academy of Sciences.

Goldring, Luin. 1988. The Power of Status in Transnational Social Fields. *Transnationalism from Below* 6: 165–195.

———. 1997. The Gender and Geography of Citizenship in Mexico-U.S. Transnational Spaces. *Identities* 7 (4): 601–637.

González, Luís. 1994. *San Jose de Gracia: Mexican Village in Transition*. Austin: University of Texas Press.

Graham, Otis L., and Elizabeth Koed. 1993. Americanizing the Immigrant, Past and Future: History and Implications of a Social Movement. *The Public Historian* 15 (4): 24–49.

Gray, Jeffrey A., and Neil McNaughton. 2000. *The Neuropsychology of Anxiety: An Enquiry into the Functions of the Septo-Hippocampal System*. 2nd ed. New York: Oxford University Press.

Grey, Mark A., and Anne C. Woodrick. 2005. "Latinos Have Revitalized Our Community": Mexican Migration, and Anglo Responses in Marshalltown, Iowa. In *New Destinations: Mexican Immigration in the United States*, ed. Víctor Zúñiga and Rubén Hernández-León, 133–154. New York: Russell Sage Foundation.

Grimes, Kimberly M. 1998. *Crossing Borders: Changing Social Identities in Southern Mexico*. Tucson: University of Arizona Press.

Gupta, Akhil, and James Ferguson. 1992. Beyond "Culture": Space, Identity, and the Politics of Difference. *Cultural Anthropology* 7 (February): 6–23.

———. 1997. *Culture, Power, Place: Explorations in Critical Anthropology*. Durham, NC: Duke University Press.

Guss, David M. 2000. *The Festive State: Race, Ethnicity, Nationalism as Cultural Performance*. Berkeley: University of California Press.

Gúzman Zavala, José. 1985. *Monografia del Municipio de Textitlán, Guanajuato*. Puebla, Mexico: Universidad de Puebla.

Hagan, Jacqueline Maria. 1994. *Deciding to Be Legal: A Maya Community in Houston*. Philadelphia: Temple University Press.

Handelman, Don. 1982. Reflexivity in Festival and Other Cultural Events. In *Essays in the Sociology of Perception*, ed. Mary Douglas, 162–218. London and New York: Routledge & Kegan Paul.

Harpur, James. 2002. *Sacred Tracks: 2000 Years of Christian Pilgrimage*. Berkeley: University of California Press.

Harris, Max. 2000. *Aztecs, Moors, and Christians: Festivals of Reconquest in Mexico and Spain*. Austin: University of Texas Press.

———. 2003. *Carnival and Other Christian Festivals: Folk Theology and Folk Performance*. Austin: University of Texas Press.

Harvey, David. 1996. *Justice, Nature and the Geography of Difference*. Cambridge, MA: Blackwell.

Hellman, Judith Alder. 1994. *Mexican Lives*. New York: New Press.

Hernández-León, Ruben, and Víctor Zúñiga. 2000. "Making Carpet by the Mile": The Emergence of a Mexican Immigrant Community in an Industrial Region of the U.S. Historic South. *Social Science Quarterly* 81 (1): 49–66.

———. 2005. Appalachia Meets Aztlán: Mexican Immigration and Intergroup Relations in Dalton, Georgia. In *New Destinations: Mexican Immigration in the United States*, 244–273. New York: Russell Sage Foundation.

Higham, John. 1974. *Strangers in the Land: Patterns of American Nativism, 1860–1925*. New York: Atheneum.

Hirsch, Jennifer. 2003. *A Courtship after Marriage: Sexuality and Love in Mexican Transnational Families*. Berkeley and Los Angeles: University of California Press.

Historic Kennett Square, Inc. 2005. "About Kennett Square." www.historicken nettsquare.com/about.htm, accessed February 11.

Holliday, Joan. 1998. Leading a Heartfelt Community Process through Principles. Path of Potential. www.pathofpotential.org/Becoming/Part%201/ leadingaheartfeltcommua.html, accessed September 30, 2002.

———. 2001a. Thoughtful Committed Citizens. *Path of Potential: A Bimonthly Reader of the Dignity Movement* 1 (3): 19–24.

———. 2001b. Presentation for Folklore 290: Ethnicity and Migration. University of Pennsylvania, February 17.

———. n.d. Notes on Bridging the Community. Unpublished manuscript.

Hondagneu-Sotelo, Pierrette. 1994. *Gendered Transitions: Mexican Experiences of Immigration*. Berkeley and Los Angeles: University of California Press.

———. 2001. *Doméstica: Immigrant Workers Cleaning and Caring in the Shadows of Affluence*. Berkeley and Los Angeles: University of California Press.

Hufford, Mary. 1992. *Chaseworld: Foxhunting and Storytelling in New Jersey's Pine Barrens*. Philadelphia: University of Pennsylvania Press.

Hutchins, Mary Skrzat. 1994. Ambit Lal, Scarlet Manor Problems Won't Go Away. *Kennett Paper*, June 9.

———. 1997a. Ribbons a Call for Unity Say Residents: Stenning Hills Reels under Accusations That a Resident's Group's Symbolic Action Was Racist. *Kennett Paper*, October 2.

————. 1997b. Yellow Ribbons Send Mixed Messages: Two Stenning Hills Residents Spoke Out on Charges That the Protest Is Racist. *Kennett Paper*, October 9.

Hymes, Dell. 1975. Breakthrough into Performance. In *Folklore: Performance and Communication*, ed. Dan Ben-Amos and Kenneth S. Goldstein. The Hague: Mouton.

Instituto Nacional de Estadística, Geografía e Informatica de Mexico (INEGI). 2000. Censo (Census).

Jackson, Bruce. 1987. *Fieldwork*. Urbana: University of Illinois Press.

Johnson, Nick, ed. 2007. *Britishness: Towards a Progressive Citizenship*. London: Smith Institute.

Johnston, Hank, and Bert Klandermans, eds. 1995. *Social Movements and Culture*. Social Movements, Protest, and Contention Series, vol. 4. Minneapolis: University of Minnesota Press.

Jones, Richard C. 2008. *Immigrants outside Megalopolis: Ethnic Transformation in the Heartland*. Lanham, MD: Lexington Books.

Karst, Kenneth L. 1989. *Belonging to America: Equal Citizenship and the Constitution*. New Haven, CT: Yale University Press.

Kashatus, William C. 2002. *Just over the Line: Chester County and the Underground Railroad*. State College, PA: Penn State University Press.

Kirshenblatt-Gimblett, Barbara. 1998. Folklore's Crisis. *Journal of American Folklore* 111 (Summer): 281–327.

————. 1989. Objects of Memory: Material Culture as Life Review. In *Folk Groups and Folklore Genres: A Reader*, ed. Elliot Oring, 329–338. Logan: Utah State University Press.

Kivisto, Peter. 2005. *Incorporating Diversity: Rethinking Assimilation in a Multicultural Age*. Boulder, CO: Paradigm Publishers.

Koch, Philip J. 1987. Emotional Ambivalence. *Philosophy and Phenomenological Research* 48 (2): 257–279.

La Grange, A., and Y. N. Ming. 2001. Social Belonging, Social Capital and the Promotion of Home Ownership: A Case Study of Hong Kong. *Housing Studies* 16 (3): 291–310.

Lamphere, Louise. 1992. *Structuring Diversity: Ethnographic Perspectives on the New Immigration*. Chicago: University of Chicago Press.

Lamphere, Louise, Alex Stepick, and Guillermo J. Grenier. 1994. *Newcomers in the Workplace: Immigrants and the Restructuring of the U.S. Economy*. Philadelphia: Temple University Press.

Laraña, Enrique, Hank Johnston, and Joseph R. Gusfield, eds. 1994. *New Social Movements: From Ideology to Identity*. Philadephia: Temple University Press.

Lattanzi Shutika, Debra. 2005. Bridging the Community: Nativism, Activism and the Politics of Inclusion in a Pennsylvania Mexican Settlement Community. In *New Destinations of Mexican Immigration to the United States: Community Formation, Local Responses and Inter-Group Relations*, ed. Zúñiga, Víctor, and Rubén Hernández-León, 103–132. New York: Russell Sage Foundation.

————. 2008. The Ambivalent Welcome: Cinco de Mayo and the Performance of Local Identity and Ethnic Relations. In *New Faces in New Places: The Changing Geography of American Immigration*, ed. Douglas S. Massey, 274–307. New York: Russell Sage Foundation.

Lawler, Edward J., and Shane R. Thye. 1999. Bringing Emotions into Social Exchange Theory. *Annual Review of Sociology* 25: 217–244.

Lawless, Elaine J. 2001. *Women Escaping Violence: Empowerment through Narrative*. Columbia: University of Missouri Press.

Leach, Neil. 2002. Belonging: Towards a Theory of Identification with Place. *Perspecta* 33: 126–133.

Lefebvre, Henri. 1991. *The Production of Space*. Oxford: Blackwell.

Legomsky, Stephen H. 2007. The New Path of Immigration Law: Asymmetric Incorporation of Criminal Justice Norms. *Immigration and Nationality Law Review* 28: 679.

Lessa, Luiz Carlos Barbosa. 1979. *O Valor e o Sentido do Tradicionalismo* (The Value and Sense of Traditionalism). Porto Alegre, Brazil: SAMRIG.

Levine, Joyce N., Ann-Margaret Esnard, and Alka Sapat. 2007. Population Displacement and Housing Dilemmas Due to Catastrophic Disasters. *Journal of Planning Literature* 22 (August 1): 3–15.

Levitt, Peggy. 2001. *The Transnational Villagers*. Berkeley: University of California Press.

López-López, J. Jesús. 1945. *Moroleón: Segunda Parte Historica (1750 a 1857)*. Moroleón, Guanajuato, México: Imp Concepcion de Maria.

Lovell, Nadia. 1996. *Locality and Belonging*. London and New York: Routledge.

Low, Setha. 1994. Cultural Conservation of Place. In *Conserving Culture: A New Discourse on Heritage*, ed. Mary Hufford, 66–77. Urbana: University of Illinois Press.

Low, Setha M. 2000. *On the Plaza: The Politics of Public Space and Culture*. Austin: University of Texas Press.

Ludden, Jennifer. 2007. Hazleton's Immigration Law Brings Suspicions. All Things Considered. National Public Radio, March 16, www.npr.org/templates/story/story.php?storyId=8959477.

Ma, Eric Kit-wai. 2002. Translocal Spatiality. *International Journal of Cultural Studies* 5 (March 1): 131–152.

MacAloon, John J. 1984. *Rite, Drama, Festival, Spectacle: Rehearsals toward a Theory of Cultural Performance*. Philadelphia: Institute for the Study of Human Issues.

Malpas, J. E. 1999. *Place and Experience: A Philosophical Topography*. Cambridge: Cambridge University Press.

Mandaville, Peter. 1999. Territory and Translocality: Descrepant Idioms of Political Identity. *Millennium: Journal of International Studies* 28 (3): 653–673.

Manzo, Lynne. 2003. Beyond House and Haven: Toward a Revisioning of Emotional Relationships with Places. *Journal of Environmental Psychology* 23: 47–61.

Mariscal, George. 1991. In the Wake of the Gulf War: Untying the Yellow Ribbon. *Cultural Critique* 19 (Autumn): 97–117.

Martin, Philip. 1995. Proposition 187 in California. *International Migration Review* 29, no. 1 (April 1): 255–263.

Massey, Doreen. 1993. Power Geometry and a Progressive Sense of Place. In *Mapping the Futures: Local Cultures, Global Change*, ed. Jon Bird, Barry Curtis, and Tim Putnam, 59–69. London and New York: Routledge.

———. 1994. *Space, Place, and Gender*. Minneapolis: University of Minnesota Press.

———. 2005. *For Space*. London: SAGE.

Massey, Douglas S. 1987a. The Ethnosurvey in Theory and Practice. *International Migration Review* 21 (4): 1498–1522.

———. 1998. *Worlds in Motion: Understanding International Migration at the End of the Millenium*. International Studies in Demography. Oxford: Clarendon Press.

———. 2000. A Validation of the Ethnosurvey: The Case of Mexico-US Migration. *International Migration Review* 34 (3): 766–793.

———. 2002. A Brief History of Human Society: The Origin and Role of Emotion in Social Life: 2001 Presidential Address. *American Sociological Review* 67, no. 1 (February 1): 1-29.

———. 2007. Understanding America's Immigration "Crisis." *American Philosophical Society Proceedings* 151 (3): 309–327.

———, ed. 2008. *New Faces in New Places: The Changing Geography of American Immigration*. New York: Russell Sage Foundation.

Massey, Douglas S., Rafael Alarcon, Jorge Durand, and González Huberto. 1987. *Return to Aztlan: The Social Process of International Migration from Western Mexico*. Berkeley: University of California Press.

Massey, Douglas S., and Nancy Denton. 1993. *American Apartheid: Segregation and the Making of the Underclass*. Cambridge, MA: Harvard University Press.

Massey, Douglas S., Jorge Durand, and Nolan J. Malone. 2002. *Beyond Smoke and Mirrors: Mexican Immigration in an Age of Economic Integration*. New York: Russell Sage Foundation.

May, Rollo. 1977. *The Meaning of Anxiety*. New York: Ronald Press.

Maye, Fran. 2009. Some Fuming over Cinco Cancellation. *Kennett Paper*, June 10.

McKay, Deirdre. 2006a. Introduction: Finding "the Field": The Problem of Locality in a Mobile World. *Asia Pacific Journal of Anthropology* 7 (December): 197–202.

———. 2006b. Translocal Circulation: Place and Subjectivity in an Extended Filipino Community. *Asia Pacific Journal of Anthropology* 7 (December): 265–278.

Melucci, Alberto. 1996. *Challenging Codes: Collective Action in the Information Age*. Cambridge: Cambridge University Press.

Merrifield, Andrew. 1993. Place and Space: A Lefebvrian Reconciliation. *Transactions of the Institute of British Geographers*, New Series 18 (4): 516–531.

Meyrowitz, Joshua. 1985. *No Sense of Place: The Impact of Electronic Media on Social Behavior*. New York: Oxford University Press.

Millard, Ann V, Jorge Chapa, and Catalina Burillo. 2004. *Apple Pie & Enchiladas: Latino Newcomers in the Rural Midwest*. Austin: University of Texas Press.

Mines, Richard, and Douglas S. Massey. 1985. Patterns of Migration to the United States from Two Mexican Communities. *Latin American Research Review* 20: 104–124.

Morgan, John. 2000. To Which Space Do I Belong? Imagining Citizenship in One Curriculum Subject. *Curriculum Journal* 11 (March): 55–68.

Mulgan, Geoff. 1998. *Connexity: How to Live in a Connected World*. Boston: Harvard Business School Press.

———. 2007. Belonging—Local and National. In *Britishness: Towards a Progressive Citizenship*, ed. Nick Johnson, 60–68. London: Smith Institute.

———. 2009. *Feedback and Belonging: Explaining the Dynamics of Diversity*. Migration Information Source. Washington, DC: Migration Policy Institute. www.migrationinformation.org/Feature/print.cfm?ID=718.

Nájera-Ramírez, Olga. 1997. *La Fiesta de los Tastoanes: Critical Encounters in Mexican Festival Performance*. Albuquerque: University of New Mexico Press.

———. 1999. Of Fieldwork, Folklore, and Festival: Personal Encounters. *Journal of American Folklore* 112 (444): 183–199.

Napier, David. 1987. Festival Masks. In *Time Out of Time: Essays on Festival*, ed. Alessandro Falassi, 211–220. Alburquerque: University of New Mexico Press.

Nast, Heidi J., and Steve Pile. 1998. MakingPlacesBodies. In *Places through the Body*, ed. Heidi Nast and Steve Pile, 1–20. New York and London: Routledge.

Nevins, Joseph. 2002. *Operation Gatekeeper: The Rise of the "Illegal Alien" and the Remaking of the U.S.-Mexico Boundary*. New York: Routledge.

———. 2008. *Dying to Live: A Story of U.S. Immigration in an Age of Global Apartheid*. San Francisco: Open Media/City Lights Books.

Noyes, Dorothy. 2003. *Fire in the Placa: Catalan Festival Politics after Franco*. Philadelphia: University of Pennsylvania Press.

Olvin, Ruben George. 2000. "The Largest Popular Culture Movement in the Western World": Intellectuals and Gaucho Traditionalism in Brazil. *American Ethnologist* 27 (1): 128–146.

Ortiz-Ortiz, Alfonso. 1993. *Distertaciones Textitlanecas* (Reflections on Textitlán). Morelia, Michoacan: IMPSEGOW.

Osterling, J. P், and S. C. McClure. 2008. Dystopia in Virginia: The 2008 Immigration Debate. *Mosaic* 1 (1): 11–21.

Park, Robert Ezra. 1930. Assimilation Social. In *Encyclopedia of the Social Sciences*, ed. E. Seligman and A. Johnson, 281–283. New York: Macmillan.

———. 1969. *Introduction to the Science of Sociology, Including the Original Index to Basic Sociological Concepts*. 3rd ed. Chicago: University of Chicago Press.

Parsons, Gerald E. 1981. Yellow Ribbons: Ties with Tradition. *Folklife Center News* 4 (2). American Folklife Center, www.loc.gov/folklife/ribbons/ribbons _81.html, accessed September 21, 2002.

———. 1991. How the Yellow Ribbon became a National Folk Symbol. *Folklife Center News* 12 (3): 9–12.

Paz, Octavio. 1961. *The Labyrinth of Solitude: Life and Thought in Mexico*. New York: Grove Press.

Pennsylvania Department of Education. 1980. Pennsylvania Department of Education Statistics. Harrisburg, Pennsylvania. www.pde.state.pa.us/ k12statistics/site/default.asp, accessed September 15, 2001.

———. 2000–2001. Pennsylvania Department of Education Statistics. Harrisburg, Pennsylvania. www.pde.state.pa.us/k12statistics/site/default.asp, accessed. January 12, 2002.

Perea, Juan F. 1997. *Immigrants Out! The New Nativism and the Anti-Immigrant Impulse in the United States*. Critical America. New York: New York University Press.

Perin, Constance. 1988. *Belonging in America: Reading between the Lines*. New York: St. Martin's Press.

Pershing, Linda. 1996. *The Ribbon around the Pentagon: Peace by Piecemakers*. Knoxville: University of Tennessee Press.

Pershing, Linda, and Margaret R. Yocom. 1996. The Yellow Ribboning of the USA: Contested Meanings in the Construction of a Political Symbol. *Western Folklore* 55 (Winter): 41–85.

Picard, David, and Mike Robinson. 2006. *Festivals, Tourism and Social Change: Remaking Worlds*. Tourism and Cultural Change 8. Clevedon, UK: Channel View Publications.

Piore, Michael J. 1973. Fragments of a Sociological Theory of Wages. *American Economic Review* 63: 377–384.

———. 1979. *Birds of Passage: Migrant Labor and Industrial Societies*. New York: Cambridge University Press.

Pocius, Gerald L. 1991. *A Place to Belong: Community Order and Everyday Space in Calvert, Newfoundland*. Athens: University of Georgia Press.

Porteous, J. Douglas. 1976. Home: The Territorial Core. *Geographical Review* 66 (October): 383–390.

Porteous, J. Douglas and Sandra E. Smith. 2001. *Domicide: The Global Destruction of Home*. Montréal: McGill-Queen's University Press.

Portes, Alejandro. 1995. *The Economic Sociology of Immigration: Essays on Networks, Ethnicity, and Entrepreneurship*. New York: Russell Sage Foundation.

Portes, Alejandro, and Min Zhou. 1993. The New Second Generation: Segmented Assimilation and Its Variants. *Annals of the American Academy of Political and Social Science* 530 (November): 74–96.

Pred, Allan. 1984. Place as Historically Contingent Process: Structuration and the Time- Geography of Becoming Places. *Annals of the Association of American Geographers* 74 (June): 279–297.

Pries, Ludger. 1999. *Migration and Transnational Social Spaces*. Brookfield, VT: Ashgate.

Probyn, Elspeth. 1996. *Outside Belongings*. New York: Routledge.

Redd, Adrienne. 1994. Eastern PA's Largest Vegetable Crop: Mushrooming. *Eastern Pennsylvania Business Journal* 5 (June 20): 19.

Rein, Lisa. 2006. A Political Newcomer's Challenge; Day-Labor Strife to Mark Herndon Mayor's Term. *Washington Post*, May 24, final edition, sec. Metro.

Relph, E. C. 1976. *Place and Placelessness*. London: Pion.

Reyes, Belinda I. 1997. *Dynamics of Immigration: Return Migration to Western Mexico*. San Francisco: Public Policy Institute of California.

Rich, Brian L., and Marta Miranda. 2005. The Sociopolitical Dynamics of Mexican Immigration in Lexington, Kentucky, 1997 to 2002. An Ambivalent Community Responds. In *New Destinations: Mexican Immigration in the United States*, ed. Víctor Zúñiga and Rubén Hernández-León, 187–219. New York: Russell Sage Foundation.

Roberts, Kenneth. 1994. Ambit Lal, Scarlet Manor Problems Won't Go Away. *Kennett Paper*, June 9.

Rodman, Margaret. 2001. *Houses Far from Home: British Colonial Space in the New Hebrides*. Honolulu: University of Hawai'i Press.

Rouse, Roger. 1992. Making Sense of Settlement: Class Transformation, Cultural Struggle, and Transnationalism among Mexican Migrants in the United States. *Annals of the New York Academy of Sciences* 645: 25–52.

Ruiz-Velasco, J. Trinidad Sepulveda. 1997. *Devocionario del Mirgrante*. (Migrant's Devotional) San Juan de los Lagos, Jalisco: Publicación de la Comisión Diocesano de Pastoral Social en su Departamento de Migrantes.

Ryden, Kent C. 1993. *Mapping the Invisible Landscape: Folklore, Writing, and the Sense of Place*. Iowa City: University of Iowa Press.

Sánchez, George J. 1997. Face the Nation: Race, Immigration, and the Rise of Nativism in Late Twentieth Century America. *International Migration Review* 31 (Winter): 1009–1030.

Santa Ana, Otto. 2002. *Brown Tide Rising: Metaphors of Latinos in Contemporary American Public Discourse*. Austin: University of Texas Press.

Santino, Jack. 1992. Yellow Ribbons and Seasonal Flags: The Folk Assemblage of War. *The Journal of American Folklore* 105 (Winter): 19–33.

Savage, Michael, Gaynor Bagnall, and Brian Longhurst. 2005. *Globalization and Belonging*. London: SAGE.

Saxton, Lisa. 1992. Cinco de Mayo Promos Hit "Gringos." *Supermarket News* 42: 126.

Schechner, Richard. 1993. *The Future of Ritual: Writings on Culture and Performance*. London, New York: Routledge.

Scott, James C. 1990. *Domination and the Arts of Resistance: Hidden Transcripts*. New Haven, CT and London: Yale University Press.

Shore, Bradd. 1990. Human Ambivalence and the Structuring of Moral Values. *Ethos* 18 (2): 165–179.

Shott, Susan. 1979. Emotion and Social Life: A Symbolic Interactionist Analysis. *The American Journal of Sociology* 84, no. 6 (May 1): 1317–1334.

Simonett, Helena. 2001. *Banda: Mexican Musical Life across Borders*. Middletown, CT: Wesleyan University Press.

Singer, Audrey. 2004. *The Rise of New Immigrant Gateways*. The Living Census Series. Washington, DC: Brookings Institution.

Smelser, Neil J. 1962. *Theory of Collective Behavior*. New York: Free Press.

Smith, Anthony. 1996. Culture, Community and Territory: The Politics of Ethnicity and Nationalism. *International Affairs (Royal Institute of International Affairs 1944–)* 72 (3): 445–458.

Smith, Robert C. 2006. *Mexican New York: Transnational Lives of New Immigrants*. Berkeley: University of California Press.

Soja, Edward. 1989. *Postmodern Geographies*. London: Verso.

Sommers, Laurie Kay. 1985. Symbol and Style in Cinco de Mayo. *The Journal of American Folklore* 98 (December): 476–482.

―――. 1991. Inventing Latinismo: The Creation of "Hispanic" Panethnicity in the United States. *Journal of American Folklore* 104: 32–53.

Spielberger, Charles D. 1966. Theory and Research on Anxiety. In *Anxiety and Behavior*, 3-22. New York and London: Academic Press.

―――. 1972. Anxiety as an Emotional State. In *Anxiety: Current Trends in Theory and Research*, ed. Charles D. Spielberger, 24–54. New York and London: Academic Press.

St. George, Robert Blair. 1998. *Conversing by Signs: Poetics of Implication in Colonial New England Culture*. Chapel Hill: University of North Carolina Press.

Staples, Kathy. 2001. Taking Back Cinco de Mayo. *Prevention File Ventura County* 16 (Spring) 2: 2–4.

Stefanou, Spiro E. 2008. *Economic Impact of the Mushroom Industry in Chester County, PA*. Department of Agricultural Economics, Pennsylvania State University. Community Awareness Committee of the American Mushroom Institute, www.mushroomfarmcommunity.org/truimg/EconomicImpact Report.pdf.

Striffler, Steve. 2007. Neither Here Nor There: Mexican Immigrant Workers and the Search for Home. *American Ethnologist* 34 (4): 674–688.

Suarez-Orozco, Marcelo M. 1998. *Crossings: Mexican Immigration in Interdisciplinary Perspectives*. The David Rockefeller Center Series on Latin American Studies. Cambridge, MA: Harvard University.

Subramaniam, Radhika. 1999. Culture of Suspicion: Riots and Rumor, Bombay, 1992–1993. *Transforming Anthropology* 8 (1–2): 97–110.

Tatalovich, Raymond. 1995. *Nativism Reborn? The Official English Language Movement and the American States*. Lexington: University Press of Kentucky.

Taylor, Charles. 2002. Modern Social Imaginaries. *Public Culture* 14 (January 1): 91–124.

Taylor, Frances Cloud. 1998. *The Trackless Trail: The Story of the Underground Railroad in Kennett Square, Chester County, Pennsylvania, and the Surrounding Community*. Kennett Square, PA: Graphics Standard Printing.

―――. 1999. *The Trackless Trail Leads On: An Exploration of Conductors and Their Stations*. Kennett Square, PA: Graphics Standard Printing.

Teske, Raymond H. C., and Bardin H. Nelson. 1974. Acculturation and Assimilation: A Clarification. *American Ethnologist* 1 (May): 351–367.

Thoits, Peggy A. 1989. The Sociology of Emotions. *Annual Review of Sociology* 15: 317–342.

Tuan, Yi-Fu. 1974. *Topophilia*. Englewood Cliffs, NJ: Prentice Hall.

―――. 1977. *Space and Place: The Perspective of Experience*. Minneapolis: University of Minnesota Press.

————. 1980. Rootedness versus Sense of Place. *Landscape* 24 (1): 3–8.

Tudor, Andrew. 2003. A (Macro) Sociology of Fear? *The Sociological Review* 51 (2): 238–256.

Turcsik, Richard. 1996. Retailers Brew Cinco de Mayo Beer Events. *Supermarket News* 46: 2A.

Turner, Victor. 1969. *The Ritual Process: Structure and Anti-Structure*. Chicago: Aldine Publishing.

————. 1978. *Image and Pilgrimage in Christian Culture*. New York: Columbia University Press.

————. 1982. *Celebration: Studies in Festivity and Ritual*. Washington, DC: Smithsonian Institutional Press.

Turque, Bill. 2007. Herndon to Shut Down Center for Day Laborers. *Washington Post*, September 6, www.washingtonpost.com/wp-dyn/content/article/2007/09/05/AR2007090502600.html.

Urry, John. 1987. Survey 12: Society, Space, and Locality. *Environment and Planning D: Society and Space* 5 (4): 435–444.

————. 1995. *Consuming Places*. International Library of Sociology. London: Routledge.

U.S. Census Bureau. 2000. "Fact Sheet: Kennett Square borough, Pennsylvania." http://factfinder.census.gov/servlet/SAFFFacts?_event=Search&geo_id=01000US&_geoContext=&_street=&_county=kennett+square&_cityTown=kennett+square&_state=04000US42&_zip=&_lang=en&_sse=on&Active GeoDiv=geoSelect&_useEV=&pctxt=fph&pgsl=010&_submenuId=factsheet_1&ds_name=DEC_2000_SAFF&_ci_nbr=null&qr_name=null&reg=null %3Anull&_keyword=&_industry.

Vangstrup, U. 1995. Moroleón: La Pequena Ciudad de la Gran Industria (Moroleón: The Small City with the Big Industry). *Espiral, Estudios sobre Estado y Sociedad* 2 (4): 101–134.

Vélez-Ibáñez, Carlos G. 1983. *Rituals of Marginality: Politics, Process, and Culture Change in Urban Central Mexico, 1969–1974*. Berkeley: University of California Press.

Walker, Francis. 1896. Restriction of Immigration. *Atlantic Monthly* 77 (646): 822–829.

Walker, Kyle. 2008. Immigration, Suburbia, and the Politics of Population in US Metropolitan Areas. Department of Geography: University of Minnesota. http://pop.umn.edu/research/mpc-working-papers-series/2008-working-papers/2008-05-immigration-suburbia-and-the-politics-of-population-in-us-metropolitan-areas/, accessed April 8, 2010.

Weigel, William Shawn. 2009. Cinco de Mayo Gets a Green Light in Kennett Square. *Kennett Paper*, February 26.

Weiss, Jeffery. 1995. Museum Tells All about Mushrooms; Kennett Square, PA.: In the Dark About Fungi? Phillips's Place Will Fill You In. *Dallas Morning News*, November 19.

Westerman, Bill. 1995. *Folklife, Bread, and Roses: The Moral Economy of Cultural Work, Political Belief, and Social Justice*. PhD Diss., University of Pennsylvania.

Wiborg, Agnete. 2004. Place, Nature and Migration: Students' Attachment to Their Rural Home Places. *Sociologia Ruralis* 44 (4): 416–432.

Williams, Michael Ann. 1991. *Homeplace: The Social Use and Meaning of the Folk Dwelling in Southwestern North Carolina*. Athens: University of Georgia Press.

Yocum, Susan. 2000. *Let's Go to a Pennsylvania Mushroom Farm*. Kennett Square, PA: Kennett Consolidated School District.

Young, Anne F., Anne Russell, and Jennifer R. Powers. 2004. The Sense of Belonging to a Neighbourhood: Can It Be Measured and Is It Related to Health and Well Being in Older Women? *Social Science & Medicine* 59 (December): 2627–2637.

Zúñiga, Víctor, and Rubén Hernández-León, eds. 2005. *New Destinations: Mexican Immigration in the United States*. New York: Russell Sage Foundation.

Index

Text: 10/14 Palatino
Display: Univers Condensed Light 47 and Bauer Bodoni
Compositor: Westchester Book Group
Indexer: Susan Park
Cartographer: Bill Nelson
Printer and binder: Maple-Vail Book Manufacturing Group